P9-BAW-768

PSYCHOLOGICAL RESEARCH IN COMMUNIST CHINA: 1949-1966

PSYCHOLOGICAL RESEARCH IN COMMUNIST CHINA: 1949-1966

Robert Chin and Ai-li S. Chin

THE M.I.T. PRESS

Cambridge, Massachusetts, and London, England

For Jeffrey, Carol, and Connie

PREFACE

The intellectual problems and premises of an academic discipline give the outsider a glimpse into some of its basic assumptions and projections about man and his world. Psychology, with its explicit theoretical statements about man's mental activities and his behavior, seems particularly suited to this type of inquiry. In Communist China, where the social sciences suffer curtailment for political reasons, psychology has remained, until recently, relatively intact and has enjoyed fairly solid standing within the limits of ideological orthodoxy. What has happened to the theory and practice of this field is therefore a valuable source for studying the evolution of an intellectual discipline in a controlled society.

This inquiry was stimulated in part, also, by the example of studies of Soviet psychology and the ensuing interchange between Soviet and Western psychologists. We wondered about the fate of the field in Communist China and were led to make a parallel study, though on a much smaller scale. Perhaps, we thought, this might help bring about a similar interchange one day between mainland Chinese and Western psychologists. There was, in any case, the plain value of exploring the unexplored and learning something of current views in Communist China about man and his role in a changing society.

To these ends, we have given a rather full description of the untranslated and until now generally unavailable material on experiments conducted in China prior to the Cultural Revolution. With the upheaval, beginning in 1966, information on psychology in China, as on many other subjects, was suddenly and sharply cut off. It has not resumed. Hence, the information on which this study is based is the latest and only information at hand. There is enough of it, we hope, to indicate the recent development of ideas in psychology in Communist China and their relationship to the sociopolitical scene.

This project was begun by Ai-li S. Chin, a sociologist, under the auspices of the East Asian Research Center at Harvard and completed at the Center for International Studies, M.I.T. Robert Chin of Boston University, the psychologist on the team, shared throughout in the organization and interpretation of the data and in the preparation of the final report. The collaboration involved in the research and writing of this work is a complex process, including the quantitative division of work, the qualitative contribution of ideas, as well as the mutual influences on each other. How can the mere listing of authorship or even an explanatory statement convey everything? Perhaps the dedication of this book to our three children reflects something of the spirit.

We wish to express our deep gratitude to the above two Centers for their generous support and stimulating atmosphere and to the Social Science Research Council for a supplementary grant for data-gathering in Hong Kong while we were in the Far East on another project under Fulbright grants. Boston University also contributed facilities and personnel in the preparation of the manuscript.

At the beginning of the fact-finding task, we spent about a month in Hong Kong, searching through the files of the

Union Research Institute. With the generous help of Lin Yü-ho, we gathered newspaper and radio items, biographical data, texts, and curriculum information on psychology. After returning to the United States, inquiries for material were sent to major libraries in North America and England with important Oriental collections. Of these, special thanks are due the Harvard-Yenching Library, the M.I.T. science collection on Communist China, the Chinese Library of Columbia University, and the Library of Congress.

The authors especially wish to acknowledge with respect and gratitude two sets of *lao shih*–teachers: Otto Klineberg and Gardner Murphy; and Florence Kluckhohn, John K. Fairbank, and Talcott Parsons. While there are many "elder brothers" who have influenced the thinking behind this work, it is possible to mention only a few for their kindness in reading parts of the manuscript at its various stages of completion. They include Mark Field of Boston University; Alexander Mintz of the City University of New York; Morton Fried, Donald W. Klein, and the late Yun Hsia of Columbia University; Benjamin Schwartz and Ezra Vogel of Harvard University; C. K. Yang of Pittsburgh University; Drs. Louisa Howe of Boston City Hospital, Ching-tiao Chien of Boston State Hospital, and Bingham Dai of Duke University; and Warren Bennis and Donald Klein of the National Training Laboratories–Institute of Applied Behavioral Science.

We want to express our special appreciation to Raymond Bauer of Harvard for implanting the idea that such a study would be worthwhile and for showing the way with his pioneer example for Soviet psychology. John Lindbeck, then of Harvard and now of Columbia, helped indispensably in getting our work under way. Completion of it would have been infinitely more difficult without the sustaining faith and encouragement of Kenneth Benne of Boston University, John Pelzel of Harvard, and Harold Isaacs and Lucien Pye of M.I.T. We also want to thank Nancy Poling of the M.I.T.

Center for International Studies staff for the editorial skill and patience with which she made many improvements in the manuscript.

Robert Chin
Ai-li S. Chin

January 1969
Belmont, Massachusetts

CONTENTS

PSYCHOLOGICAL RESEARCH IN
COMMUNIST CHINA: 1949-1966

CHAPTER ONE

INTRODUCTION

One of the consequences of the political revolution of 1949 in China was an intellectual revolution in all scientific and humanistic fields. Almost immediately after the revolution, the Marxist-Leninist mode of thought was adopted for all academic and professional activities, scarcely two or three generations after an even greater wrench away from the Confucian tradition toward the twentieth century Western mode of thought. The discipline of psychology was no exception: its modest beginnings in the days of the Republic had to be scrapped, and it had to be re-established and relegitimized under the Chinese People's Republic. A discipline having scientific claims had to be integrated with Marxist-Leninist doctrines and the thought of Mao Tse-tung, and a new science built that could provide a psychological basis for the "new socialist citizen." The fate of psychology must be studied as a fluctuating process of adjustment between ideological pressure and political movements on the one hand and methodology and the maturation of ideas on the other. For even within the confines of ideological orthodoxy and political correctness, there is some room for variation in the form of theory and research. And conversely, the logic of a science can push the investigation of problems to the borderline of ideological correctness. By studying the emergence of a new academic tradition, or the revamping of an old one, we hope to obtain some insight into the influence of ideology and politics upon knowledge building, which in turn may help toward an understanding of the total society.

The present study might be considered one example of a number of inquiries into the interaction of intellectual life and the evolving Chinese ideology. There have been worthy precedents in these efforts, including Li Cho-ming's work on the use of economics and economists, Merle Goldman's research into the fate of literary men and women, and the work of Albert Feuerwerker and others in historiography in mainland China.[1] In the behavioral sciences, we have only a very sketchy idea of what has taken place.[2] Sociology was abolished in the very first years of the present regime, while social anthropologists, who flourished briefly in community studies just before the Communists came to power, are now largely restricted to the study of minority problems related to the implementation of government policy. Psychology, by comparison, enjoyed some degree of acceptance as a scientific field and some scope to function and grow. This study of psychology in mainland China thus has to assume the burden of discovering what was happening to the ideas and applica-

[1] Li Cho-ming, *Economic Development of Communist China* (Berkeley, Calif.: University of California Press, 1959); Merle Goldman, *Literary Dissent in Communist China* (Cambridge, Mass.: Harvard University Press, 1967); and studies in Chinese Communist historiography by Albert Feuerwerker and others in various issues of the *China Quarterly*, several of which have been collected in a volume entitled *History in Communist China* (Cambridge, Mass.: The M.I.T. Press, 1968). See also Albert Feuerwerker and Sally Cheng, *Chinese Communist Studies of Modern Chinese History* (Cambridge, Mass.: Harvard University Press, 1961), especially the Introduction, "Chinese Communist Historiography," pp. vii–xxv.

[2] See, for example, Maurice Freedman, "Sociology in China: A Brief Survey," *China Quarterly*, No. 10 (April–June 1962), pp. 166–173, and "A Chinese Phase in Social Anthropology," *British Journal of Sociology*, No. 14 (March 1963), pp. 1–19.

tions in the behavioral science of man up to the onset of the Cultural Revolution.

As a profession, psychology was small in terms of absolute numbers or by Western standards. Its actual or potential influence on policy matters cannot be documented; our impression is that it was slight and indirect. As for scientific accomplishments, Chinese psychologists were at a rudimentary stage, unlike Soviet scientists who have made internationally recognized advances in certain areas, such as work on the orienting reflex in perception. Nevertheless, the ideas, concepts, and researches in mainland Chinese psychology may be considered a crystallization of the prevalent ideological views on man. For both psychological knowledge and the thinking of national leaders were partly derived from the same doctrinal source, the same ideological orthodoxy. Spelling out these psychological concepts may serve as a screen upon which theories implicit in the political control and redirection of individual and mass behavior can be viewed in a clearer, sharper form.

From the Marxist-Leninist tradition, there was derived a particular psychological view of man characteristic of Communist China's men of power. Their belief, indeed almost mystical faith, in the efficacy of correct ideas or the power of doctrine was evident behind mass campaigns such as the Great Leap Forward and the Cultural Revolution. As John W. Lewis demonstrates in his analysis of the Secret Military Papers, internal dislocations and economic disasters are typically met with doctrinal revival:

> In the Chinese scheme of things, revolutionary doctrine, if "properly" carried out, moulds the society and policy into an operative unit. When in 1960, Party leaders became fully aware of the domestic upheaval that confronted them, they turned with missionary-like zeal to doctrinal positions which first had been given meaning in the years of revolutionary war. Indeed Party cadres who express themselves in the *Bulletin* recall other near-fatal periods — 1927–29, 1934–35, and 1941–42 — in which adherence to doctrine sup-

3

posedly saved the day and out of which came a sharper understanding of the tools of revolution. The desire to duplicate the doctrinal revival of earlier years thus came to dominate the elite after 1960.[3]

In psychological theory, a parallel reliance is placed on the function of knowing or of correct "recognition," which, it is assumed, in turn motivates socially desired behavior.

Once a system of knowledge attains legitimate status in a new society, it can be used as post-factum justification of policy. In psychology, the one example of such use was the rationale for thought reform spelled out in detailed psychological terms and steps. It is clear that, historically, Chinese psychology could not have contributed to the practice of thought reform in mainland China, for thought reform there antedated the new Soviet-style psychology by at least a decade. All the evidence we have shows that, aside from their Soviet origin, techniques of thought reform were perfected by party cadres through practice without benefit of academic psychology. Yet after the field reached a stage of readiness, a psychologist came forth with a scientific explanation of the desirability and efficacy of thought reform. And as we shall note in the discussion of treatment procedures in medical psychology, thought reform is one manifestation of the general process of re-education and therapy.

This study will begin with a discussion of the importation of Soviet psychology into mainland China and will attempt to trace Chinese modifications in the ideas and practices in light of the new national and political setting. We hope to accomplish this by examining the research and teaching activities of the Chinese psychologists, by outlining the main branches of the discipline, and by analyzing the major issues of the developing psychology.

[3] John L. Lewis, "China's Secret Military Papers: 'Continuities' and 'Revelations,'" in Roderick MacFarquhar, ed., *China Under Mao: Politics Takes Command* (Cambridge, Mass.: The M.I.T. Press, 1966), p. 67.

ROOTS OF WESTERN PSYCHOLOGY IN PRE–1949 CHINA

Psychology in China before 1949 was almost entirely American in nature and in origin. During the intellectual and social ferment in post–World War I China, disciples of Dewey looked to his functionalism and pragmatism as a powerful weapon with which to implement ambitious programs of social reform. While the actual impact of Dewey's psychology on larger reform schemes is difficult to assess, it did have pervasive influence on educational circles.

Psychology was introduced in the Chinese universities as early as the mid-teens of this century, and leading works such as those of William James, the psychological parent of Dewey, were already being translated. Shortly thereafter, the first department of psychology was established at Nanking Teachers' College under the leadership of Lu Chih-wei and Ch'en Hao-ch'ien, soon to be followed by departments at Peking, Tsinghua, Yenching, and Futan Universities. A psychological journal was started by Chang Yao-hsiang. When the original Academia Sinica was established in 1928, it included a unit on psychology headed by T'ang Yueh. The Chinese Association of Psychological Testing was founded in 1930, and the Chinese Psychological Society came into being in 1937. By this time, a few Chinese texts were available and the translation program of Western works continued. General psychology was being taught in a number of colleges, and educational psychology was rapidly gaining popularity.

During the thirties, a great deal of national attention was focused on education and language reform as a primary means of modernizing China. Psychologists therefore devoted much energy to studying how one learns and, in particular, how the Chinese language is learned. Great hopes were pinned on psychology as a science, for it was thought that it could solve many of the perplexing problems of modernization.

5

In a general sense, it could be said that John Dewey created psychology in China through his works, his students, and his personal presence. Dewey was lecturing in China on and off for two years in 1919–1920. Coming at the height of the intellectual revolution that was to encompass every aspect of China's cultural life, Dewey's ideas in philosophy and psychology were promulgated with great enthusiasm. Indeed, T'sai Yuan-p'ei, Chancellor of Peking University, introduced Dewey to a Chinese audience in 1918 as a thinker greater than Confucius.[4] The majority of the early Chinese educational and experimental psychologists were trained at either the University of Chicago, where Dewey first worked with the psychologists Angell and Carr, or at Columbia University, where Dewey continued to develop his theories.

Chan Wing-tsit, in his history of modern Chinese philosophy, noted that pragmatism was the first Western philosophy to become a concerted movement in China: "It was the guiding philosophy of the renaissance set in motion by Dewey's pupil, Hu Shih. . . . Its philosophy of ideas as instruments to cope with actual situations and its emphasis on results had special appeal to the reformers."[5] As for the content of what was to be studied in psychology, Dewey advocated a "functional" definition. Dewey did not believe human responses to be passive, isolated reflexes. Mental and behavioral processes, he insisted, could not be disengaged from their conditions and, more significantly, their consequences. What was to be considered "stimulus" and what was to be considered "response" were not abstract entities but depended on the part each played in the coordinated efforts of the organism to reach a goal or adapt to the environment.[6] These views implied a favorable attitude toward

---

[4] Joseph R. Levenson, *Modern China and Its Confucian Past* (Garden City, N.J.: Doubleday Anchor, 1964), p. 147.

[5] Chan Wing-tsit, "Trends in Philosophy," Chapter XX, in Harley MacNair, ed., *China* (Berkeley, Calif.: University of California Press, 1946).

[6] John Dewey, "The Reflex Arc Concept in Psychology," *Psychology Review*, July 1896, pp. 357–370.

the applied branches of psychology. Indeed, Dewey had already committed himself to a combination of psychology and education prior to going to China.[7]

Under Dewey's influence, educators in China began to take an interest in the child as an individual; and there was an increased emphasis among educational psychologists on studying those factors that the child brought to the learning situation: his aptitudes and his capabilities. The old, established educational practices of rote learning characterizing the classic Chinese education were now to be judged according to their results for the individual child. In time, the viewpoints of functionalism permeated other technical concepts of educational philosophy and such specialties as testing and teacher training.

Functionalism fitted into the mood of the times; and complemented by the traditional Chinese tendency toward pragmatic behavior, it might be said that Dewey's pragmatic philosophy became an ideology in China. More important, the new philosophy not only allowed but insisted on revamping and reconstructing no less than all of the behavioral and cultural patterns, subjecting them to the tests of usefulness and adaptability in contemporary situations. With the elaboration of these doctrines into a methodology of "scientific testing" of the functions and consequences of a pattern of acting, there was, indeed, a rallying point for all the revolutionaries in China. The reconstructionists in philosophy represented a methodology and a set of substantial values on how people should act. Social reformers of all kinds in China could find their home in these views. Thus, Dewey inspired Chinese intellectuals in finding a philosophy of change and reform.

With the main course of development defined by func-

---

[7] In his presidential address before the 1899 convention of psychologists, Dewey argued for the application of systematic psychological knowledge to the school and the educative process. See "Psychology and Social Practice," in Joseph Ratner, ed., *Philosophy and Social Practice* (New York: Putnam Brothers, 1963), pp. 295–315.

tionalism in psychology and pragmatism in education and social reform, other schools of psychology were introduced, too, although in very minor ways. Gestalt psychology, with its abstract emphasis on the whole and on organization, did not have many proponents. Psychoanalysis was present in very circumscribed ways in a few quarters. The other points of view that did take some root were experimental psychology, industrial psychology (the Taylor system), and behaviorism.

Behaviorism came into China via Kuo Zing-yang (Z. Y. Kuo), probably the Chinese psychologist best known to the West for his contribution to psychology. Influenced by J. B. Watson at the University of Chicago, Kuo assumed an even more extreme behaviorist position than Watson's. In the post–World War I period, when the concepts of instinct and innate human nature and behavior were being attacked by many, including Boas in anthropology and Floyd Allport in social behavior, Kuo moved in 1921–1922 forthrightly to insist on discarding the concept of instinct altogether. Among his arguments, he pointed out that the concept was based on the old exploded notion of innateness and the operation of a mental or spiritual force. He insisted that all so-called instincts were learned and that even reflexes were acquired. At an international meeting of psychology in the twenties, he exclaimed, "There are only one and a half true behaviorists in this world; Watson is the half. I am the only true behaviorist."

Following the line of Kuo, Watson, in his next book on behaviorism, came out strongly for a psychology without instincts. Kuo continued publishing his empirical research on embryonic behavior and reflexes through the early thirties.

Two psychologists who were better known in China in this period were C. W. Luh and Chou Siegen. Luh later became administrator for Yenching University and is known for his replications of the massive and classic studies of Ebbinghaus on learning nonsense syllables. Chou Siegen is noted for his work in assessment and personnel selection. Other active psychologists included Ts'ai Loh-seng in comparative psychology, William K. C. Ch'en in attitude measurement, and Randolph Sailor, an American psychologist trained at Teacher's College, Columbia University, who taught at Yenching University for many decades.

The onset of the war with Japan halted all developments. Although the teaching of psychology continued on a reduced scale in the refugee universities in West China, and to some extent on some of the occupied campuses, growth of the field was not to be resumed again in the same direction. At the end of World War II, some of the Chinese psychologists abroad joined the few colleagues who remained in China, but 1949 marked the end of the era of Western psychology on the mainland, and a new one began.

In 1949, as the National Government moved to Taiwan, many of the psychologists came to the United States, but psychology and its associations were reconstituted on the island, including its journal now known as *Acta Psychologica Taiwanica*. National Taiwan University, along with other schools, offers a major in psychology with some attention to educational psychology. The Chinese Psychological Association and the Association for Testing have also continued. A full story of the development of psychology on Taiwan has not been written, but Su Hsiang-yü, a leading psychologist there, has published a summary of the developments.[8]

ROOTS IN SOVIET PSYCHOLOGY

There was no discernible Soviet influence on Chinese psychological circles before the changeover. After 1949, however, the budding Western-inspired psychology in China

---

[8] Su Hsiang-yü, "Development of Psychology in China in the Last Decade" (in Chinese), *Acta Psychologica Taiwanica: Science Reports of National Taiwan University*, pp. 112–115.

was deliberately obliterated and systematically reconstructed on the premises of Soviet theories and methodology.

"Soviet psychology," at the time it was introduced into mainland China, had itself undergone considerable change. While the changes do not directly concern us here, there are strands and issues of this early history that found their echoes in the debates accompanying the retraining of Chinese psychologists. In these pages we shall not presume to give a comprehensive summary of early psychology in the Soviet Union but will only touch upon those developmental elements that help us understand the formation of a Communist Chinese psychology. This discussion of Soviet roots is based on the scholarly work of such American psychologists as Gregory Razran, Ivan London, Raymond Bauer, Alexander Mintz, and Josef Brozek.

The Soviet psychology that Peking modeled itself upon was a Marxist-Leninist psychology with a philosophical base in dialectical materialism and a newly added label, Pavlovianism. This new Soviet psychology leaned heavily on Lenin's theory of reflection, which was unearthed in his two volumes posthumously published in 1924. Toward the late twenties, a group of Soviet research psychologists headed by Vygotskii, along with Luria and Leont'ev, laid the groundwork for a Marxist-Leninist approach to psychic development. Man's psyche was viewed by this group as a historical, developmental product, with emphasis on the social roots of different aspects of man's consciousness. Thus, the Soviet psychology that China imported in the fifties proposed dialectical materialism as the only position that truly unites the subjective and objective worlds; image and reality were presented as inseparable parts of the same reflection process. Here, Soviet psychology contrasted itself with Western "idealistic" psychology in which, it is maintained, consciousness or the image in man's mind comes first and objective reality is secondary.

When Lenin's theory of reflection became popular in the

10

thirties, it provided the philosophical bridge between Pavlovian physiology and psychic processes. In fact, Pavlov was wooed by Lenin and, later, Stalin for many years with awards and sinecures, but during most of his lifetime he expressed contempt and disdain for the Soviet regime and ill-concealed rejection of its interference with science. In 1952, in a seminar sponsored by the Academy of Pedagogical Sciences and attended by over 400 psychologists, it was officially promulgated to build psychology on the philosophical base of dialectical and historical materialism as well as on Pavlov's teachings on the higher nervous system.

Pavlov considered his major work on the conditioned reflex to belong to neurology and physiology, defining his proper concern as problems of sensation and perception and the origin of consciousness. In fact, he dissociated himself from psychology for most of his life. During the three years before his death in 1936, he became interested in verbal behavior and the function of consciousness. These activities of the higher nervous system he called the second signal system. The second signal system — in Chinese, *ti-erh-hao hsin-hsi* — refers to those reflexes in man that respond to verbal stimuli; it is specific to man and is distinguished from the first signal system by the capabilities of abstraction and generalization. This concept enabled Pavlovian physiology to be linked up with psychology, for the physiological process of nervous excitation and inhibition could be applied to mental activity involving language. Nevertheless, psychology in the Soviet Union was never revamped completely into Pavlovian schemes; and certainly, by the late fifties, a good deal of the work there went beyond Pavlov's original position and interest.

Besides Pavlovianism, a few other strands in the Soviet psychological heritage should be mentioned, although officially their status was vanquished by the joint position of dialectical materialism and Pavlovianism. The faint shape of their ghosts was evident at the criticism-debate meetings of the Peking psychologists, which will be discussed in Chapter Two. What Pavlovian psychology displaced, in a sense, was Bekhterev's *reflexology* and Kornilov's *reactology*. Reflexology, which flourished in the Soviet Union in the twenties, was comparable to American behaviorism, struggling with the same sort of issues and in the same terms of reference as the psychological dispute then current in America. Reactology also stressed motor activity but added the study of human personality. Both these strands stood in opposition to Pavlov's physiological explanation of behavior and they gained temporary ascendence. In time, however, Bekhterev and Kornilov came to be criticized as examples of "vulgar materialism" or "mechanistic materialism." Their views were attacked because they saw the human brain to be on the same level as other matter, giving only a mechanical response to outside stimuli, while the acceptable Soviet position maintained that the brain is autogenetic and is capable of setting its own direction, of integrating responses on a higher level. This new position, although still based on materialism, focused on the "class theory" of social behavior, a theory that required the active intervention of the human brain.

Reflection (*fan-she*) is the basic Leninist statement of relationship between man and his external world. This concept provides the link between objective reality and psychological reality. The human brain knows the world because it mirrors objective reality. What distinguishes man's reflective activity from that of lower forms of matter is psychological or mental activity. Thus, reflection of the external world, including the social world, by the human brain in the form of various psychic phenomena constitutes subjective activity. It is this process, by which objective reality is translated into such subjective activities as sensation, perception, memory, attention, thought, and so forth, that forms the definition of psychology. Since the process of reflection itself is a neutral process, all conditions in external nature can be reflected on the human brain, including contradictions. What provides moving power for *human* reflective processes is consciousness.

When the Soviet concept of consciousness was introduced into Communist China, it resulted in three corresponding Chinese terms. The simplest and most direct rendering of consciousness into *i-shih* was in accordance with existing and commonsense usage of ideographs. More often, however, the complex term "active consciousness," or *tzu-chueh neng-tung-li,* was used, thus emphasizing the energy or moving power of consciousness. This concept appears to have been used interchangeably with that of *chu-kuan neng-tung-li,* "subjective consciousness" or "subjective initiative," although the latter is less often found. One Chinese psychologist compared the moving power of the active consciousness with man's positive nature, creative nature, voluntary nature, spiritual nature, purposive nature, and predictive nature (*chi-chi hsing, ch'uang-chao hsing, chu-tung hsing, ling-huo hsing, mu-ti hsing, yü-chien hsing*). It was said to be manifested in subjective hard work, willful behavior, or struggle that is necessary to overcome difficulties.

In man, the process of reflection pivots on the function of consciousness. The concept of consciousness is almost coterminous with the subjective aspect of man, since no unconsciousness or subconsciousness is accorded theoretical status. Understanding the world and acting purposefully on it are inseparable processes. As the highest form of psychic activity, consciousness is unique to man and distinguishes him from lower forms of animals. Consciousness is derived from human society, representing a socially conditioned reflection of reality. Language, which is also a product of human society, is inseparable from consciousness. Consciousness is conceived as formed by the activities of man in society in concrete actions. Thus, mental processes cannot be studied in the abstract but only in the setting of concrete activities.

The other characteristic of this active consciousness, besides its autogenetic quality, is that it is conscious of itself, or possesses the ability to reflect upon its own process. Thus, the moving power of the active consciousness is not absolutely free, mysterious, or uncontrolled by any regulations. It is said to work according to its own understanding of reality, utilizing objective principles to reach specified goals.

What distinguishes this concept of consciousness from the equivalent Western concept is that here consciousness is the supreme force governing man's behavior, unchallenged by competing forces such as the unconscious or the subconscious. Thus, the implication is that "correct" consciousness leads automatically to "correct" behavior. The other unique feature is that the goals to which correct consciousness leads are *ipso facto* the socially defined ends. At times, a certain automatic character is implied to the sequence that consciousness leads to socially desirable, goal-directed behavior. A fuller statement of this position would be that man strains toward correct consciousness, which tends to lead to desirable, goal-directed behavior. A further assumption is that *individual* goal-directed behavior automatically adds up to desirable *societal* goals. Little or no conceptual attention is paid to group pressures or to the individual's need to belong as intermediary between the individual and society.

Within the framework of active consciousness, the Chinese psychologists made most frequent use of the concept of recognition, paying only passing attention to the other two aspects of will and emotion. "Recognition," *jen-shih,* was the English term used by the Chinese psychologists themselves to refer to the function of understanding or knowing. The Chinese made a noun out of the verb "to recognize," thus giving the concept "recognition" a connotation that is closer to the circumlocution "way of recognizing or conceptualizing things." The concept of recognition was broader than the Western idea of cognition, for the former included not only the function of knowing but also a goal orientation. In fact, recognition implied the *acceptance* of the socially defined goals, for nonacceptance was called "incorrect recognition." There was no conceptual distinction between "knowing and not accepting" on the one hand and "not knowing and not accepting." In Communist theory, it was self-evident that all men, when enlightened, would follow the party line, since the party *ipso facto* showed the correct road to the ideal socialist society.

Another frequently used concept borrowed from Soviet psychology was *individuality* or individual character, *ko-hsing chu-i*; man develops a habitual or repeated way of reflecting objective reality — which is his individuality. One's recognition function and the self-consciousness of goals form the core of this individuality. The concept also included emotion and will, ability and temperament, but these factors were decidedly subordinate. Ability and temperament as used by Chinese psychologists were not static entities but could change according to man's reflective activity, that is, according to experience. Individuality is not self-moving but is moved by activity of consciousness. Class individuality is a repeated tendency of reflection common to members of a social class, a counterpart on the class level to individuality. Individuality may or may not have been viewed by mainland psychologists as completely class-bound, depending upon whether one belonged to the scientific faction or the activist faction of psychology. If one emphasized the abstract processes of the brain, one would point to the universal quality of the processes as well as to individual differences cutting across class lines. But if, as the activists maintained, man's existence was entirely class conditioned, then individuality would be inseparable from class individuality. It must be stated here that these concepts were not treated by mainland psychologists as research tools to be operationally defined in each study. Rather, they were concepts in a basic theoretical system, employed as ways of categorizing phenomena or of explaining events. As such, these concepts were not subjected to revision on the basis of empirical findings; at times, they were only implicit in research writings.

With this brief history in mind, the major components of

15

the Soviet psychology introduced into China can be described in more detail.

In addition to outlining the basic positions that went into the making of a Sovietized Chinese psychology, a word should be said about Soviet research methods, the ways in which Soviet psychologists choose relevant topics for study and define new directions for the field. These also had their impact on Chinese slants and approaches developed since the inception of the Soviet-inspired psychology. The Soviet psychologists have been less heavily experimental than their American colleagues, if we classify the early Pavlovian work under neurology and physiology rather than psychology. Instead of the deliberate creation and manipulation of different states of the variable under "artificial" conditions, the Soviet model of experimentation makes use of a more "natural" setting, controlling one or a few variables at a time. Perhaps related to this leaning has been the avoidance of complex statistical techniques. Rudimentary forms of statistics are used, supplemented by descriptive notations; inferential or probability statistics have not been developed.

The Soviet approach to selecting areas for investigation has not been one of *laissez-faire* but rather a careful canvassing for ideological and practical requirements. There is also a characteristic style of determining direction and achieving consensus in psychology through meetings or "open discussions" that signal major alternations in line and approach. Whether or not an area of empirical work is to be tackled depends upon arguments pro and con, on the basis of derivations from basic Marxist-Leninist theories. Problems are not always chosen from scientific requirements intrinsic to the field; that is, results of the testing of hypotheses, concepts, or theories. Rather, the basic conceptual framework is a set of assumptions not to be constantly challenged or replaced through empirical testing.

They have been succinctly summarized as follows: [9] (1)

[9] While earlier versions of these principles are reported in Soviet

the principle of materialist monism — that mental phenomena are a property of the brain, upon which the psychological activities are superimposed; (2) the principle of determinism — that there is constant interaction between processes of higher nervous activity and the external environment; (3) the principle of reflection — that consciousness is a subjective reflection of an objective reality; (4) the principle of unity of consciousness and activity — that man's mind is formed in activity and manifested in activity; and (5) the principle of historicism — that mind develops in the process of the historical development of man.

In the next chapter, we shall discuss how Soviet psychology and the needs of the new Communist state changed the shape of Chinese psychology after 1949, as reflected in the organization and activities of government institutes, psychology departments, and professional associations. Chapters Three, Four, and Five describe and evaluate in more detail the experimental and theoretical development of medical psychology, labor psychology, and educational psychology; and Chapter Six, on moral character and individuality, attempts to discern in the emerging psychology indications of sociocultural limitations. We shall conclude with an assessment of the position and character of psychology in China as of the beginning of the Cultural Revolution.

------

writings in the early forties, we have used P. R. Rudik, *Psichologia* (Psychology), Moscow Fizkul'turai Sport, 1958, as reported by Josef Brozek, "Soviet Psychology," in Melvin Marx and William Hillix, ed., *Systems and Theories in Psychology* (New York: McGraw-Hill, 1963).

CHAPTER TWO

EVOLUTION OF THE PROFESSION: 1949-1966

Since 1949 there has been a constant pull in China between internal scientific pressures in psychology, complicated by the introduction of Pavlovianism, and such external pressures as the anti-rightists movements and the Great Leap Forward. These tensions were expressed at times as organizational realignments, and we shall begin this chapter with a discussion of the post-1949 history of the Institute of Psychology, the teaching of psychology, and the Chinese Psychological Society. The cross-pressures of the first decade of Communist rule came most sharply to light in the criticism-debate meetings of 1958–1959, which preceded the Great Leap phase in psychology, a period when psychology was most clearly responding to state needs. We will describe these debates here as background for our subsequent accounts of psychological activity during the Great Leap period.

THE INSTITUTE OF PSYCHOLOGY IN THE ACADEMY OF SCIENCES

The field of psychology was given formal recognition in 1950, when the newly established Chinese Academy of

18

Sciences, a direct organ under the State Council, set up a preparatory committee for psychology. The structure of the National Academy was a carryover from Nationalist days, though its function was more like that of its Soviet counterpart. The Nationalist Academia Sinica was a society in which members enjoyed the privilege of research under government subsidy, while the new Academy of Sciences had the responsibility for setting directions for the field under Party surveillance. As a student of Soviet psychology pointed out, each Academy institute developed a coherent program of research dominated by a senior figure, much in the tradition of European laboratories.

A first aim of the centralized Academy in Communist China was to give psychologists of established reputation the task of rebuilding the discipline. To judge by the general goals of the Academy, this preparatory committee was (1) to reorganize and consolidate the research institutes of the country; (2) to provide for a continuation of research activities and plans, relating them to requirements in industry, education, and national construction; (3) to compile a national roster of scientists and work out assignments for them on a planned basis; (4) to develop plans to increase China's scientific manpower in cooperation with the universities through training programs, foreign education, and recruitment of Chinese scientists abroad; and (5) to educate research workers in Marxism-Leninism.[1]

In 1951, the Academy of Sciences established the Psychology Research Office, which expanded into the Institute of Psychology five years later. At that time, it absorbed the personnel and equipment of the Psychology Department at Nanking University. (Subsequently, all psychology courses at Nanking were offered under the physiology department.) Establishment of the Institute points to an over-all policy in

[1] John M. H. Lindbeck, "The Organization and Development of Science," in "Science in Communist China," *The China Quarterly,* No. 6 (April–June 1961), pp. 98–132, especially pp. 104–105.

the early years of concentrating scarce scientific resources into a central organ for research. The Institute was placed under the Department of Philosophy and Social Sciences, one of the five departments of the Academy. As the central governmental organ for the pursuit of basic research, the Academy appointed to its various institutes the nation's most eminent scientists in each field. The Institute of Psychology therefore had on its staff top specialists in each branch of psychology. P'an Shu, a Ph.D. from the University of Chicago (1926), was director of the Institute from its inception at least until the Cultural Revolution, and Ts'ao Jih-ch'ang, chief theoretician, with a Ph.D. from Cambridge University, England (1948), was its deputy director. These Institute leaders were, as of 1966, also top men in the Psychological Society and its professional publication.

Besides P'an Shu and Ts'ao Jih-ch'ang, four of the six other known members of the Institute of Psychology had been educated in the United States and another in Canada. In the list of 78 eminent psychologists prepared by P'an Shu,[2] 51 had received their advanced degrees in the United States, 12 in other countries abroad, and only 15 in Chinese universities.

The role of leadership of the Institute of Psychology was heightened in 1956 when it undertook the training of postgraduate students. (Two other institutions were giving graduate courses in psychology at this time, Peking University and Hua-tung Normal University.) At the Institute, advanced students, besides taking prescribed scientific and ideological courses, were assigned in small numbers to in-

---

[2] Given by P'an Shu to a European psychologist, coeditor with Eugene Jacobson, for the *International Directory of Psychologists* (Washington, D.C.: National Academy of Sciences, National Research Council Publication No. 520, 1958), pp. 94–99. This list is highly selective; many psychologists holding responsible positions or with important publications are not included. However, it is the only available list prepared by Communist Chinese psychologists themselves.

dividual senior staff members for training and guidance.[3] In 1956, the Academy announced a plan to begin granting a four-year *fu-po-shih* degree, or associate doctorate, but no further information has been published on this program. The strong influence of the Institute scientists in the early years is further suggested by its program of research inspection. A Central Inspection Committee delegated inspection teams to examine research organization both within and outside the Institute, which was the main granting agency of awards and prizes for scientific achievements.[4]

Retraining in Soviet Psychology

P'an Shu, head of the Academy psychologists throughout the period of this study, has written: "During the first few years, members of the Psychology Research Office spent most of their time learning Marxism-Leninism, engaging in thought remolding, learning Russian, Pavlov, and Soviet psychology, and translating Soviet works of psychology." [5]

A central program of the professional's retraining was a summer seminar in 1953 for the study of Pavlov, sponsored jointly by the Ministry of Public Health, the Academy of Sciences, the Central Physicians Board, and the All-China Federation of Natural Scientists. About twenty leading psychologists took part, along with the nation's top physiologists and physicians. This nucleus of twenty psychologists in turn

[3] A calculation of the rough proportion of senior staff to younger professionals in the Academy as a whole would give us about a dozen students of psychology at the Institute in the mid- to late fifties.

[4] See L. A. Orleans, *Professional Manpower and Education in Communist China* (Washington, D.C.: National Science Foundation, 1961), especially pp. 77 and 112.

[5] All historical data in this section on the organizational structure and change of psychology in the Academy are taken from the following article by P'an, unless otherwise stated: P'an Shu, "Chung-kuo hsin-li-hsueh ti hsien-chuang ho fa-chan ch'ü-hsiang" (A general review of psychology in China), *Hsin-li-hsueh-pao* (*Acta Psychologica Sinica*), No. 1 (1958), pp. 3–8. This reference is to p. 5.

conducted a shorter, two-day discussion meeting with other psychologists. Psychology was officially launched along its new Pavlovian line and brought in a closer theoretical congruence with the biological sciences.

That psychologists were asked to meet with the natural scientists and the medical profession for theoretical rehabilitation indicates that the authorities viewed psychology as a science, or at least closely allied to science, and accorded it the academic status and privileges of a scientific field. Indeed, in 1956 the Scientific Planning Commission of the State Council asked the Academy psychologists to produce a 12-year Scientific Development Plan. Major directions of this plan were stated in terms of conventional academic divisions of the field: (1) origin and development of the mind; (2) basic stages of the mind; (3) psychology of individuality; (4) basic theories and history of psychology; and (5) special branches in education, medicine, art and literature, and physical culture. When P'an Shu reported on the plan, he called psychology "one of the basic sciences," undoubtedly echoing an official definition.

Indeed, in the course of the retraining, Western psychology was denounced as a form of idealism without foundations on a materialistic basis and therefore without scientific validity. More specifically, educational testing came under heavy attack in light of the socialist faith in the perfectibility of man through environmental alteration. Western testing was said to be the measurement of inborn capacities, and a "fatalistic" belief in heredity was attributed to the testers. Following Pavlovian methodology closely, an experimental, laboratory approach to psychological studies was sanctioned. Because of a simultaneous emphasis on consciousness, subjective data also were permitted; but a thin line was drawn between the permitted use of subjective data and Western "introspection," for the latter was associated with "unscientific" Western idealism.

By 1956, psychologists in the Academy and in institutions of high learning were just beginning to turn their attention to original research, for hitherto, what little "research" they did was described by P'an Shu as incidental to their Pavlovian learning, "a by-product of the professional re-redirection," aimed at "familiarizing themselves with Pavlovian research methods, testing of Pavlovian theories, or the re-examination of past psychological studies from the Pavlovian point of view."

Psychology in the Ministry of Education

In addition to the State-sponsored Academy, the State Ministry of Education also apparently had some responsibility, either directly or indirectly, for professional activities in the field of educational psychology. In 1957, the Ministry planned to open an Educational Science Research Institute (*Chiao-yü k'o-hsueh yen-chiu so*),[6] with a section on educational psychology. This section was supposed to share research responsibilities with the Educational Psychology Division of the Institute of Psychology and develop research on (1) children's psychological age, (2) educational psychology, (3) psychology of character development, (4) psychological factors in the training of productive techniques, and (5) history of educational psychology and criticism of capitalist educational psychology.[7] Thus, there seems to have been a great deal of overlap in assignment between these two organs. But whereas the Institute group has published much of what we know about educational psychology research, almost nothing is known about the output of its counterpart under the Ministry of Education. We know that Ch'en Yuan-hui, a leader in educational psychology and an empiricist method-

[6] This may have been later renamed *chiao-hsueh chi k'o-hsueh yen-chiu ssu* (Office of teaching and scientific research), reported by Chi Wang in 1961 to be under the Ministry of Education. See *Mainland China Organizations of Higher Learning in Science and Technology and Their Publications* (Washington, D.C.: U.S. Government Printing Office, 1961), p. 70.

[7] P'an Shu, "Chung-kuo hsin-li hsueh . . . , p. 6.

ologically, was an original member or perhaps head of the Ministry psychologists. It is possible that the Ministry group served mainly as an administrative or coordinating agency for local interdisciplinary organizations dealing with education workers, including psychologists, for we found references to provincial or city "Pedagogical Institutes." [8]

THE TEACHING OF PSYCHOLOGY

In the revamping of academic departments in the early fifties, psychology was preserved as a discipline and was allowed to expand and develop in certain directions. By comparison with other social sciences, psychology stood somewhere in the middle between importance and neglect, between independence and strict surveillance. Sociology had been eliminated and anthropology had been severely curtailed. History, however, was numerically much stronger, both because of its traditional strength and because of the central place of history in the study of Communist ideology. Since history is intrinsically linked to dialectical materialism, the content of history courses and texts had been continually under official scrutiny.[9] Philosophy as an academic field was perhaps closer to psychology in size. Philosophy was also centralized; only one of the 12 to 15 philosophy departments that existed in Nationalist China survived, and that one department was to specialize in the teaching of Marxism.[10]

To assess the place of psychology in the undergraduate curriculum, we must first differentiate the main categories of institutions of higher education. These categories were created soon after the changeover as the result of a systematic

[8] *International Directory of Psychologists*, p. 95.

[9] O. Briere, S.J., "Philosophy in the New Regime," *Soviet Survey*, No. 24 (April–June 1958) (special China issue), pp. 10–15.

[10] See Albert Feuerwerker and Sally Cheng, *Chinese Communist Studies of Modern Chinese History* (Cambridge, Mass.: Harvard University Press, 1961), Introduction: "Chinese Communist Historiography," pp. vii–xxv.

reorganization of higher education. Some colleges and universities, largely the foreign-supported missionary institutions, were either abolished or consolidated and nationalized; new ones were established. Leaving technical institutes out of consideration, there were four main categories: comprehensive universities (*tsung-ho ta-hsueh* — total of 16 in 1958); four-year normal universities (*shih-fan ta-hsueh* — three in 1958 and increased to four in 1960); four-year normal colleges (*shih-fan hsueh-yuen* — 47 in 1958); and two-year teachers' academies (*shih-fan chuan-k'o hsueh-hsiao* — 15 in 1958).[11]

Peking University and the Normal Universities and Colleges

Although there have been several psychologists on the faculties of many of the comprehensive universities and medical colleges, the undergraduate and graduate training of academic and research psychologists has been concentrated in Peking University. Peking introduced the first course in psychology in China in the first decade of this century, and as early as the twenties established a Department of Psychology. It was in continual existence until 1952,[12] when it was reclassified as a specialty and placed in the Department of Philosophy. One could get a bachelor's degree in the Psychology Specialty, Department of Philosophy. This is one of the three or four institutions that in 1958 had an "ade-

[11] Based on a survey of annual issues (1953–1958) of the *Kao-teng hsueh-hsiao chao-sheng sheng-hsueh chih-tao* (Registration bulletin for institutions of higher education), ed. by Ch'uan-kuo kao-teng hsueh-hsiao chao-sheng wei-yuan hui (Committee for the nationwide registration in institutions of higher education (Shanghai: Commercial Press, annual issues 1953–1958).

[12] According to the registration bulletin of the Ministry of Higher Education, this Department was not changed into a Specialty until 1954, but P'an Shu wrote in "Chung-kuo hsin-li-hsueh . . ." that the Specialty was established in the 1952 reorganization of academic departments.

quate" collection in psychological literature or in research literature.[13]

The Psychology Specialty at Peking University had a fairly strong faculty, with at least ten psychologists on its staff in 1957. To indicate the range of subject matter covered, the following courses were offered by the Psychology Specialty at Peking University in 1958: political theory, biology, human anatomy, human and animal physiology, foreign languages, Chinese philosophy or Western philosophy, logic, neurology, foundations of Pavlovian experimentation, general psychology, history of psychology, and child psychology.[14] The basic science courses were added in 1958, at which time there was a call for increased enrollment.

It is interesting to note two liberalizations in the curriculum for psychology majors between 1953 and 1958. The first was a lessening in the load of political courses. In 1954, students had to take foundations of Marxism-Leninism, political economy, dialectical materialism and historical materialism, and history of modern Chinese revolution (changed in 1955 into history of Chinese revolutions). All of these were later combined into a single course called political theory. The second change, in 1957, was an expansion of language electives beyond Russian. These changes coincided with the period of rapid expansion in psychology.

Peking University was among the first to respond to the call for Pavlovian experimentation in the mid-fifties when it set up an animal laboratory for the study of conditioned reflex; similar installations were made in a few other teaching centers, all with the aid of Soviet experts.[15]

Four Soviet psychologists are known to have lectured

[13] P'an Shu, "Chung-kuo hsin-li-hsueh. . . ."
[14] Kao-teng hsueh-hsiao . . . , 1958.
[15] P'an Shu, "Fa-hui chi-ti li-liang wei fa-chan fu-wu yü wo-kuo wei-ta ti she-hui chu-i ti k'o-hsueh erh fen-tou" (Develop group strength, struggle to expand scientific psychology to be of service to our great socialist construction), Hsin-li hsueh-pao, No. 1 (1956), pp. 1–10.

on Pavlovian psychology.[16] At that time the Education Ministry also had a Soviet adviser, who gave lectures to some Education Departments.[17] No further mention of Soviet advisers has been found since that period. Collaborative efforts in research between Soviet and Chinese psychologists appear very limited; we know only of a joint study on motor and vegetative components of conditioned feeding and defense responses.[18] We can assume that the Soviet or heavily Pavlovian period subsided in 1957, when the Great Leap Forward spirit took over.

At the time of our study, although the training of psychological specialists was concentrated at Peking University, the training of psychology workers was spread out among many normal institutions, both geographically and according to academic levels. Trained in psychology and education for teaching in secondary schools and other posts, the psychological workers were expected to help the masses "cultivate a superior character" and "develop their utmost capacities" for socialist construction. In prestige and intellectual level, the four normal universities appeared to stand closer to the better comprehensive universities than to the provincial normal colleges. It is unlikely that the kind of psychology taught at Peking Normal University was very different in quality from that of the degree program at Peking University. The great spread in psychology curriculum was between the top normal universities and the small normal colleges in remote areas.

Although there was no separate degree in educational psychology, there was an education department in each of the original three normal universities: Hua-tung Normal University at Shanghai, Tung-pei Normal University at Ch'ang-

---

[16] We know that they lectured at Peking Normal University — perhaps at other institutions as well.

[17] "Chiao-yü yen-chiu," *Kuang-ming jih-pao*, May 16, 1955.

[18] Yvonne Brackbill, "Research and Clinical Work with Children," in Raymond Bauer, ed., *Some Views on Soviet Psychology* (Washington, D.C.: American Psychological Association, 1962).

ch'un, and Peking Normal University. (It was not discovered whether the newer Shih-chia-chuang Normal University had an education department.) Of the 50 four-year normal colleges in 1958, 10 had education departments. It seems reasonable to assume that a more extensive psychology curriculum was offered in those institutions with education departments than in those without. The required psychology courses in education departments were general psychology, child psychology, and anatomy. In addition, the practicum of the teacher-training program included 34 hours of laboratory work in general psychology, according to regulations set up by the Ministry of Education in 1954.[19] Because of this wide penetration, it may be fair to assume that the practical implications of psychology were given some degree of recognition and that psychology had a certain role within the educational system through teacher training, though we found no direct evidence of its influence on educational policy.

TEACHING MATERIALS

Popular Lectures on the Learning Process

What psychology has to say about children and ways of handling them of course has to be considered in conjunction with the dictates of ideology, as well as society's store of commonsense assumptions and the natural selection process that attracts certain personality types to the teaching profession. In the Soviet Union, for example, American psychologists and educators have observed a remarkable degree of personal warmth and motherly attitude among those who handle the very young, in spite of the rigorous institutional routine concerning their physical care and exercise. Aside from glimpses of the formal program in day nurseries, we do not have any sophisticated firsthand observations of the teacher-pupil relationship in Communist China. The teacher-

[19] P'an Shu, "Chung-kuo hsin-li hsueh. . . ."

pupil relationship in pre–Communist China was a solemn one in which the maintenance of respect was paramount. Although children might have been treated with warmth and indulgence outside the school situation, such an atmosphere had no place in the classroom. Children were viewed as rational beings, little adults who were able to control themselves. It is doubtful that this picture has changed fundamentally under Communist rule, although the position of children has been elevated in relation to the rest of the adult world, and the activities and views of children have been taken into serious consideration. What we can provide here are some indirect indications of the trained outlook among teachers, based on the pedagogical view that once children are taught what is good — that is, once they have the correct recognition — desirable behavior will follow. There is little room in current psychological thinking on the mainland for the role of emotions, which, if considered, would make the task of training the child more elusive.

The psychological concepts supporting current Chinese educational practice were discussed in a series of "popular psychology lectures" published in *Chiao-shih pao, The Teachers' Newspaper,* in 1957. Since this semiweekly publication was aimed at the rank-and-file teacher, including the older teachers who would not have gone through the new teacher-training system, the lectures could bring the ordinary teacher up to date on some sort of scientific psychological basis for his teaching methods. The series presented in simplified form the contents of the new Communist psychology in its early phase, along with practical advice on teaching procedures based on these principles.

This popular psychology series came to be published because, according to the editors, many teachers wrote letters to *Chiao-shih pao* complaining of their lack of knowledge of psychology and consequent inability to deal with many problems in teaching. The paper responded by inviting three psychologists to write on 12 different topics in general psychology. The resulting 17 lectures can be taken as an indication of the kind of influence psychology indirectly exerted on methods of classroom teaching in the fifties; the contents thus warrant a review.

Pavlovianism and an emphasis on consciousness and will were apparent throughout. Some of the more obvious ways in which the psychological assumptions behind these lectures differed from Western conceptions included the distinction made between "intentional attention" and "unintentional attention" and the assertion that "belief in the Communist morality" constituted "energy to push behavior." No other factors were mentioned as motivation for behavior. The opening lectures dealt with the nature of children. Character, they said, was not inborn, as Mencius and Hsun-tzu believed, but was formed by experience, society, class origin, family, and school. Children who had not yet matured in body and mind were unable to understand clearly their own strengths and shortcomings. "They are not yet adept at controlling their own behavior." Psychology was the study of the reflection of the objective world on the brain. Reflection was a complex process, going through the child's sensory organs, including the brain. The brain could store reflections, could understand them, and could use language to utilize other people's knowledge and add the child's own understanding.

Infants were born with unconditioned reflexes, and they learned conditioned reflexes. Education consisted of eliminating undesirable conditioned activities and building desirable ones. As the brain developed, conditioned reflexes built up sensations and perceptions. Since children's perceptual ability was limited, the teacher must, as concretely as possible, using models and demonstrations, show the children how to differentiate one thing from another. The question-and-answer method should be used, and training in observation should be pushed.

Children's psychological problems relevant to the educator were divided into two areas: (1) the general processes of learning, feeling, and volition (the process of knowing was to be subdivided into sensation, perception, image, thought, attention, and memory); and (2) individuality (*ko-hsing*), which was broken down into temperament, ability, interest, and character. The various aspects of the two areas were then taken up in detail.

Imagery, one lecture said, arose out of sensation and perception, gradually becoming abstract and being transformed into thought and knowledge. A rich imagery led to complex thinking. The teacher must therefore cultivate imagination and creativity through organization of science clubs and handicraft groups. Thought, or the generalization of concrete imagery into abstract ideas, depended on language. In leading children from concrete examples into abstract ideas, teachers should use comparisons and train children to apply ideas to many situations. Independent thinking and problem-solving abilities must be encouraged.

In teaching children to memorize something, the lectures continued, understanding must come first. When memory was linked up with language, it built upon existing knowledge. However, mechanical memorization had its place, and the teacher could help this process by pointing out characteristics of the material to be memorized or by pointing to analogies. Review was recommended as important for retention. In short, children should be taught to use memory consciously and effectively, with frequent reviews and self-examinations.

Attention was the next psychological process covered, from which concrete lessons for the teacher were drawn. When attention went through conscious will, it became "intentional attention." To rouse the latter, the teacher must instill in children their sense of responsibility. Teachers were advised to make use also of "unintentional attention" in small children and to vary the method of teaching as well as to use other devices to hold attention. The teacher must eliminate all distractions from the classroom, including "hidden distractions" such as "pampering at home, looking forward to play after school, or heavy burden of thought due to beatings at home."

The lectures recommended that the teacher encourage in children a love of the country and a firm belief in the Communist morality. This belief and feeling constituted energy to push behavior (*t'uei-tung hsing-wei ti li-liang*).

Volition was said to be evident when children used active participation to change environment. The most important component of volition was consciousness (*tzu-chueh hsing*). The teacher must train children to persevere in purposeful behavior and to carry out verbal promises. Lack of self-awareness in volition showed up either in being easily swayed by others or in being stubborn about one's own way of doing things. Good volition was demonstrated by ability to tell right from wrong and to be decisive. Resolution and self-control were qualities to be cultivated in school. To achieve this one must first build a scientific world view and rich moral feeling, for these motivate purposeful behavior. Fear of punishment may lead to superficial fulfillment of required behavior; this was not enough. Only children with the correct motivation would really work hard. To teach children the correct world view, verbal instruction must be supplemented by concrete examples and models. Teachers must at the same time raise the level of knowledge of children, increase their self-awareness of will, and cultivate the habit of overcoming difficulties. All this must be based on strong bodies.

It was said to be the duty of teachers to build up good moral character in children so that they would have correct attitudes toward labor, toward the group, and toward self. Teaching correct moral views by words was not enough; children must be shown the connection between correct moral views and their own concrete behavior. Teachers could use model heroes and organize student groups for the cultivation of good character.

Teachers should observe differences in individuality among children and teach them accordingly, the lectures allowed, but it was considered neither feasible nor desirable to test children. Differences in original endowment (*su-chih*) were viewed only as potentialities. This original endowment could influence children's ability but it could not determine individual development, which depended on experience and environment. Just as those born with sensory defects could be trained to use substitute organs, the original nature of one's higher nervous activity could also be changed by later experience. Children develop at different rates due to early or late training. The teacher's primary duty was to rouse children's interest and attitude toward learning. It was possible, the lectures asserted, to raise the level of attainment of all children to one of excellence. There were already model classes of "all good children." (This position was to be modified in the late fifties.)

The basic group activity of primary school students was described as *hsueh-hsi huo-tung*, or the study group. From it the child started to learn the responsibility of all *hsueh-hsi* (learning) and to be concerned about the results of learning for himself and others of the group. Gradually, children would build up a sense of responsibility toward those around them and become adept at conscious, organized behavior. Other than *hsueh-hsi,* games and socially useful labor also served a function in character building. Participation in student organizations such as the Young Pioneers taught children a sense of duty and of organization and regulations, and trained them for independent work, initative, and creativity. The final goal was to produce spontaneous, happy, forward-looking children, full of feeling for the group and love of friends.

These popular lectures represented one of the pragmatic aspects of academic psychology. The other aspects will be discussed in later sections on research. Although there was an organizational separation between research and the teaching of psychology, there was an attempt to bring the applications of the discipline directly to bear on everyday life.

College Textbooks

The writing and translation of new college textbooks in psychology began almost simultaneously with the retraining of psychologists; in fact, these activities may have been viewed as part of the rehabilitation. We know that by 1953 a Chinese version of Teplov's *Psychology* was already in existence.[20] The earliest known original Chinese text on the new psychology was written by Yuan Kung-wei in 1953.[21] Yuan, who had been teaching psychology since the change-over, used several Soviet references and wrote a new text containing the following material: (1) a simplified introduction to Pavlov; (2) child psychology based largely on Kornilov's *Higher Psychology*, secondarily on Leont'ev; (3) psychology of learning taken entirely from Pavlov and excluding Western learning theories; and (4) concrete, illustrative studies drawn mostly from medical and educational psychology. In Yuan's introductory remarks, the central task of psychology was seen as thorough change in people's psychological consciousness. As he saw it, the Communist program of national social reform required large-scale psychological reform (*she-hui kai-tsao* and *hsin-li kai-tsao*). He cited the Soviet example in the thirty-five years since the October Revolution and saw the Chinese counterpart as just beginning. Such psychological reform, he pointed out, would not come about automatically; it must be systematically carried out along with political and economic revolution. The central task of psychology was thought to be a concerted fight against the old psychological consciousness and the development of the new. This conception of the role of psychology in the new society appears, in retrospect, to be highly presumptuous and grandiose. No such ambitious claims have been found since. It must be remembered that Yuan was

[20] P'an Shu, "Fa-hui. . . ."
[21] Yuan Kung-wei, *Hsin hsin-li-hsueh* (A new psychology) (Shanghai: Kuang-hsieh Book Co., 1953).

writing in the early years of expanding national and revolutionary horizons.

In the next few years, several general psychology texts were turned out by group effort in teacher-training institutions. Peking Normal University prepared some teaching material with the help of Soviet specialists around 1953 to 1956.[22] Sometime in the early fifties, the Education Ministry had published specifications for required psychology courses. In response to this, the first Congress of the Chinese Psychological Society in 1955 prepared a "tentative outline for the required course in normal institutions and teachers' academies," [23] an outline that was subsequently adopted by the Education Ministry. Based on these specifications, the Psychology Staff Research Group of Kaifeng Normal College produced a volume in 1957, a result of two-years' group labor. This book made use of two Soviet texts and a Soviet adviser. An examination of the contents shows that the main body follows traditional topics in general psychology. What distinguishes this book as Communist psychology are the two early chapters on the philosophical foundation on dialectical materialism and natural science foundation in Pavlovianism. At the end are two more chapters with a Communist or Soviet slant: "the psychological analysis of games, *hsueh-hsi*, and labor," and "the study of individuality." If we can judge from this and the earlier Yuan text, the teaching of introductory psychology remained along fairly conventional lines except for the addition of Pavlovian and ideological appendages. Political ideology had not yet penetrated into the body of basic psychological principles.

Another text on the teaching of psychology for teacher-training schools was prepared by the Shanghai branch of the

[22] P'an Shu, "Fa-hui. . . ."

[23] Chu Man-shu, Shao Jui-cheng, *Hsin-li chiao-hsueh ti chi-ko wen-t'i* (Some problems in the teaching of psychology), ed. by the Shanghai Branch of the Psychological Society) (Shanghai: Hsin-chih-shih ch'u-pan she, 1958), p. 71.

Psychological Society in 1958. This book showed a higher degree of integration between the conventional method of viewing psychological processes and new elements derived from two sources: the Communist theory of reflection and of consciousness and Pavlov's conditioned reflex and second signal system. The basic processes of sensation, perception, memory, and imagination were presented as aspects of the reflection process, while volition was tied to a physiological base as the regulation of motor conditioned reflex by the second signal system. The remaining topics of emotion and feeling and of individuality were also treated in terms of reflection of social reality. This text represented an intermediate position on the continuum of the politicizing of psychology. Under this scheme, future teachers were taught to observe character traits in children in terms of desirable or undesirable traits, according to that part of society which was reflected. For example, attitudes toward physical labor and group activities would be viewed as either stable or wavering, diligent or lazy, earnest or *ma-hu* (lackadaisical). Attitudes toward people would be either courteous or rude, friendly or selfish, sociable or solitary, and so on, while attitudes toward self would be frank or deceiving, modest or conceited, with or without self-control, and straightforward or crafty. These are clearly value-laden, politically derived dichotomies.

After the criticism-debate and Great Leap periods, more political challenges intruded into the preparation of teaching materials for introductory psychology. Such were the circumstances surrounding the cooperative writing of a 1959 text in general psychology by Hua-tung Normal University and Shanghai Normal College. In the first place, this task was undertaken "with the encouragement of" the party secretary of Hua-tung Normal University, intended for the use of seven teacher-training institutions. Meetings were held in which questions were raised on two issues: class nature of the mind and class nature of will. The first point had been debated at great length during the previous year or so and was carried over to the preparation for this textbook. The second question raised in this context — whether everyone possessed a will — had not been found elsewhere. The political activists in this group denied it, but others present maintained that will was universal. Some argued that "the act of reactionaries is not an act of will, otherwise the destructive activity of the counter-revolutionaries would also be a strong expression of will power." [24] Others wanted the inclusion in the text of ways of training young Communists for work in the Great Leap, while those who disagreed felt training processes should be studied elsewhere. Another group project in text writing was the 1964 plan of Nanking University to prepare a draft on educational psychology.[25]

The extreme position of politicizing the subject matter of basic psychology was found in Cheng Chün-chieh's article in the journal of Shansi Normal College,[26] offering some preliminary suggestions on an outline for general psychology. This article, although it was published in 1957, anticipated the criticism of 1958–1959 by charging that psychology not only had not improved but had adopted "capitalist" viewpoints by stressing the pan-human nature of psychological phenomenon and the biological foundation of behavior. He accused some psychologists of "transferring the results of dog experiments to humans," and of stressing brain functions as determining psychological phenomenon. This, Cheng said, was "putting secondary things first" and was therefore against Marxism-Leninism, which would treat the brain itself as a product of human social history. Cheng went on to present

---

[24] China News Analysis No. 388, September 8, 1961. "Psychology 1959–1961," quoting *Wen-hui pao*, August 13, 1959.

[25] *Kuang-ming jih-pao*, January 6, 1964.

[26] Cheng Chun-chieh, "Tui pien-ting p'u-t'ung hsin-li-hsueh chiao-hsueh ta-kang ti ch'u-pu i-chien" (Preliminary suggestions on preparing an outline for the teaching of general psychology), *Shansi shih-fan hsueh-yuan hsueh-pao* (Shansi Normal College Journal), No. 1 (1957), pp. 85–97.

his idea of a proper text for general psychology, consisting of three parts. Part I would define the proper concern of psychology as the study of the formation and development of red and expert workers through misunderstanding the processes of socialist consciousness. The method of study should be historical materialism and class analysis, written from the workers' point of view. Social reality, especially productive labor, formed and developed man's psychological organization and provided man with knowledge, technology, will power, and consciousness. Part II in Cheng's proposed outline was entitled "psychological processes for understanding the world and reforming the world." In this section, sensation and perception, memory, thought, attention, and volition were all treated from the standpoint of social, historical, and class determination. Volition was defined as the "psychological process for world reform." Part III dealt with "individuality and the characteristics of red and expert workers" toward *hsueh-hsi* and labor. The special characteristics of the red and expert worker were listed in detail and proposed as the model for all citizens of new China: patriotic, determined, dare-to-think, dare-to-speak, dare-to-do, both expert and *to-mien-shou* (can-do-anything), possessed with love of Party and love of labor, self-respect and self confidence, groupism and revolutionary optimism, and, finally, with both proletarian standpoint and world view.

Cheng's views represented one extreme logical development of Chinese "Communist psychology," with politics and ideology serving as both the basic premise and the sole criterion for defining the limits, methods, and content of the discipline. Psychology should cease being a science and become a technology for implementing politically defined ends. Psychology in Communist China, up to the Cultural Revolution of 1966, had not taken this road of development. What had emerged, even at the popular teacher-training level, was not a completely politicized psychology, as Cheng would have wished, but a partially traditional yet Pavlov-based psychology, with particular stress on rational control and supremacy of the active consciousness. Many aspects of Western psychology were not included in either the texts or the curriculum. The teaching of psychology tended to be more "scientific" and academic at the leading universities, and more political and "practical" in the provincial normal institutions.

THE CHINESE PSYCHOLOGICAL SOCIETY

The psychologists were encouraged by the new regime to start preparing for their professional organization immediately after the takeover. In 1955, the Chinese Psychological Society was formally inaugurated, and its First National Congress was held that August. The "preparations" lasted about five years, during which ideological training and professional redirection took place. By 1958, the association had 585 members, a tenfold increase in membership over the pre-1949 association, although a majority of this number were psychologists teaching at various pedagogical institutions.[27] P'an Shu, chairman of the Board of Directors, and Ts'ao, deputy chairman, headed the Society as well as the Institute. The executive secretary was Ting Ts'an through 1958; he was later replaced by Shang Shan-yu, probably at the 1960 Second Congress of the Society, which elected a new council of 24 and a standing committee of nine.[28] The main office of the Society was in Peking, with 26 branches in Shanghai, Nanking, Canton, and other cities and regions.[29] Beginning at least in the sixties, these branches were grouped

[27] P'an Shu, "Chung-kuo hsin-li hsueh . . . , p. 5.
[28] Ch'en Ta-jou, "Chung-kuo Hsin-li-hsueh hui ti-erh-tz'u tai-piao hui-i" (Second Congress of the Chinese Psychological Society), *Hsin-li hsueh-pao*, No. 2 (1960), p. 131.
[29] These were Tientsin, Wuhan, Peking, Hangchow, Foochow, Lanchow, Taiyuan, Kunming, Changsha, Changchun, Kweilin, and Hsian; additional ones were later opened at Soochow, Kaifeng, Tsinan, Chungking, and Kweiyang.

into seven cooperative districts.[30] Thus, the new psychology, unlike its predecessor, penetrated deep into the interior, provincial centers of learning.

The Psychological Society had an editorial committee headed by Ts'ao Jih-ch'ang, with Ch'en Yuan-hui, another board member, as assistant editor.[31] This committee put out four series of publications. The *Hsin-li hsueh-pao*, also known as *Acta Psychologicol Sinica*, was the only journal for psychology proper. The first issue appeared in 1956, and it came out irregularly thereafter until 1959, when it became a quarterly. We have no knowledge of its status since the Cultural Revolution. Circulation in 1958 was about 8,000, more than 10 times its membership-wide influence. The *Hsin-li-hsueh i-pao*, or *Journal of Translations in Psychology*, was under the editorship of Wu Chiang-lin, and lasted from 1956 to 1958. It began with a circulation of 3,000, and later increased to 8,000.[32] The *Hsin-li-hsueh t'ung-hsin* was a newsletter; it was not available for this study. The *Hsin-li-hsueh wen-che* contained selected translations of foreign works in psychology. In 1960, there was mention of a new publication on the teaching of psychology, *Hsin-li-hsueh chiao-hsueh*.[33] In addition, the Society also sponsored the translation of longer works. A "12-year publication schedule for psychology" prepared by the Society was to outline "urgent subjects" to be written by Chinese psychologists, as well as to plan translation of 140 titles from Soviet Russia and "socialist brother countries," and selected works of English and French

---

[30] "Hsin-li-hsueh Hui chao-k'ai chiao-yü hsin-li chuan-yeh hui-yi" (Psychology Society called meeting of educational psychology specialty), *Kuang-ming jih-pao*, March 9, 1962.

[31] Other members of the editorial committee were Chu Chih-hsien of Peking Normal University, Wu Chiang-lin of the Institute of Psychology, and T'ang Yueh of Peking University.

[32] Shinkuro Iwahara, "Oriental Psychology," Appendix C in Melvin Marx and William Hillix, *Systems and Theories in Psychology* (New York: McGraw-Hill, 1963), p. 464.

[33] Ch'en Ta-jou, "Chung-kuo Hsin-li-hsueh hui . . . ," p. 131.

psychologists.[34] The preparation of teaching material was a task entrusted to the Society by the Ministry of Education. Thus, the Society had a major hand in the dissemination of psychological knowledge as well as in the guidance of research.

At the time of our study, there had been three national conferences of the Society. The First National Congress condemned the capitalist heritage in the old Chinese psychology and specified directions for the new. P'an Shu's opening speech viewed psychology in the previous twenty years as "blind imitation of the capitalist countries," singling out in particular psychological testing — especially intelligence testing — and the "wrong" application of language research. He then outlined tasks facing the Society: (1) emphasizing practical work in education, labor, public health, and medicine; (2) struggling against reactionary thinking, such as the ideas of Hu Shih and Hu Feng; (3) criticizing capitalist psychology and past psychology in China; (4) learning from Soviet psychology, cultivating talent, and developing research; (5) taking part in socialist construction, such as the Five-Year Plan; and (6) summarizing past historical experiences relevant to psychology, such as the 30 years of revolutionary history in arousing the masses, the process of organizing the people, and the techniques for conducting educational campaigns.[35]

The first item, practical work in education, labor, and medicine, anticipated the new direction of research after the 1958–1959 criticism-debate meetings. Similarly, the next four items foreshadowed the increasing political emphasis of the coming years. Of particular interest is the last item, in that, if followed through, it would have touched upon the central sphere of activity of the Communist Party, past and present. Since no subsequent mention was found on this sub-

[34] P'an Shu, "Chung-kuo hsin-li hsueh. . . ."
[35] P'an Shu, "Fa-hui. . . ."

ject, it might be concluded that such a delicate topic was quietly dropped.

The Second Congress, in January 1960, signaled the existence of a national community of psychologists; 61 members representing 25 local chapters gathered to read papers and discuss research and teaching. A total of 142 papers were submitted, out of which 19 were read during the sessions.[36] This was a small showing compared to the mammoth American conventions, but in light of similar professional meetings before 1949, this Congress, a short five years after the Society's inception, showed rapid progress as the organ for the direct exchange of ideas and research findings on the national level.

The research picture at this time was still dominated by the Institute, although six other institutions of higher education also presented papers. The main thrust of work at the Institute was in education, particularly on the problems of entrance age for school and psychological factors in the teaching of specific subject matters. In the area of labor psychology, the Institute reported a study on creativity; in medical psychology, it gave its main attention to a psycho-medical approach to neurasthenia. In addition, the Institute announced trial studies in control theory and information theory and the completion of a brain-wave analysis.

The other educational institutions presenting research papers were widely dispersed geographically: Hangchow University, Hunan Normal College, Southwest Normal College (Chungking), Kweiyang Normal College, Harbin Medical College, and Shanghai Normal University. Research areas in these institutions ranged from specific learning problems to motivation in the school situation. The question of changes in the methods and materials for the teaching of psychology was discussed by members of Peking Normal University, Tientsin Normal College, and Peking University.[37]

[36] Ch'en Ta-jou, "Chung-kuo Hsin-li-hsueh hui. . . ."
[37] Ibid.

To our knowledge, there has been no third congress, but a relatively large meeting took place from December 6 to 15, 1963, known as the "First Annual Academic Meeting of the Chinese Psychological Society." Eighty-five delegates gathered in Peking, representing 27 provincial, autonomous regional, and municipal branches of the Society, together with 200 persons engaged in Peking's psychological, educational, and public health work. The 203 papers submitted covered general, child, educational, medical, labor, and physiological psychology, as well as history of psychology. (Eleven of the papers were presented in assemblies, and 41 were read in four section meetings.[38])

At this Annual Meeting, Ts'ao Jih-ch'ang, who delivered the main address due to the illness of P'an Shu, reported on the publication by various psychologists of a total of about 300 articles in academic or other journals since 1960,[39] or an average of 100 a year, a definite increase in rate since the Second Congress. There was also a continued concentration on the educational sphere; of the 203 papers submitted to the meeting, he characterized 75 percent to be in the combined categories of child and educational psychology. Yet, in Ts'ao's opinion, both these papers and the articles published in the past three years showed insufficient emphasis on individual differences and character development in children, or on emotion and volition as compared to perception and sensation. He also felt more should be done on psychological theory and methods as well as on dialectical materialism. Finally, quoting Pavlov himself that "science will progress as methods are improved," Ts'ao declared: "We must continue to adopt the conditioned reflex method but must also *create new research methods*" (italics added).[40]

---

[38] Ch'en Ta-jou, "Chung-kuo Hsin-li-hsueh hui 1963 nien hsueh-shu nien-hui" (The 1936 annual academic meeting of the Chinese Psychological Society), *Hsin-li hsueh-pao*, No. 1 (1964), pp. 109–112.

[39] Other journals mentioned by Ts'ao are *Hsin-chien-she* (New Construction), *Hsueh-shu yen-chiu*, and university journals.

[40] Ts'ao Jih-ch'ang, "Kuan-ch'e li-lun lien-hsi shih-chi, k'o-hsueh yen-

From Ts'ao's address and a breakdown of the papers submitted to the 1963 meeting, we can see some patterns. Educational psychology, including child psychology, clearly emerged as the most popular branch, but not much of the work was innovative, either in methodology or in exploring the hitherto ignored areas of emotion or volition. Pavlov's name still had prestige and conditioned reflex still carried methodological weight, but much of the actual research was only tenuously related to it. In the whole area of character development, the concepts of consciousness and recognition remained paramount. However, the question of why individuals with similar education and moral teaching develop in different directions was barely tackled. In other words, psychologists were now faced with the problem of explaining the low development of moral character in children raised in the socialist society. These developments look like the result of both political demands for practical research in moral education and the maturation of a science.

When the Psychological Society called a special meeting on educational psychology in Peking in February, 1962, it not only brought together scattered psychologists interested in education but also integrated and gave greater leadership to the uncoordinated local research efforts. This special meeting drew over 200 representatives from 16 provincial, municipal and regional branches of the Society, along with members from some 40 organizations in Peking that dealt with education and child care. There were more than 100 submitted papers, which were subsequently published in a volume.[41] Deputy Director Chang P'an-shih of the Propaganda Section of the Party came "for exchange of conversation," and lead-

---

chiu wei she-hui chu-i chien-she fu-wu ti fang-chen t'i-kao hsin-li-hsueh kung-tso ti shui-p'ing" (Raising the scientific level of psychological research: Address to the 1963 annual meeting of the Chinese Psychological Society), *Hsin-li hsueh-pao*, No. 1 (1964), p. 1–18. Quotation from p. 5.
[41] See Chapter Five, pp. 138–139.

ing newspapers carried accounts of the proceedings for several days.

This meeting marked the stage of organizational unity and programmatic coherence in educational psychology. Besides P'an Shu's statement of goals, the conference also created the Educational Psychology Specialty Committee under the Psychological Society. This committee, headed by Ch'en Yuan-hui of the Educational Science Research Institute and including P'an Shu, Chu Chih-hsien of Peking Normal University, and Liu Ching-ho of the Institute of Psychology,[42] was apparently entrusted with the task of overseeing and perhaps coordinating the educational research program envisioned by the Society. Creation of this body was possibly the alternative solution to staffing a working institute, which would have required pulling the much-needed teaching personnel out of the universities and teacher-training installations. Thus, the functions of planning and organizing research left unfulfilled by the Educational Psychology Section of the Educational Science Research Institute were now put in the hands of this committee, whose members could simultaneously teach and undertake research. The size of this committee (26 members) may also indicate an attempt to broaden the base of research activities, as published articles in the following years tended to show. The *Hsin-li hsueh-pao*, which all through the fifties, had been heavily dominated by papers from the Institute of Psychology, began in the sixties, to publish many educational articles by psychologists from provincial normal colleges. In addition, more works on educational psychology began to appear in university journals, such as the *Hua-tung shih-fan ta-hsueh hsueh-pao (Journal of East China Normal University)* and *Hua-nan shih-fan ta-hsueh hsueh-pao (Journal of South China Normal University)*, and provincial normal college journals, such as the *Shansi shih-fan hsueh-yuan hsueh-pao (Journal of Shansi Normal College)*.

[42] *Kuang-ming jih-pao*, March 9, 1962.

The 26 local branches of the Chinese Psychological Society became increasingly active. In the early sixties, there were local or regional "annual discussion meetings"; we know of 10 specific ones in 1963.[43] This may have been part of a decentralization move to take the place of national congresses. A particularly active branch was the southern regional group, especially in applied and educational work. For example, the teachers of psychology in Kuangtung province organized a teachers' *hsueh-hsi* class in 1959 to discuss psychology, and five research teams to work in the village, factory, school, and army, producing 27 research reports.[44] A south-central district meeting, in cooperation with education research workers, in 1963 prepared an outline on the teaching of psychology and a guidebook on experimentation in educational psychology.[45]

POLITICAL MOVEMENTS AND PSYCHOLOGY

The formation of a profession or the growth of a body of ideas in Communist China must be seen against the backdrop of political campaigns and movements, for these embody in sharp, dramatic form the main outlines of the changing intellectual and ideological atmosphere. Psychology and psychologists were affected at various times in varying degrees by the political currents sweeping across the country. Sometimes, the effect was indirect and difficult to demonstrate; at other times, the involvement was direct and intimate, penetrating into the core of the profession. Because the Institute and the Society had such strategic positions in the field of psychology in China, they were the focus for the interplay of politics with the discipline.

The first and most general point to be made is the spirit of "politics taking command," a spirit that pervaded all

[43] Ts'ao Jih-ch'ang, "Kuan-ch'e li-lun. . . ."
[44] *Kuang-ming jih-pao*, June 12, 1959.
[45] *Nan-fang jih-pao*, January 22, 1963.

intellectual endeavors since 1949. Under this overarching principle was the "red versus expert" controversy, which periodically raised the question of the fundamental status of all specialized personnel. The early thought-reform campaign of intellectuals in 1951–1952 can be considered the first concrete step toward pulling down the unchallenged supremacy of specialists of ideas. While we have no information on major psychologists being singled out for the more serious forms of attack and reform, the message of the campaign was nevertheless apparent. In a real sense, the Pavlovian seminars for the re-education of psychologists were a special form of thought remolding, although their contents were focused on the technical, scientific level of correct theory and method, rather than strictly on political knowledge and attitude.

There were a few other important movements in the early fifties that had indirect relevance for the new psychology in defining the extreme limits of anti-Americanism in intellectual ideas and in setting the moral tone for later character studies by the psychologists. They included the "Hate America" campaign during the Korean conflict; the land-reform program; the three anti's aimed at bureaucrats — anticorruption, -waste, -bureaucratism, and the five anti's aimed at business groups — antibribery, -tax evasion, -fraud, -stealing of state property and -stealing of state economic secrets.

Even after the entrenchment of the profession, there were no retrospective studies by the psychologists on the form or processes of these campaigns. They remained the exclusive concern of the Party, a sacred ground beyond the reach of academic specialists.

The Hundred Flowers and Anti-Rightists Movements

One year after the Institute of Psychology under the Academy of Science and the Chinese Psychological Society were formally established in 1956, the Hundred Flowers movement of 1957 signaled a brief period of relaxation ideologically. Then the anti-rightist movement followed immediately to clamp down the voice of dissidence. From all indications, psychologists were not deeply implicated in either campaign, but neither were they entirely unaffected.

Although some intellectuals spoke out during the Hundred Flowers movement against aspects of the bureaucracy and society, psychologists did not produce any significant criticism on national issues, as far as available sources would indicate. The only instance we can cite was a complaint against government policy affecting psychologists, by the director of the newly created Institute of Psychology. What P'an Shu expressed was his dissatisfaction regarding academic arrangements and the use made of psychologists. The ambiguous academic status of psychology was evident. P'an's feeling was that psychology should be given greater importance, perhaps as an independent specialty in more schools. P'an also implied criticism against the use of psychologists when he bemoaned the lack of trained specialists in the field and added that existing psychologists should be "shifted and made better use of." [46] These were minor administrative complaints, and nothing further was heard about them. Since we found no written recantations by psychologists, we may surmise that leading psychologists did not speak out with undue freedom in the period of relaxation.

During the anti-rightist movement that immediately followed the Hundred Flowers movement, no psychologist was accused of political plotting, as were some other leading social scientists. This could mean either that psychologists were less outspoken or that the authorities regarded the profession with greater favor. The other social scientists did not

[46] P'an Shu, "Wo-kuo hsin-li-hsueh ti hsien-chuang ho fa-chan fang-hsiang" (A review of psychology in our country), *Jen-min jih-pao*, July 2, 1957. The title of this news article is almost exactly the same as that of another, previously cited, article by the same author, but the contents are not the same.

fare so well. At the two five-day criticism meetings held by the Academy of Sciences against "rightist" intellectuals, plus smaller departmental meetings, some members of the Academy were put through "the struggle." Prominent among the social scientists under attack were anthropologist Fei Hsiao-t'ung, sociologists Wu Ching-ch'ao and Li Ching-han, economist Ch'en Cheng-han, population expert Ch'en Ta, and historian Lei Hai-tsung.[47] One of the charges against Fei was his alleged opposition to the policy of the Education Ministry, while the other intellectuals were accused of plotting with minority parties in various ways against either the policy of the government or its record of achievement.[48] No psychologist was involved in these published charges.[49]

However, a few psychologists were criticized for rightist leanings and capitalist influences in their teaching and research activities. The psychology being attacked was the "bourgeois" Western approach based on "idealism" — more specifically, the schools of behaviorism, gestaltism, and psychoanalysis. Available evidence points to greater criticism of this sort in the provincial teacher-training institutions, where in the fifties politics tended to intrude more into academic psychology than it did in the central universities of the Academy.

[47] *Jen-min shou-ts'e* (People's Handbook) (Peking: Ta-kung-pao Publishing Co., 1958), pp. 156–175.

[48] For documents giving detailed accounts of charges and criticisms against these members of the Academy, see *Jen-min shou-ts'e*, 1958, p. 162.

[49] At the same time, it might be noted that Sun Kuo-hua, one of the deans of Chinese psychology, died suddenly of a heart attack on February 2, 1958, at the age of 56. He was chairman of the Specialty of Psychology and vice-chairman of the Philosophy Department at Peking University, hotbed of criticism and debate. The obituary, which appeared in the journal (July 1958), briefly traced changes in his political attitude: he was said to have "resisted" joining the Kuomintang and to have declined the profitable sale of his private library to the Japanese during wartime, and after 1949 to have "changed his hatred for politics." Later, he was said to have "improved his attitude after the *cheng-feng* and anti-rightist movements." "Ching-tao Sun Kuo-hua hsien-sheng" (Obituary for Mr. Sun Kuo-hua), *Hsin-li-hsueh-pao*, No. 1 (1958), p. 1.

49

For example, the Hua-tung (or East China) Normal University journal published two student articles attacking the "capitalist psychology" of the Western-trained Chang Yao-hsiang, and a third one objecting to capitalist viewpoints in a course on "higher psychology" taught by a team of five psychologists.[50] This kind of criticism aimed at selected targets had the effect of "purifying" the content of psychology, rather than discrediting psychologists as a professional group.

Criticism-Debate Meetings: 1958–1959

The more general effects of the anti-rightist movement on psychology were not felt until a year or two later, when a series of criticism-debate meetings was convened for psychologists both in the capital and elsewhere to examine "erroneous tendencies in past work." These meetings, which began in the spring of 1958 and lasted well into the summer of 1959, were held at the direction of the Party, for as P'an put it, "The Party showed us the road; the Party laid down the policy: education should serve the proletarian government; education should be united with productive labor." [51] The Institute of Psychology began by criticizing itself for capitalist tendencies and for neglecting concrete research on socialist construction. Beginning in August, Peking Normal University students raised criticisms against capitalist standpoints and methods in the teaching of psychology, leading to criticism and self-criticism meetings of the faculty and students in psychology "under the guidance of the Party." [52] Soon, psychology units in other institutions followed suit, and criticism meetings in psychology became nationwide.[53]

[50] *Hua-tung shih-ta hsueh-pao*, No. 4 (1958), pp. 40–53.
[51] P'an Shu, "Mien-tui keng-ta ti yueh-chin hsing-shih, p'an-teng hsin-li-hsueh ti kao-feng" (Responding to the Great Leap, scaling the peaks of psychological science), *Hsin-li hsueh-pao*, No. 2 (1960), pp. 63–66.
[52] *Ibid.*
[53] Detailed documentation on this section is on file.

There were indications that the Party was not satisfied with the results of the early round of meetings in 1958, for in 1959 meetings were resumed for a "deeper airing of views," and again "under the leadership of the Party." All the major organizations dealing with psychology were again involved: members of the Institute, psychologists in the teaching institutions, and officials of the Chinese Psychological Society. There were meetings in large intellectual centers and in remote provincial university towns. In the less important meetings, topics for discussion were often couched in oversimplified terms of the issues explored at the major meetings. For example, some of the local topics were: "Is Pavlovian theory necessary?" "Should psychology only study the awakened, cultured working class and pay no attention to the exploiting class?" or "Psychology is a social science full of Party nature."

These meetings were widely publicized in several leading dailies, the first time psychologists as a group received national attention. P'an Shu called this the first "mass movement" in psychology (it was the only one up to 1966). Although most psychologists who attended these meetings were members of the Chinese Psychological Society, the Society took no stand on the meetings at its Second Congress in 1960. Chairman P'an simply described the debate proceedings. Local debate-criticism meetings were organized by branches of the Society. Many of these meetings involved fairly large groups. One meeting in Peking was attended by some 80 psychologists from the Institute of Psychology, the Educational Research Institute, and universities and colleges; a second meeting was national in character, its 200 participants including psychologists and education workers from as far as Harbin, Changchun, Canton, Lanchow and Hu-ho hao-t'e.

Apparently, the meetings started out in a rather tense and hostile atmosphere, but it gradually improved. Ts'ao Jih-ch'ang described participants in the early sessions as being "divided into two camps: the attackers were all correct and the attacked all wrong." During the second round in 1959, however, "free discussion and exchange" occurred and the meetings became "more fruitful." He went on to quote Premier Chou En-lai as supporting free scientific discussions.[54] P'an Shu in 1959 also pleaded for a renewed Hundred Flowers spirit in the discussion meetings: "If comrades are afraid to speak up, how can psychology progress? 'Hundred schools of thought' should mean not only the airing of different views, but also that each should work according to his own angle and method." [55] Two years later, the "blooming and contending" motif was reiterated and directly attributed to Party policy.[56] Perhaps this is further evidence of the Party's watchful nurturance of psychology as a new science.

The criticism-debate meetings of 1958–1959 embodied the themes of several political campaigns. The spirit of rectification was mixed with some belated atmosphere of "blooming and contending," while at the same time, the pressures from the Great Leap Forward program to produce concrete research on practical problems were already being felt by the profession.

Yet the phrasing of the controversies and the evidence marshalled by the opponents were scientific and intellectual rather than blatantly political. Political polarization did not occur at that time in the profession of psychology; the year-long debate ended on a politically inconclusive note. The atmosphere was one of exploration into theoretical issues of the field; views were exchanged on the nature of psychology and the proper methodology for studying it. The discussions served three important functions: (1) recapitulation in a microcosmic form of some of the philosophical issues of dialectical materialism and methodological principles in

[54] *Jen-min jih-pao*, June 10, 1959.
[55] *Wen-hui pao* (Shanghai), October 1, 1959.
[56] *Kuang-ming jih-pao*, June 9, 1961 (Joint Publications Research Service No. 4937).

Soviet psychology (see brief statement in Chapter One); (2) public overthrow of the heritage of capitalist psychology in China; and (3) presentation by the regime of the demand for a more activist and society-oriented discipline. These activities can be interpreted as a continuation of the retraining of psychology, but more appropriately as the beginning of a new phase: the trend away from strict adherence to the newly imported Pavlovian brand of Soviet psychology.

The criticisms raised first against Peking Normal University and then against other teaching institutions in Peking and Shanghai were the "lack of class analysis," "biological reductionism," and "abstractionism" and "other capitalist viewpoints and tendencies deviating from Party leadership." The teachers were also attacked for their neglect of the masses and their concrete problems and for "neglect of reality."

The basic charges are closely interrelated. By "abstractism" was meant the tendency of the laboratory psychologists to isolate aspects of mental processes for study, such as perception or memory, instead of the functioning of the whole individual. "Biological reductionism" was the label used against those who approached the higher or more complex level of psychological phenomena in terms of simpler, lower level, physiological processes. The "lack of class analysis" of course referred to the fact that psychologists were looking at universal principles affecting psychological processes and were ignoring the relevance of class membership. Together, the three charges were aimed at the pull toward science of the new psychology, which was perhaps intensified by its identification with Pavlovian methodology. Ironically, the earlier political remolding of the psychologists in the Pavlovian seminars gave the profession a solid and respectable new status, for the strength of the new theoretic foundation became apparent as the debate sessions progressed. The Party was applying pressure to make psychology more political. Its accusation was that while the fundamental Marxist creed stated that "psychology is the activity of the brain and reflection of objective reality," some psychologists only "grasp the first half and neglect the second half." These charges apparently expressed the concern of the Party that psychologists were more interested in examining abstract principles of behavior than in serving a political ideology. Perhaps the charges also revealed a dissatisfaction with Soviet psychology and the new emphasis of Pavlovianism. Another issue involved may have been that of elitism in the profession, for the stronghold of scientific methodology was the Institute of Psychology of the Academy of Sciences, which was also the repository of the more elaborate laboratory equipment and the center for the highly specialized brain research.

Several intellectual issues were explored at length: the proper subject matter of psychology; whether psychology was a natural or a social science; and the appropriate methods of studying psychological phenomena.

Members of the Institute of Psychology maintained that psychology was the study of reflection. Psychologists should concentrate on the origin, development, and laws of the process whereby the brain reflects objective reality. This meant, above all, a biological emphasis on the mechanism of reflection and therefore on the universal, pan-human nature of psychological processes and laws of development. It followed that psychological phenomena *could be* treated independently of class analysis, although proponents of this view did not deny that *some* psychological phenomena were affected by class. However, they pointed to such universal human sensations as heat, cold, or pain, the reactions to which had on class distinction, and to the fact that perception, thought, emotion, and aspiration did not necessarily take on class coloration. Speed of learning was used as an illustration of individual differences, not of class differences. Some, for example, stressed the abstract *process* of reflection as opposed to the *content* of the reflection process. Others tried to separate the study of "social consciousness" from the psychological concern of "individual consciousness" so that the field could preserve its separate identity.

The group from Hua-tung Normal University criticized psychology for not paying enough attention to the class nature of psychological phenomena, for not making enough of a contribution to socialist construction. They argued that content and form were inseparable, or that content determined form; that "psychological consciousness *is* class consciousness," or that "the essence of mind *is* class mind." A somewhat more moderate statement was that "the core of psychology is class determined." [57] This group would deny the validity of studying pan-human psychological phenomena. To study human psychology without class consideration was termed "abstractism." As one psychologist proclaimed, "only when the communist society is achieved and classes are abolished can you have a common human psychology." The main duty of psychology, therefore, was the study of the *content* of reflection — in other words, social reality as "reflected" in individual consciousness, with all the concrete class factors and social conditions. This approach would focus on the process of internal contradictions between the subjective and objective aspects or within the subjective process.[58] To concentrate on brain processes would be to neglect individuality. Instead, psychology should devote its attention to the psychological processes of live, concrete individuals.[59]

An attempt to arbitrate the opposing sides was an inclusive scheme that divided human consciousness into four aspects: individual consciousness, general consciousness, social consciousness, and class consciousness. Pychologists

[57] *Kuang-ming jih-pao*, March 26, 1959, and China News Analysis No. 338, September 8, 1961, quoting *Hsueh-shu yueh-k'an*, No. 3 (1959), p. 55 ff.

[58] *Kuang-ming jih-pao*, March 26, 1959.

[59] *Jen-min jih-pao*, June 10, 1959.

were urged to pay special attention to those aspects of individual psychology that had social reality.

The second issue was the academic status of psychology: Is psychology a natural science, a social science, or an in-between science? The position of psychology as a social science was bolstered by the Marxist axiom, "Man is the product of social relations." Psychologists of Peking Normal University defined the discipline as the study of consciousness. Man was the sum of social relations; his consciousness was born of labor. Social experience was the origin and basis of psychological consciousness. What was reflected was social life, not simple nature — at least, it was nature full of social meaning.

There was a compromise position that argued that psychology was an "in-between science leaning toward the social sciences" including both the study of *psychological processes* belonging to natural science, since in origin and mechanism brain was natural matter, and the study of *individuality* belonging to social science, since the content of psychology reflected material conditions of social living. Those who specialized in the *origin* of consciousness or the process of reflection were natural scientists. Others who concentrated on the *direction* of consciousness or the influence of social life on individual psychology were social scientists. However, since psychology ought to emphasize processes of reflection in general, it should lean toward the natural sciences. This position came close to a rejection of the relevance of politics for psychology; psychology as a science should be above politics.

The third issue was one of method. Western-style introspection was unanimously condemned. Everyone did agree that experimentation should be one of the methods of study for psychology, but opinion was divided as to its relative importance. Members of the Institute, of course, argued for the supremacy of experimentation, including the use of electronic techniques, especially for the study of communications theory and control theory. Many felt that experimentation should be combined with other methods.

Foremost among other methods proposed was the use of class analysis on psychological problems, although what was meant by class analysis was not specified. The politically oriented who defined psychology as a social science argued for the use of class analysis on all psychological problems, while others did not want to see such restricted methodology. A more moderate position, adopted by most psychologists, including the scientifically oriented Institute men as well as some normal college psychologists, agreed on the adoption of class analysis "in principle," and the preservation of the "class viewpoint" both in teaching and in research. At least, it was pointed out, class analysis and the conditioned reflex were not contradictory.

One or two psychologists, however, spoke out against class analysis entirely as an appropriate method for psychology. They maintained that class analysis should be the method of the social sciences, not of psychology, which was the study of individuals. Another took an empiricist point of view, saying that in conducting research with children, one must do "concrete work," one must "observe, observe, and again observe."

The psychologists' views on the three main issues could consistently be predicted by their institutional affiliation. It is obvious that the Institute of Psychology was most interested in studying abstract psychological processes regardless of particular content of social experience; in particular, they were interested in brain experiments, employing advanced technological equipment. On the side of the Institute were nearly all the psychologists attached to Peking University, except one who took a moderate stand. The psychologists at Hua-tung Normal University of Shanghai, with support from Peking Normal College, asserted the class nature of all or all major psychological phenomena and pushed for class analysis in every kind of research. The psychology faculty of Peking Normal University (different from Peking Normal College) was split in thirds, with equal numerical strength supporting the Institute, Hua-tung Normal University, and a middle position. The smaller normal institutions, such as Shanghai Normal College and Hua-nan or South-China Normal College, maintained a middle position. It is apparent that the alignment took shape between the academic tradition represented by the Institute and the comprehensive university (including the leading normal university), on the one hand, and the practical interests of the teacher-training institutions, on the other.

The debate meetings began with simple either-or statements on both sides: whether psychological phenomenon was or was not determined by class position, whether class analysis should or should not be the main method in psychology, and whether psychology was a natural or social science. Gradually, after the different views became more complex and the positions more refined, the debate spurned either-or solutions in deference to degrees of emphasis; for instance, they began to consider the *manner* of interaction between physiological and social factors, and the choice of problems for research. A distinction was now made between social effects in the physical make-up of man, on the one hand, and biology as the product of social relations, on the other. Again, as in psychological research in the classroom, a plea was made not to duplicate the concerns of educators but rather to determine psychological rules concerning discipline, the learning process, and age characteristics. Similarly, the objectives of medical psychology were judged to be not merely solving certain concrete problems but investigating the relationship between psychological conditions and pathology, psychological types among patients, or various substantive adjustment functions. In other words, the discussion became a matter of phrasing the proper questions. However, no conceptual system or methodology emerged at these meetings, and the controversy over scientific beliefs reached no settlement. Even late in 1961, P'an Shu wrote,

There are people who laugh at us because we are still discussing what is psychology. . . . The question of class character is very important, but in the whole field of psychology this is but one particular question and not one that is all-inclusive.[60]

Perhaps there was some merging of views, or perhaps the agreement was to let some differences remain. What emerged was a rather broad, inclusive statement of psychology within the ideological confines of Marxism-Leninism-Maoism, paying lip service to Pavlovianism. There was enough theoretical room left for psychology to develop in more than one direction.

Preparations for Research During the Great Leap Forward

After these meetings, psychology did, indeed, look different; it changed from a laboratory-centered, Pavlov-inspired type of academic science into a problem-oriented action program in the Great Leap spirit. Psychologists put aside their conventional divisions of labor according to classic psychology and pooled their resources to attack concrete problems in answer to the contemporary needs of the society, all in the spirit of "going to the masses" (*hsia-fang*). Concrete groups were studied and practical solutions to problems were sought, although "class analysis" was not specifically an issue.

The most visible sign of this new trend was the reorganization of research units into three interdisciplinary teams oriented toward practical problem areas: (1) labor psychology, (2) medical psychology, and (3) educational psychology. Thus, Institute psychologists departed from their conventional academic mode of subdivisions and prepared to leave the laboratories for team research in the factories and classrooms in response to the socialist call. In the same spirit of diversified, concrete research, the Academy set up branches in many provinces and municipalities between 1957

[60] China News Analysis No. 388, quoting *Kuang-ming jih-pao*, September 9, 1961.

and 1959, with the slogan "walking on two legs." Several of them included educational psychology units or combined psychology with educational research.[61]

Along with the redirection of research in the Institute, the 12-year plan of development for psychology also came under thorough revision in 1959. The original plan was found to place too much emphasis on theory and not enough on "relations between theory and reality" and on "contributions of psychology to socialist construction."

Actually, even before the Great Leap Forward and the debate of 1958–1959, a beginning was made by psychologists at the Institute and leading teaching centers to engage in practical research problems. Beginning in 1956, the various ministries concerned with production, the Ministries of Transportation, Public Health, and Physical Education, all made requests for psychological research. The state of affairs in the summer of 1958 was roughly as follows: work was reportedly begun for the ministries of production on accident prevention, increasing work efficiency, and minimizing waste. The Institute had the prime responsibility for coordinating and planning research, while cooperating with appropriate units in the Ministry of Machine Industry, the Psychology Specialty of Peking University, Chekiang Normal College Psychology Study Group, and an agency for the study of technological and industrial organization. Three lines of psychological research were under way in transportation, two under the auspices of the Institute and one in which the Institute took part. The Ministry of Public Health called the first National Conference on Mental Health in 1958. Work for the Ministry of Physical Education was a little slower in getting started. As P'an said, they were "not clear how to begin." Educational psychology was greatly expanded.

This account of progress in research plans, although perhaps somewhat optimistic, was on the whole substanti-

<hr>

[61] P'an, "Mien-tui. . . ."

ated by later publications. Possible exceptions are research on transportation and physical education, on which no published reports are available. There is no indication, either from the nature of the problems tackled or from subsequent accounts, of the extent to which research findings were made use of in administrative decisions. It may be said, however, that at that point (1958), psychology was given a modest and limited role by the government apparatus. In the first decade of Communist rule, it had not been an important academic discipline, but neither had it been a completely neglected or suppressed profession. Available accounts of the research done by the three reorganized teams suggest that the government gave it cautious sponsorship.

MEDICAL PSYCHOLOGY

INTRODUCTION

The long-range or ideal conception of medical psychology in Communist China has been described by Ting Ts'an, a psychologist with prewar psychiatric training in Peking Union Medical College, as "the utilization of psychological knowledge based on dialectical materialism to assist the medical profession in the prevention and cure of disease and the preservation of the health of the people." [1] He further stated that medical psychology thus conceived is not only closely related to medical practice but is, indeed, an indispensable part of modern scientific medicine, and that psychologists should address themselves to the psychological problems in the diagnosis, treatment, and prevention of illness, both somatic and mental, and to the carrying out of educational programs toward building a healthier nation. Writing in the psychological journal to present his case for medical psychology, Ting gave some specific examples of the need to study psychogenic factors (*hsin-yin-hsing*) in instances of internal medicine such as high blood pressure and digestion,

[1] Ting Ts'an, "Tsen-yang tsai wo-kuo k'ai-chan i-hsueh hsin-li-hsueh ti kung-tso" (How to develop medical psychology in China), *Hsin-li hsueh-pao*, No. 3 (1959), pp. 146–150.

obstetrics and pediatrics, and "even dermatology." As we shall later indicate, other psychologists stressed the importance of understanding the psychological aspects of the doctor-patient relationship, such as "the effect upon it of the doctor's speech or attitudes" and "the patient's thought and individuality." [2]

This range of topics was to be treated, of course, within the Marxist-Leninist theory of reflection and the Pavlovian system of psychological activity, which are in this view the first true bases for unifying the historically separate theories of body and mind. Psychosomatic medicine was conceded as the only Western attempt at linking psychology with medicine, but this was rejected as highly unsatisfactory and doomed to fail because of its philosophical "dualism" and close affinity with Freudian psychology. The latter was denounced, in turn, as basing the origin of illness upon the "physiological reaction to the manifestation of mysterious sexual drives." [3]

A very limited place was reserved for traditional Chinese medicine in the post-1949 medical psychology.[4] At the time of this study, a wide variety of Chinese herb medicines, as well as some traditional medical techniques, had been adopted in psychiatric treatment. However, the theoretical thinking and empirical research in medical psychology did not encompass traditional doctrines of mental illness or the psychological makeup of man. Efforts to integrate the two areas were limited to the reinterpretation of some historical documents on medical knowledge and lore.

The seminar in dialectical materialism and Pavlovianism in the summer of 1953, which was discussed in Chapter Two, laid the groundwork and opened up channels for collabora-

---

[2] Ch'en Ta-jou, *Jen-min jih-pao*, June 26, 1959.

[3] Ting Ts'an, "K'ai-chan wo-kuo i-hsueh hsin-li-hsueh ti kung-tso" (Developing a program in Chinese medical psychology), *Chung-hua shen-ching ching-shen k'o-hsueh ts'a-chih* (*Chinese Journal of Neuropsychiatry*), No. 4 (1956), pp. 322–325.

[4] *Ibid.*

tion between medical psychology and the medical sciences. However, Soviet precedents did not support such collaboration. Although the original conception for such a specialization is traced back to the Soviet physiologist Sechenov, not much had been built up in the Soviet Union by the mid-fifties. Ting Ts'an quoted a Soviet source of 1956 as complaining that little psychological experimentation was being carried on in Soviet hospitals and that leadership in "certain Soviet organizations" held "mistaken notions" about psychology.[5] Thus, when the Chinese psychologists presented the argument for the inclusion of psychology courses in the curriculum of Chinese medical schools, the retort came back that there was no such precedent in the Soviet medical program. Ting attributed the lack of appreciation for the possible contribution of psychology to medicine in his own country to the compartmentalization of academic life as well as the lack of an example in the Soviet situation.

The relationship between psychology and psychiatry apparently rested on firmer ground, at least conceptually. Soviet psychiatry declared its aherence to Pavlovian principles at the 1950 meeting of the USSR Academy of Sciences and Academy of Medical Sciences.[6] Specifically, a connection was pointed out between psychiatric practices and Pavlov's physiological theory of hypnotic sleep, defined as a form of protective inhibition. Psychotherapy, which did not win immediate acceptance, gained respectability when the theoretical justification was presented in terms of Pavlov's second signal system—that is, psychotherapy was then viewed as a form of manipulating behavior change through language in the place of other external stimuli.[7]

The Chinese psychologists saw psychogenic factors as among the important factors, and often the chief ones, in the

[5] Ting Ts'an, "Tsen-yang. . . ."
[6] Ivan D. London, "Therapy in Soviet psychiatric hospitals," *American Psychologist*, No. 2 (Feb. 8, 1953), pp. 79–82.
[7] Conversation with Professor Mark Field of Boston University.

complex origins of mental illness. They urged that diagnostic tools of a psychological nature, such as the determination of the level of mental developmental or retardation, or of disturbances in the thought process, or of fantasy life, are "indispensable" to psychiatry. Ting Ts'an also wanted psychotherapy to become an integral part of the treatment program along with pharmacotherapy, physical therapy, and occupational-recreational therapy.

In the area of preventive mental health, medical psychologists saw a wide-open field in which they had a special role. To give people knowledge of the laws of development of individuality and origins of illness was judged the foremost duty of medical psychology.

A word may be appropriate here on the evaluation of information regarding mental health, especially of figures and percentages. Since the collaborative projects were undertaken as part of the Great Leap program in 1958, with all that this implies in the hasty expansion of personnel and facilities and in the spirit of the sudden exertion of effort for maximum results, all data must be treated with extreme caution. Much can still be learned, however, about the characteristic modes of approach of psychology to the problems of mental illness, as well as underlying assumptions regarding these problems. Our primary interest lies not in discovering the extent of mental illness or the adequacy of ways of coping with it, but rather with the manner in which these problems were conceptualized, and with the growth of a scientific discipline through the activities of its members, both in practice and in research.

How much research, then, was going on in medical psychology? Since around 1958, when medical psychology became an active branch of psychology, roughly one out of ten professional articles in the journal could be classified in this category. These works ranged from the study of the etiology of neurasthenia [8] and schizophrenia, and the evaluation of

[8] To be defined later in this chapter.

treatment programs, to the use of EEG (electroencephalo-grams), and experimental measures of memory, time estimate, and discrimination. After an initial trial period, research of the late fifties tended to be of a broader scope; then, in the mid-sixties, psychologists again turned to work of a more technical, narrow sort, such as the use of EEG on different types of individuals, both normal and disturbed.

PARTICIPATION OF MEDICAL PSYCHOLOGY IN PSYCHIATRIC PROGRAMS

Before the changeover, China had a small tradition of psychiatric practice and research centered in Peking, Shanghai, and Nanking, with limited participation by psychologists. In those years, a number of American personality tests were translated into Chinese and put to use in psychiatric settings, and some joint research programs were undertaken by psychiatrists and specially trained psychologists. Since 1949, however, little evidence of collaboration was found until the Great Leap period, when the medical profession and the psychologists joined efforts to cope with problems of mental health, either as preparation for or as a result of the extraordinary demands being made on the people.

Mental health then was considered "one of the three largest subjects for scientific research," according to an official review of medical achievements.[9] Preventive work was especially emphasized as the result of a directive from the Party. An important milestone in Communist China's mental health program was the first National Conference on Mental Health, called by the Ministry of Health in June 1958. Workers in the psychiatric field from all over the country met in Nanking to "formulate goals and regulations in the pre-

[9] Wu Cheng-i, "New China's Achievements in Psychiatry," pp. 614–615, in *Collection of Theses on Achievements in Medical Sciences in Commemoration of the 10th National Foundation Day of China*, Vol. II, "Mental Health," pp. 594–699. Joint Publications Research Service No. 14829.

vention and healing of mental illness." [10] This conference launched the Great Leap program on mental health, and was undoubtedly responsible for a broadened conception of mental health and the inclusion of psychologists in a new, coordinated attack upon these problems.

Psychiatric Facilities and Personnel

To analyze the significance of the role of medical psychology in psychiatric programs, it is first necessary to present a brief account of the state of psychiatry in Communist China: its psychiatric facilities and personnel, modes of classifying mental illness, and methods of treatment.

Some idea of the growth of psychiatric services and personnel up to 1959 can be gathered from the following figures presented in a review of the first ten years of achievements in the medical sciences.[11] It was claimed that during the ten-year period, 60 new hospitals for the mentally ill were built throughout the 21 provinces and autonomous regions, and some old facilities were enlarged. The total number of psychiatric beds was said to have increased 14-fold from pre-1949 days. The number of such beds in 1950 was 1.1 percent of the total capacity of hospitals and wards, as compared to 3.6 percent in 1957.[12] The same report pointed out that the increase in doctors dealing with psychiatric problems during the ten-year period was 16 times, and that of nurses was more than 20 times.

A Czechoslovakian source [13] summarizing materials in several languages on Chinese psychiatry stated that there were 100 neuropsychiatrists in 1952, but that that number had grown to 436 in 1957. In the four psychiatric hospitals

---

[10] *Ibid.*

[11] *Collection of Theses on Achievements in Medical Sciences . . . ,* pp. 594–699.

[12] Compare with approximately 50 percent in the United States and 10 to 12 percent in the U.S.S.R.

[13] Jan Cerny, "Chinese Psychiatry," *International Journal of Psychiatry,* Vol. I, No. 2 (1965), pp. 229–247.

in Peking, Shanghai, Canton, and Nanking, there was an increase from 1,000 beds and 60 psychiatrists in 1949 to 20,000 beds and 400 psychiatrists in 1957.

The biggest expansion in the broad field of psychiatry was undoubtedly the establishment of mental health clinics in different parts of larger cities as well as outpatient mental health clinics attached to hospitals. Such psychiatric services were said to be found as far as Inner Mongolia and Sinkiang.[14] Among the major cities, Peking had the first mental health clinic, known as the East City Area Psychopathic Clinic.[15] This was followed by 12 other such installations, which were joined with birth control agencies in the 13 districts of Peking. Some of these organizations had apparently grown into small-scale hospitals. Shanghai had such outpatient mental health clinics in 14 districts, and Nanking placed similar clinics in district hospitals and "equipped more than 200 sick beds in various homes." Nanking also boasted of the first outpatient clinic for children suffering from mental disorders, established in 1956. In 1957, the Nanking Mental Hospital added a children's ward.

We have no information on changes in facilities after 1959. However, we do know that the training of psychiatrists was stepped up during the Great Leap. The National Conference of Psychiatry adopted a resolution in 1958 to use the "double track method" of training psychiatric staff, whereby intensive training was to be given to an elite group, while a shorter training program was to produce a larger number of "medium-level" psychiatric workers. Five geographic areas were mapped out, each with an assigned quota of experts to be trained. To give some indication of the size of the training program, Shanghai and Nanking turned out 375 high- and medium-level specialists between 1953 and 1958.[16] Concerning advanced training, a firsthand Western

[14] Cerny lists three clinics in Yu Ching Hsiang, Inner Mongolia, and Urumchi in Sinkiang-Uighur Autonomous Region.
[15] Ting Ts'an, "Tsen-yang . . . ," pp. 146–147.
[16] Wu Cheng-i, "New China's Achievements. . . ."

observer reported that there was a formal postgraduate and intensive one-year training course for psychiatry in Shanghai in 1960, possibly the first such arrangement. The same report also stated that ordinary medical students in their fourth year must spend two weeks in a psychiatric hospital.[17] Other specialists include those trained in law schools on legal aspects of the mentally ill, based on Soviet works on the subject. The criminally insane were said to be subjected to psychiatric examination, and the opinions of the specialists in these cases were reportedly "decisive." [18]

Psychiatric Classification and Terminology

Psychiatric classification and terminology in Communist China suffered from the lack of precision and theoretical systematization, as was to some extent true of the situation in the West. A leading psychiatrist, Wu Cheng-i, once listed the major mental illnesses of Communist China as follows: (1) schizophrenia, (2) neurasthenia (psychasthenia [19]), (3) manic-depressive, and (4) paralytic mental stupor. With the three major types of psychoses: schizophrenia, manic-depressive, and paralytic mental stupor, the Chinese terms and the English translations appear to correspond to Western usage. The same cannot be said of *neurasthenia*, the term given in the English titles of the Chinese Journal for the mental disorder known as *shen-ching shuai-jo cheng,* or nervous weakness, which is the only type of neurosis discussed to any extent in writing. Historically, the term *neurasthenia* has had varying definitions and usages in Western psychiatry, ac-

[17] This is a very short period. See, Denis Lasure, "Politics and Mental Health in New China," *The American Journal of Orthopsychiatry*, Vol. XXXIV, No. 5 (Oct. 1964), pp. 925–933.

[18] Wu Cheng-i, "New China's Achievements . . . ," p. 597 ff. See also Lasure, who wrote in the earlier cited article, "Each criminal brought to Court is examined by a psychiatrist and, if found mentally ill, is sent to a psychiatric hospital."

[19] Li Hsin-t'ien, "Jen-shih huo-tung tsai shen-ching shuai-jo chih-liao shang ti tso-yung" (The effect of recognition in the treatment of neurasthenia), *Hsin-li hsueh-pao*, No. 1 (1960), pp. 36–45.

cording to different systems of classification. However, since it is no longer in current use in the West, it is impossible to find its equivalent entity.

The concept of neurasthenia in China is based on the Pavlovian theory of neurophysiology, according to which unfavorable external conditions can bring about tension in the higher nervous system in excess of its capacity, thus causing a weakening in the functioning capacity of the brain tissues and a lack of balance or confusion in nervous activity. Li Hsin-t'ien, a member of the Institute of Psychology and a leading medical psychologist, defined neurasthenia as "the lack of regulation of tissue nervous excitation and inhibition. Its manifestation is in serious disturbances in the tissue nervous activity relating to work, *hsueh-hsi* (study), society and family." The most prominent behavioral symptoms were reported to be insomnia, headache, dreams, and pains. A fuller operational definition, based on Pavlov's theory of neurasthenia and the symptomatic description of V. A. Gilyarovsky, is as follows.[20]

(1) When objective reasons for exhaustion were eliminated, and the pathological symptoms persisted, and even became more severe for over a month, we diagnosed the symptoms as neurasthenia, otherwise not. (2) When other physical disorders were present (tuberculosis, high blood pressure, rheumatism, syphilis, stomach or duodenum ulcers, overactive thyroids, severe anemia or malnutrition, and chronic diseases of the eye, ear, nose or throat), we did not diagnose the patient to be suffering from neurasthenia. (3) If there was no clear indication of emotional causes, and yet the

[20] The translation by the Joint Publications Research Service of this major category of mental illness is *psychasthenia*. From internal evidences in this document, such as definition of the disease and some overlap with other documents in the evaluation research cited, we have no doubt that it is the same disease entity that the English titles of articles in the *Hsin-li hsueh-pao* give as *neurasthenia*. Nowhere else in our data have we found the term *psychasthenia*, although both terms stem from the changing vocabulary of Western psychiatric tradition. We shall henceforth use only the term *neurasthenia*.

typical symptoms of neurasthenia were present, and no physical disorders were discovered, we diagnosed the illness as neurasthenia. (4) If the patient complained about headache or other organic malfunction without suffering from other general symptoms of a weak suppressing process (such as extreme irritability, lack of patience and reduced self-control, inability to concentrate, lack of memory, and insomnia), we did not diagnose the trouble as neurasthenia. (5) When symptoms of other mental diseases, such as compulsion or hysteria were present along with the characteristics of neurasthenia, we did not diagnose it as neurasthenia." [21]

The problem of neurasthenia was prominently recognized during the State's concentrated attack upon it during the Great Leap Forward. Neurasthenia is a rather large and amorphous category of mental illness, with boundaries that must be difficult to draw in practice. As a result, diagnosis and definition of cure were probably interpreted with a high degree of flexibility during the rapidly expanded program of 1958–1959. Neurasthenic patients were apparently treated as a group, with no further subclassifications. This appears to be the only type of mental disturbance that received much attention either in treatment programs or in research.

Mental Health Surveys

During the Great Leap, in the spirit of carrying the knowledge of experts to the people to solve their concrete problems, teams of medical and psychiatric personnel, psychologists, and others cooperatively carried out mass surveys of mental health in several leading cities. A total of at least 18 million persons were thus covered in these surveys. We

---

[21] Li Ch'ung-p'ei, Hsu Yu-hsin, Keng Chen-mei, Wang Ming-te, Graduate Study Group, Mental Health Department, Peking College of Medicine, "Some problems concerning the cause of psychasthenia and attempts to find quick treatments," in *Collections of Thesis on Achievements in Medical Sciences in Commemoration of the 10th National Foundation Day of China*, Vol. II, "Mental Health," pp. 652–670.

have some information regarding at least three such undertakings, two in Peking and one in Nanking; and three other cities, Shanghai, Ssu-p'ing, and Chengtu, are known to have had similar surveys. In these primarily urban studies, a few cities, such as Nanking, Ssu-p'ing, and Peking, included their surrounding farm villages as well. The surveys sought first to discover those who were suffering from mental illness and, in addition, to determine the different rates between various social or occupational groups, the "causes," and the preventive measures that could be applied.

The methods for conducting these community surveys and the techniques for screening potential patients were characteristic of the mass movement approach of the Great Leap period, and are worth quoting in some detail:

> The doctors specializing in mental diseases, the nurses and mental health social workers organized themselves into small groups. They checked with the local police offices, the residents' councils, and block committees to gain some knowledge of the condition of mental diseases in each area. Then they made door to door visits, and collected information concerning each patient (including potential patients). They gave these patients mental and physical check-ups, made diagnoses, and kept the files.

> For the purpose of making the survey a success, the groups organized the masses, families of the patients, and the Red Cross Committee of the block. Meetings were held, and informative literature was distributed. They began a program of mental health education, and helped the residents to correct their past misgivings about mental diseases, so that all of them may not only take good care of the afflicted, but also report new cases quickly.[22]

Similar procedures took place in universities, factories, and organizations; speeches were made at meetings explaining the meaning of the investigation, the usual or typical symptoms were described, and voluntary registration was asked for. Furthermore, through Young Communist Leagues

[22] Wu Cheng-i "New China's Achievements . . . ," pp. 615–616.

and other student bodies, lists of potential patients were drawn up "from every class and every group." In farm areas, door-to-door visits were made. These lists were also screened by specialists, with students in these fields doing the bulk of the preliminary work.

Additional surveys were conducted for the screening of neurasthenia sufferers. In Peking, the first such study of neurasthenia was undertaken between June and December of 1958. It took in workers of one factory and the student bodies of two universities, by the combined efforts of the Graduate Study Group of the Department of Mental Health in the Peking College of Medicine, the Division of Medical Psychology of the Institute of Psychology, the Psychology Specialty of Peking University, the Medical School of Peking University, and the hospital of Shih-ching-shan Iron and Steel Company. The second Peking survey, apparently a separate one, was carried out by the Peking College of Medicine during the first half of 1959 on a total of more than 25,000 persons in "eight factories, one commune, two colleges, two high schools, three art groups, one state-operated department store, and three people's district committees." [23] In Nanking, the city's own Mental Health Institute made a similar neurasthenia survey of 4,000 people in schools and hospitals in 1958.[24]

Incidence and Etiology

Information on the distribution of different types of mental disorders is highly selective and incomplete. Since the main concern of this study is not the extent of mental illness needs, the lack of comprehensive numerical data is not crucial. Nevertheless, due to the general inaccessibility of such information, the available data will be presented here.

Among the four major types of mental illness listed by

[23] Li Ch'ung-p'ei and others, "Some problems concerning the cause of psychasthenia . . . ," pp. 653–654.
[24] Wu Cheng-i, "New China's Achievements . . . ," p. 606.

Wu, schizophrenia was reported to be the most serious. Wu quoted a study of 3,875 hospitalized mental patients as concluding that 35 to 40 percent were schizophrenics, and that they made up 50 percent of all the hospitalized mental patients. About half of them were between the ages of 21 and 30. Second in frequency were manic-depressives, found most often in the 16 to 25 age group and next between 26 and 30. The proportion of manic-depressives varied from 7 to 14 percent of all mental patients in four cities (Hsian, Nanking, Peking, and Heilungkiang). The rate of paralytic mental stupor was reportedly about 2 percent of hospitalized mental patients in three cities (Nanking, Heilungkiang, and Peking), which Wu compared to a pre-1949 figure of 10 percent. As for neurasthenia, it accounted for 60 percent of the admissions to the outpatient mental-health department of the Peking College of Medicine.[25] By way of rough comparison, a study of first admissions to outpatient neuropsychiatric dispensaries in Moscow showed that in 1956 about a third fell into a comparable classification.[26]

Some further data on neurasthenia, produced by a survey in 1959, is given in Table 3.1, which shows the proportion of different population groups classified as neurasthenics. Since no figures are available to indicate the total number of neurasthenics, we cannot report incidence rates. However, we are told how the types of people found among neurasthenics compared with the same types in the total population surveyed.

Of the total population surveyed, roughly 54 percent of the residents were classified as "mind" workers—primarily high school, college, and medical students, agency officials, actors, and stage workers—and 46 percent were physical la-

[25] *Ibid.*, p. 599 ff.
[26] Regrouped from information contained in Mark G. Field, "Soviet and American Approaches to Mental Illness: A Comparative Perspective," *Review of Soviet Medical Sciences*, Vol. I, No. 1 (1964), p. 31, Table 6. (Alcoholic psychoses loom large in the Soviet Union, a category probably of negligible importance in Communist China.)

TABLE 3.1. SURVEY OF PEKING RESIDENTS, 1959 [27]
Distribution among Neurasthenics

Classification	Percent Among the Neurasthenics (total unspecified)	Percent in Total Survey (N = 25,491)
Age		
16–40 years	90.2	—
below 15, over 40 years	9.8	—
Type of worker		
"Mind" worker	86.7	54.4
Physical laborer	13.3	45.6
Physical laborers		
Heavy laborer	13.6	68.7
Light manual	86.4	31.1
One textile factory — by sex		(N=494)
Males	21	25
Females	79	75

borers. Yet 86.7 percent of those who suffered from neurasthenia worked with their minds as opposed to 13.3 percent physical laborers. Thus, while only about half of the total surveyed were mind workers, they made up almost seven-eighths of all the sufferers. (The figures indicate that neurasthenia sufferers were primarily young adults: 90 percent were between the ages of 16 and 40.) This finding supports the ideological emphasis on physical work. There is a further consistency in the breakdown between light and heavy labor: light laborers contributed proportionately much more to the patient group than heavy laborers. What is of interest is the conclusion drawn from this differential rate and the prescription for cure of the mind workers. Work of the mind was said to cause "tension of the cerebrospinal nervous system.

[27] Data from Wu Cheng-i, "New China's Achievements . . . , pp. 652–670.

This became excessive not because of 'too much mind work' but because of 'too little physical labor.' " As remedy, large numbers of the mind workers were "sent down" to work as physical laborers, and subsequent improvements in their condition were noted. Two experiments with a group each from Shanghai and Peking were supposed to have shown improvement in 57 percent and 51 percent of the cases, respectively.[28] A male-female breakdown among 494 workers in a textile factory showed hardly any sex differences in rate. Another comparison revealed that farmers did not differ from laborers engaged in loading and unloading work. Among medical students, those taking basic courses contributed two or three times more neurasthenic patients than those practicing in hospitals. Similarly, it was reported that the graduating classes in high schools have a higher proportion over the other classes, but we have no information on the proportions of these classes surveyed.

A study of neurasthenia among Peking University students and workers in the Shih-ching-shan Steel Mill, conducted by the Division of Medical Psychology of the Institute of Psychology, showed students to be six times as likely to suffer from neurasthenia as steel workers.[29]

The theoretical assumptions implicit in the Institute's approach to the problem of etiology, that is, the mode of classifying the origins of neurasthenia, reveal the conception of mental illness. In August 1959, 283 patients under treatment for neurasthenia were examined; they included students, workers, and members of a "certain military organ." [30]

[28] *Ibid.*, p. 605.
[29] "Kang-t'ieh kung-jen shen-ching shuai-jo k'uai-shu tsung-ho chih-liao kung-tso tsung-chi" (A summary of practices in speedy synthetic treatments of neurasthenics among the steel workers), Chung-kuo k'o-hsueh-yuen, Hsin-li yen-chiu-so, I-hsueh hsin-li tsu (Division of Medical Psychology, Institute of Psychology, Academy of Sciences), *Hsin-li hsueh-pao*, No. 4 (1959), pp. 256–263.
[30] Wang Ching-ho and Li Hsin-t'ien, "Shen-ching shuai-jo ping-yin wen-t'i ti ch'u-pu t'an-t'ao" (Preliminary study of the etiology of neurasthenia), *Hsin-li hsueh-pao*, No. 1 (1960), pp. 46–54.

Causes leading to neurasthenia were classified, first, according to the usual view of major life activities, work, *hsueh-hsi,* and daily life, as follows:

(1) Excessive nervous tension arising from the work situation. This type of tension reportedly accounted for 48.8 percent of neurasthenia in the military organ. It was argued that the functioning capacity of brain tissues was lowered either when the physical body was weakened by somatic disease or when pressures of work and *hsueh-hsi* became too great. Thus, 30 percent of the factory workers suffering from neurasthenia had just gone through recent illnesses, and 12.8 percent of the neurasthenics in the military organ showed symptoms of nervous exhaustion prior to becoming neurasthenic. However, the main instigating cause of neurasthenia was seen to be located in the individual's faulty "recognition process," whereby inadequate perception of reality leads to inability to respond appropriately. Concrete types of faulty recognition were given:

(a) Work responsibility beyond the limits of self-estimated ability. When a person's sense of responsibility is strong, he can temporarily overcome excessive work demands and carry on. But when the situation persists and tissue cells get no chance to recuperate, neurasthenia results.

(b) Difficult and unfamiliar work combined with high pressure. Examples were given of old workers promoted to cadres, or semi-literates suddenly faced with the demand to prepare reports. These two reasons together accounted for 35 percent of the neurasthenia cases in the military organ.

(c) Individual recognition falling behind objective demands, such as when someone loses interest in his work or complains of fatiguing burdens or lack of appreciation by others.

(d) Overconcern with responsibility of work.

(2) Excessive nervous tension arising from *hsueh-hsi.* This cause was attributed to 41 percent of neurasthenic students and 19.8 percent of the afflicted military persons.

(a) Excessive self-demands combined with heavy load in *hsueh-hsi.* Most people in this category came from worker or peasant families. They reportedly showed impatience to learn and lacked knowledge of mental hygiene.

77

A minority also felt too proud, too competitive, or too afraid of losing face.

(3) Unfortunate events in life. Unforeseen tragedies in life were thought to be responsibile for 45 percent of neurasthenia among students, 39 percent of workers, and 31 percent in the military organ. Such incidents included loss of love or unhappy marriages, blame for errors, lack of harmony with work associates, death of loved ones, overconcern with physical impairment, temporary financial difficulties, and so forth.

A basic assumption of this theory was that no matter what the external circumstances may be which exert pressures upon the individual, they must "go through" his psychological activity, especially the recognition process, before they can become internal causes for neurasthenia. This view of mental illness placed heavy emphasis upon the concept of active consciousness.

Psychiatric Treatment and the Speedy Synthetic Method

Psychiatry in Communist China by the end of the fifties was making use of a combination of several Western and Chinese drugs and techniques, with the addition of a kind of mass movement approach. Among the drugs and technical procedures in use were insulin, Novocain, hydroxyzine, electric shock, heat treatment, artificial hibernation (via lowering of body temperature), and hypnotherapy (or various ways of artificially induced sleep). Psychotherapy was apparently not widely used until the Great Leap period,[31] when it became a routine part of a packaged treatment known as the "speedy synthetic method" (to be discussed later).

[31] An examination of the *Chinese Journal of Neuropsychiatry* during 1956 and 1957 (8 issues) revealed not a single article on psychotherapy. Neither were there any contributions from psychologists on any testing or other aspects of the diagnostic and treatment program. The only work by a psychologist was the piece by Ting Ts'an quoted previously, pleading for the relevance of psychology for medicine and psychiatry.

The use of traditional Chinese medical practices for psychiatric patients was widespread, especially acupuncture and ignipuncture [32] (also known as moxipuncture, which involves the infliction of small burns on the skin). Acupuncture, the insertion of needles into the skin in various specified zones of the body, is known to have been used on mentally ill children as young as three years of age.[33] A variety of herb medicines were tried on several types of mental patients. Among neurasthenia patients, some experimentation accompanied the use of these herbs: in one test a mixture of six different types of herbs was given to 115 cases, and in another instance a different mixture was administered to 640 such patients. The results were reportedly "beneficial."

The environment in which the patient underwent treatment also saw some changes in the late fifties. Proclaimed in 1958 in the spirit of the Great Leap was a campaign to show greater concern for the well-being of mental patients as fellow socialist citizens. Humane considerations were to govern the handling of patients. All "harmful" practices such as isolation and physical restraints were to be abolished, and a therapeutic aura was to be established, with the motto: "No shrieking in the adult wards and no crying in the children's wards." [34] A strong component of what is called in the West "social milieu" therapy was introduced, in which the entire social environment of the patient became a therapeutic situation. This program included patient self-government, work therapy, and the organization of physical and cultural activities such as choruses, dances, and evening parties, as well as study groups and discussion meetings.

In 1958, a quick, packaged method of treating neurasthenia was evolved, known as the "speedy synthetic method"

[32] Wu Cheng-i, "New China's Achievements . . . ," esp. pp. 612–614.

[33] T'ao Kuo-tai, "Healing and Preventive Work in the Field of Childhood Mental Diseases," in *Collection of Theses on Achievement in Medical Sciences* . . . , pp. 692–693.

[34] Cerny, "Chinese Psychiatry."

or *k'uai-su tsung-ho liao-fa.* This innovation was put to use on large groups, and it excited considerable attention in medical and psychological circles. The treatment, made popular during the Great Leap, persisted for a few years afterwards, but references to it tapered off in the sixties. Creation of the speedy synthetic method is attributed to Li Hsin-t'ien and Li Ch'ung-p'ei. Li Hsin-t'ien was a leading member of the Division of Medical Psychology of the Institute of Psychology. Li Ch'ung-p'ei, presumably a psychiatrist, was at the Mental Health Department of the Peking College of Medicine. The method was a combination of all procedures and resources available to medical and psychological personnel, with no systematic attempt to differentiate the effectiveness of the separate elements of treatment. An important part in the speedy synthetic treatment was still played by drugs and physical therapy. The use of insulin, Novocain, "Pavlov's mixture of bromine and caffeine," and herb medicines was frequently mentioned, as well as acupuncture, ignipuncture, electric shock, electric stimulus, and a variety of techniques of inducing artificial sleep. Separately, these techniques and drugs were not new to Communist China; neither was psychotherapy on an individual level, although it was apparently not widely practiced, since Wu Cheng-i wrote in 1959 that "treatment with drugs is still preferred by most doctors." [35]

The speedy synthetic method was novel in that it (1) packaged all measures as a unified program of treatment; (2) was invariably accompanied by psychotherapy; and (3) consistently used the collective setting. It is worth recounting in some detail because it demonstrated the accommodation of a technical, scientific method to the political and ideological needs of the time. The program had elements of the "total push" characteristic of mass movements. The sequence, typically lasting about a month, would begin with a pre-cure mobilization assembly, sometimes couched in military phraseology, for all neurasthenic patients of a particular

[35] Wu Cheng-i, "New China's Achievements . . . ," p. 604.

group. A lecture would be given on the nature of the treatment procedure, benefits of the drugs, reasons why attempts at cures in the past had failed, and reasons why patients should have confidence in the present treatment. Subsequent lectures would take up the nature of the nervous system, function of the brain tissue and scientific origins, and prognosis of neurasthenia. The lecture courses varied from five sessions of a fairly academic and detailed nature to a simplified and shortened series for factory workers or other less-educated groups. Sometimes information on such things as the nature of sleep was added to correct a particular symptom, such as insomnia, with advice on the instillation of correct attitudes toward sleep and the use of "positive aids." Exhortation and pep talks were interspersed among the more technical material presented. Undertaking the speedy synthetic treatment was urged first of all as a political duty. Personal optimism, considered a central element in the cure, was linked with revolutionary optimism and duty to socialist construction. National accomplishments were extolled to heighten individual revolutionary zeal.

After the lectures, patients were organized into small discussion groups of 8 to 10 to talk over the material and to exchange their personal reactions. These *hsiao-tsu* (small cell) sessions, sometimes organized along "temporary Party cell lines," may have been attended by medical personnel, but their role was kept in the background. Leaders elected from among the patients "ran" these sessions. In addition, there was individual therapy, usually lasting one to four sessions, with the psychiatrist taking a directive role. These sessions, as well as group therapy meetings, again included a good deal of didactic material, although the building of a patient-doctor relationship of trust was also valued. An additional element in this relationship, not found in Western or even Soviet psychiatric practice, was that of inspiration through the personal example of the psychiatrist. His own determination to make the treatment effective and his ex-

81

pression of confidence in the cure sometimes took the form of a written testimonial posted outside his office. The therapist was further described in one account as a devoted, tireless worker, "covering the patients at night," "buying food for them," and "replacing hot water for cold," much as the idealized local Party official serves his people.[36]

Other aspects of this psychosocial therapy included health contests, self-government by the patients, work therapy, physical exercise, and cultural activities. Traditional forms of exercise were included, such as *t'ai-chi-ch'üan* (popularly known in English as shadowboxing) and Buddhist breathing exercises. In addition to the organized therapeutic measures, each patient was also encouraged to work out for himself a "sensible daily schedule" while in the hospital, to be modified and followed after discharge. This, too, became part of the material for discussion between doctor and patient and in patient groups.

While this description of the speedy synthetic method applies to both hospitalized treatment and clinic care, some special arrangements for outpatient programs may be mentioned here. In Peking University, for example, 80 of the "more serious" neurasthenic students during this Great Leap program were housed in a special dormitory and were given treatment before 9 A.M., between 11:30 and 2:30, and again in the evening. Neurasthenic patients among industrial workers, such as those in the Shih-ching-shan Steel Mill, were assigned either to live and take treatment in after-work rest centers or to attend mental health clinics. Thus, the patients were not removed from their normal work environments; therefore, there was minimum interference of the therapy in their work or study. Since the mental health clinics were throughout various districts in the larger cities, access to them presented no great problem. In this decentralized approach to mental illness, the Soviet precedent was undoubtedly helpful.

[36] Cp A.S. Chen, "The Ideal Local Party Secretary and the 'Model' Man," *The China Quarterly*, Jan.–Mar. 1964, pp. 229–240.

Some Indications of Rates of Cure

The rate of cure or improvement in neurasthenic patients under the speedy synthetic treatment was generally placed at about 75 percent or better. For example, 30 neurasthenic patients at the Peking College of Medicine clinic took the speedy synthetic treatment for three weeks and were tested by psychologists under the direction of Li Hsin-t'ien. Among them were 18 cadres, 2 workers, and 10 students, all between 16 and 43 years of age, with an average length of illness of five years, five months (ranging from two months to 21 years). Main symptoms were insomnia and headache. At the end of the course of treatment, 73.7 percent were said to be "all cured or basically cured." [37] In another study by the same Division of Medical Psychology under Li, 80 of the more serious students suffering from neurasthenia were treated in August of 1958. Everyone was said to have showed improvement at the end of the four-week treatment. Of the total, 81.2 percent were either "cured or were greatly improved." Among this group, 3 had a history of ten years of illness, 17 had five to ten years, 11 had under one year.[38] In still another study of 117 unspecified neurasthenia patients by the same team of psychologists, the results of the speedy synthetic cure were 34 percent cured, 43 percent basically cured, 16 percent greatly improved, and 7 percent improved.[39] Another report of research on 401 "older neurasthenia patients" with medical histories of five to fourteen

[37] Chang Tseng-hui, Li Chiu-lin, Feng Heng-ts'an, "Kuan-yu shen-ching shuai-jo tsung-ho k'uai-shu chih-liao chung ping-jen chu-kuan neng-tung-hsing ti ch'u-pu t'an-t'ao" (The role of active consciousness of neurasthenic patients in the speedy synthetic treatment) *Hsin-li hsueh-pao*, No. 3 (1961), pp. 163–178.

[38] "Hsin-li chih-liao tsai shen-ching shuai-jo k'uai-su tsung-ho liao-fa chung ti tso-yung). (Function of psychotherapy in a speedy and synthetic treatment of neurasthenia), *Hsin-li hsueh-pao*, No. 3 (1959), pp. 151–160.

[39] Li Hsin-t'ien, "Jen-shih huo-tung tsai shen-ching shuai-jo chih-liao shang ti tso-yung" (The effect of recognition in the treatment of neurasthenia), *Hsin-li hsueh-pao*, No. 1 (1960), pp. 36–45.

83

years showed that the combination method was also effective.[40]

In some of the cases just cited, follow-up studies were made from three months to a year after the treatment ended. Usually about three-quarters of those "cured" of neurasthenia claimed to have maintained the cure. Thus, of 58 former university patients who answered a written questionnaire, 46 (79.3 percent) said conditions remained stable. Among 69 cases of "cured" patients in a steel mill and power plant, 53 (76.8 percent) reported no relapse half a year later. As for the elderly patients studied by Kung, 114 cases were investigated again after four months, and 77 percent remained cured.

While major attention of the combination treatment was focused on neurasthenia, the same technique was tried on an experimental group of chronic schizophrenics in 1961–1962, although the name *speedy synthetic method* no longer appeared. The experimental group, consisting of three groups of 30 patients each, evenly divided between men and women, underwent the combined medical and psychosocial therapy for 16 weeks, a much longer treatment program than for neurasthenia. In other respects, the procedure appears to have been the same: assembly lectures on reasons for the treatment, the nature of psychological activities and of the illness, and ways of preventing recurrence of the illness; small group discussions; and, finally, open ward meetings for more exchange of informal talk among patients and physicians. After discharge, patients returned to the clinic on specified days for continued small group discussions, and the physician made home calls or visited the patient at work. Successes similar to those for neurasthenia were claimed but more cautiously stated.

One significant development emerged in this treatment

[40] Kung Yao-hsien, "Lien-hsiang shih-yen chi-ch'i lin-ch'uang ying-yung, I, II" (Free association test and its clinical application, I, II), *Hsin-li hsueh-pao*, No. 2 (1963), pp. 130–145.

program for schizophrenia: the increased emphasis placed upon psychotherapy, particularly on the doctor-patient relationship. Li Hsin-t'ien, who conducted this study, tried to counter skeptics who maintained that contact with the doctor was of no avail during the stage when schizophrenic patients had active delusions. Li said that even during early stages of the treatment, the patient characteristically hoped for more contact with the doctor, and that the doctor must not begin by direct attacks on the delusions. In later stages, Li continued, the patient would accept more direct criticisms from the doctor. Thus, he wrote, "When patients can grasp knowledge of psychology and the nature of the illness, they can shed delusions. But their capacity for coping with reality is limited, so they must continue to receive help and guidance during and after recovery, they must be shown which reactions to the environment are appropriate, which not, in order to maintain harmonious relations with the environment." [41] Li, in experimenting with the effectiveness of psychotherapy for chronic schizophrenics, attempted to demonstrate that the doctor-patient relationship was fundamental in the recovery process. This represented one of the efforts of medical psychology to contribute to an interdisciplinary approach to mental illness.

RESEARCH IN MEDICAL PSYCHOLOGY

The conceptual gains of medical psychology may be discussed under three topics: (1) contribution to current therapeutic thinking in Communist China, particularly in psychotherapy and the doctor-patient relationship; (2) clarification of the concept of active consciousness in mental illness, and the role of its components—recognition, will, and

[41] Li Hsin-t'ien, "Hsin-li chih-liao tsai man-hsing shen-ching fen-li cheng chung ti ying-yung" (The application of psychotherapy in the treatment of chronic schizophrenia), *Hsin-li hsueh-pao*, No. 1 (1963), pp. 55–64.

emotions; and (3) investigation into some physical and psychological correlates of certain mental disorders, using the EEG and a free-association test.

Although the speedy synthetic treatment for neurasthenia may have been launched as much for political reasons as for scientific-theoretical ones, its therapeutic approach nevertheless included innovative conceptual elements. It has already been mentioned that most psychiatrists in Communist China were in the habit of relying solely on drugs and physical measures in their treatment of mental illness. Here, instead, organized lectures, discussion groups, and work and recreational groups made controlled use of the entire environment of the patient, a method somewhat similar to the concept of milieu therapy of the West, although that term was not adopted in Communist China. One might say that the over-all atmosphere of the speedy synthetic treatment, including its mass mobilization techniques, constituted the managed social environment in the broadest sense, while the various social organizations of the patients made up the planned milieu in the more conventional sense. Advocates of the speedy synthetic method did conceive of the entire packaged plan rather than any specific measure or combination of measures as the effective treatment for neurasthenia and, to some extent, also for schizophrenia.

This use of the entire social environment for therapeutic purposes might well have become the main object for scientific study and evaluation by medical psychologists, but this did not take place. There were just a few isolated observations on this subject, such as the desirability of maximizing the influence of the group through cell organization and the favorable effect of one patient's cure upon another in the same group. This failure to make a rational study of a major social movement directly relevant to a scientific specialty is repeated in other branches—in labor psychology, for example. Of course, the group in its various forms was fully utilized in practice, but its effect upon the individual, or on different types of patients, was not systematically analyzed. Medical psychologists chose mainly to theorize about the functioning of the active consciousness within the entire speedy synthetic package, and to evaluate only one type of interpersonal relationship: the patient-therapist relationship. Psychotherapy was based entirely on the functions of consciousness, using mainly the methods of suggestion (*an-shih*) and reasoning (*shuo-li*). Medical psychologists consistently argued against the Freudian type of therapy involving the unconscious, which was said to "degrade the functions of consciousness."

Medical psychologists in China defined psychotherapy as "everything that goes through the patient's psychological activity which has a curative effect." In the narrower sense, psychotherapy was defined as "everything that goes through the second signal system" or that employs linguistic symbols; in other words, the influence of symbols and language on the functioning of the nervous system. Thus defined, this touches upon many aspects of organized group activities in the therapeutic setting as well as the formal lectures. Li Hsin-t'ien, in connection with the use of psychotherapy on chronic schizophrenic patients, pointed out that the patient-therapist relationship was critical for the recovery process, for it facilitated the physiological effects of drugs.

Aside from broadening the concept of therapy for mental illness from the predominantly physical and pharmaceutical to that of control over the total psychosocial situation, some conceptual clarification was also made on the nature of the active consciousness and the functioning of its components. In a study of 30 neurasthenic patients in a Peking clinic in the winter of 1960, Li Hsin-t'ien and his assistants investigated the three components of the active consciousness: recognition,[42] will, and emotional attitudes.[43] Their methods of investigation were chiefly case study, clinical

[42] See definition on page 14.
[43] Chang Tseng-hui, *et al.*, "Kuan-yu shen-ching shuai-jo. . . .

observation, and individual conferences. The research workers took direct part in the treatment in order to "build up good relations with the patient, gain his confidence and cooperation . . . and deeply understand his thinking, behavior and emotions." The purpose of this study was to measure changes in different aspects of the active consciousness during treatment and to study the role of improved active consciousness in the recovery process.

In our attempt to trace the development of concepts, this research is important for two reasons: (1) it shows the efforts of the medical psychologists to break down the much-used concept of active consciousness into observable and even measurable elements; and (2) it is the most explicit statement by psychologists on the theoretical supremacy of the rational component of recognition in the psychological activity of the individual. It was stated that of the three components, recognition and will were much more important in determining the behavior of the individual than emotion; and of the first two, recognition was the foremost.

Recognition was observed through its manifestation in the patient's understanding of his own illness and his confidence for a cure. Thus, patients were divided into three groups: Group I had comparatively correct and complete understanding and confidence in a cure; Group II had partial understanding and lacked an optimistic attitude toward a quick cure; and Group III had defective understanding and was chronically under the control of the illness. Purposive behavior was observed in terms of the patient's ability to persevere in his work, to plan his leisure activities, and to carry out his personal interests. Finally, the emotional dimension was assessed through such qualities as pessimism, restlessness, irritability, calmness, or elation. To demonstrate their theoretical position that recognition was the most important component of consciousness, the investigators showed that the quality of recognition was crucial in affecting an eventual cure.

Changes in the recognition component were noted as follows: during the first phase of the treatment, there were 8 patients in Group I (in this group, 6 were completely cured and 2 showed marked improvement); in the second phase 17 had attained Group I; and at the end of the treatment, 18 were classified in Group I. The proportion of cured or improved patients rose with each phase. Purposive behavior was rated in such activities as the patient's ability to follow regulations, take medicine, participate in *t'ai-chi-ch'üan* (shadowboxing), "voluntarily eliminate" causes of neurasthenia, arrange his own schedule, cooperate with the doctor, and show concern for the group and fellow patients. Ratings of this component also rose during the treatment. As for the emotional component, the number of pessimistic patients steadily declined during the course of the treatment. Those patients who were classified in Group I in recognition were shown to have preserved this high rating throughout the treatment and to have achieved either complete cure or "basic cure." Those with poor recognition (Group II) produced only one "basic cure," the rest showed either improvement or marked improvement. Among the 14 who started the treatment with average recognition, 9 increased their recognition to the level of Group I, and 6 of these were able to raise their level of cure. It was argued from these results that the recognition function was of fundamental and critical importance in the psychological balance of the individual.

According to the authors of this research report, although the individual's class background and social environment colored his thinking, a person's individuality was also relevant. For instance, neurasthenia patients were observed to be impatient, anxious, oversensitive, and dogmatic. But active consciousness was, in this view, subject to change, depending on the severity of the problem, elimination of precipitating causes, and effectiveness of treatment measures, including the attitude and efforts of medical personnel.

In another investigation,[44] Li Hsin-t'ien probed into the fluctuating nature of the recovery process of neurasthenia and the development of secondary symptoms, leading him to note "contradictions" in the recognition function. He plotted the curve of improvement into three kinds: straight curve up, gradual curve up, and wavy curve up. "The straight curve up had the highest percentage of cures." Sometimes in the course of treatment, Li observed, new interests were cultivated in the patient, which led him to lose interest in the treatment program. Or a patient would become over-concerned with his own illness, or oversensitive to the ups and downs of the cure. Li wrote:

> The original external causes in work or *hsueh-hsi* may have disappeared, but due to neurasthenia, changes occur in work or *hsueh-hsi* which make the patient turn his attention to his own illness, becoming in turn associated with the new illness. . . . Therefore, it is unavoidable that after inception of illness, new causes arise out of incorrect management of work, *hsueh-hsi,* or living. Thus in four weeks, one third of our patients showed new waves of symptoms.

These phenomena were observed and recorded but were given no theoretical explanation in terms of the internal dynamics of the components. Undoubtedly, the lack of conceptual refinement on the connections between self-attitudes and relationships to others hampered the systematization of these clinical observations. The concept of recognition was thus used to cover a broad range of phenomena, including this additional dimension of the complex adjustment process of the neurasthenic patients. As Li stated elsewhere, the interrelationship among the three elements of the active consciousness was an unexplored subject that needed deep study.

The second component of the active consciousness, will or volition, was less explicitly developed. Nevertheless, the element of will was generally assumed to be necessary in the treatment program, especially in psychotherapy, although it

[44] Li Hsin-t'ien, "Jen-shih huo-tung . . . , pp. 36–45.

was not always analytically segregated from the operation of the recognition component. It sometimes appears from the writings of medical psychologists that correct knowledge would automatically lead to desirable change. At other times, we found statements such as this: "Armed with knowledge gained from the doctor, the patient can *voluntarily undertake struggle* with his own disease." [45] The source or motive power of this will is seen to be socialist society itself. As one medical psychologist put it, "The only source of unlimited motivation to fight mental illness is the sense of responsibility toward socialism." [46]

There had been almost no research on the emotional component of the active consciousness at the time of our study. When Li Hsin-t'ien observed the three components in neurasthenia patients, he wrote that the patients' emotional condition was used "only for reference." However, this emotional element, especially in interpersonal relationships, apparently became an increasing concern of Li's, for in a subsequent project applying psychotherapy to schizophrenics, he went at length into the importance of the doctor-patient relationship. On the basis of his experience with a variety of mental patients over a number of years, Li stated that he had come to the conclusion that this relationship was of crucial importance. Medicine, Li pointed out, could remedy only some malfunctioning in the physiology of the brain, with just passive effects on the original abnormal psychological conditions, leaving the patient still ill at ease in coping with the people around him. He must be shown which reactions to the environment would be appropriate. Through positive relationships with the patient, the therapist could, in Li's opinion, build a foundation for new social relationships and thus exercise active influence in the patient's ability to deal with others. The benefits of this relationship would,

---

[45] Li Ch'ung-p'ei, *et al.,* "Some problems concerning the cause of psychasthenia," p. 656.
[46] *Ibid.,* p. 665.

in turn, affect the will of the patient to struggle with his own illness.

This view of the emotional aspect of the therapeutic situation and its critical role in recovery is not very far from the Western concept of transference. In fact, for this particular study, Li Hsin-t'ien cited twice as many English-language sources as Russian.[47] These remarks by Li indicate a line of thinking that might eventually challenge the primacy of the recognition process, and perhaps bring about refinements in the theory of the active consciousness. Of course, there were other manifestations of the emotional dimension of the individual's total functioning: notably, his relationship with his fellow patients — the small group as well as the total therapeutic environment or movement. These had remained unanalyzed by medical psychologists.

Several psychologists began working in this area after the Great Leap period, when work of a more "scientific" rather than "activist" nature became more prominent. They used both the free-association test and electroencephalographic (EEG) measurements.

Parallel to the investigation of the functioning of the active consciousness in mental disorders was a different type of study on the correlates of nervous disorders, which was more directly in line with the Pavlovian experimental tradition and Soviet precedents.

Kung Yao-hsien was one of these more strictly Pavlovian psychologists. What is of special interest is the fact that Kung approached his research on mental illness both from the cognitive side and from the physiological side, although he made no mention of Li's use of the concept of recognition. To investigate the mental correlates of nervous

---

[47] Li appears to have been making an extensive study of this subject, for unlike most psychology publications, which have short lists of references, largely Chinese and Soviet, this article by Li listed 48 sources, of which 30 were in English, predominantly by American authors. (The remainder: 3 Chinese, 1 Japanese, and 14 Russian.)

disorders, Kung created and standardized a free-association test of 50 stimulus words, which he used first on 496 normals and then on 198 mental patients.[48] The reaction time and the responses were analyzed and compared with foreign as well as previous Chinese results. His conclusion — that sex of the experimental subjects did not produce a difference in reaction time or response but that age and educational level did — was based strictly on Pavlovian theory. He explained the shortening of reaction time from childhood to adulthood in terms of the gradual development of the second signal system. Furthermore, he interpreted the similar trend in rising educational level as the cumulative establishment of temporary nerve connections in the learning situation, thus producing a ready supply of connections to react to the stimulus words. With increasing age beyond adulthood, the reaction time again lengthened. The concepts of nerve excitation and inhibition were evoked to explain this trend. During the growth period, Kung pointed out, excitation and inhibition were both being developed, but within this, voluntary inhibition was the last to mature. In old age, however, the strength and activity of nervous processes declined. Thus, the slower reaction in childhood was due to low development of the excitation function, while in old age, voluntary inhibition accounted for the same phenomenon.

Kung then applied the free-association test to a group of mental patients (198 neurasthenics, 29 hysterics, 17 cases of obsessional neuroses, and 26 hypertension and peptic ulcer patients) and compared the results. The test reported reactions of all the mental patients to be slower, fewer, and less complete, with each type of illness showing a characteristic pattern. For example, the reaction time of neurasthenics and obsessional neurotics turned out to be the longest, with neurasthenics omitting more responses and obsessional neurotics giving more delayed responses. Again, Pavlovian concepts were employed. Neurasthenics were said to have weak-

[48] Kung Yao-hsien, "Lien-hsiang. . . ."

ened excitation in the second signal system. The reaction times of patients with clinical symptoms of heightened excitation were slower than normals but faster than patients suffering from involuntary inhibition. In this theory, when both excitation and inhibition functions were weakened, with voluntary inhibition especially so, the net effect was fairly high excitation. The characteristic reaction pattern of patients with obsession neuroses — slow in the beginning but with increasing speed and increasing repetitions — was explained in terms of the development of inertia (*to-hsing*), not the weakening of tissue processes. Hysteria patients were described as showing a gradual increase in reaction time due to weakening of nerve processes. Compared to neurasthenic patients, although there were some similarities in symptoms, their patterns of mental reactions were different. The obstructions in the nervous functioning of the patients with hypertension or peptic ulcers were said to be less severe, since they originated from the lower level tissues, involving less of the higher, psychological functions. Further differences were pointed out between the patterns of patients with obsessional neuroses, whose reactions to concrete and abstract words were not different, and hysteria patients, who had longer reactions to abstract words than to concrete ones.

Finally, a concept of "illness center" (*ping-tien*) was invoked by Kung to explain the spreading of effect from the emotion-laden words in the test to the adjacent neutral words. The reasoning offered was the spreading of effect from one signal system to another. Kung proposed this concept to explain the obstinate outlook of obsession neurotics and the self-centeredness of neurasthenics. In adopting his conceptual scheme for the mental activities of normals and psychological deviants, Kung relied chiefly on such Soviet authors as Pavlov, Smirnoff, and Ivanov-Smolenskii. Kung saw the free-association test as revealing two major types of deviations, and he wanted to promote the test as a useful indication of different abnormal conditions and as a tool for evaluating the effectiveness of treatment.

Besides working on the mental correlates, Kung was also interested in physical correlates of the mentally ill.[49] He investigated these using the EEG, with an eight-pen Ediswan-Mark II recorder. His subjects were 150 neurasthenia patients, most of whom were college students and cadres between 25 and 30 years of age, and a control group of 30 normals. Kung found that the EEG reactions to external stimuli were unusually quick and the after-effect reactions delayed among neurasthenic patients. Kung accounted for this difference from the normals not on the basis of inertia of the nervous system but rather on a weakening in its tensile strength, leading to a directness in responding to external stimuli and difficulty in returning to the state of normalcy.

The EEG (Ediswan 16-channel recorder) was used in a different way in connection with mental defectives (106 subjects), carried out under the leadership of Liu Shih-i,[50] a specialist in the study of brain mechanisms. Liu hoped to come to some theoretical conclusions on the effect of brain damage at various ages. He interpreted his experimental results on the brain waves of mental defectives of different ages to show the intimate connection between the level of mental development and the growth or damage of the brain. Injury or delay in brain development during early childhood would produce mental defects; but while similar occurrences in older people might result in amnesia or related illnesses, their EEG would not be too different from that of normals. Liu claimed that this developmental approach was a seldom-studied subject.

Other studies in the physical correlates of mental illness included the measurement of reactions to sound stimuli among

[49] Kung Yao-hsien, "Shen-ching shuai-jo huan-che p'i-ts'eng kuo-ch'eng chang-ai ti nao-tien-t'u yü lin-ch'uang ti yen-chiu" (An EEG and clinical study of the cortical function of neurasthenics), *Hsin-li hsueh-pao,* No. 1 (1963), pp. 65–74.

[50] Liu Shih-i, Wang Nei-i, "Chih-li fa-yu pu-ch'uan wei-che ti nao-tien-t'u yen-chiu" (An electroencephalographic study of mentally deficient patients), *Hsin-li hsueh-pao,* No. 3 (1963), pp. 194–202.

schizophrenic patients,[51] and the use of the psychogalvanic reflex (PGR) on neurasthenics. The PGR measures minute changes in the electric resistance level of the body.[52] A study in the use of the PGR was reported by Ch'en Chung-keng, who was interested in physiological indications of emotional states, particularly what he called the "self-sensitivity" of neurasthenia patients. The results of his experiments showed some degree of correlation between self-sensitiveness and the PGR. He also found that two types of neurasthenic patients — those who were restless, emotionally anxious, and oversensitive and those who were excessively tired — showed different curves (resting scores) than normals but similar greater reactivity. This seemingly paradoxical characteristic was explained by Ch'en in terms not of the oversensitivity of the receptive organs but rather of the weakening of the tensile strength of brain tissues, which caused the brain to lose selectivity.

Before concluding this discussion on research gains, a brief word must be said on the place of traditional concepts. Ch'en's work is of special interest because he may have been attempting to provide a bridge between strictly experimental psychology and traditional medicine. In addition to the numerous references to Western sources and Soviet theory in his writings, he also cited works from journals devoted to traditional Chinese medicine. In addition, he made a study of the psychopathological thoughts in the 2,000-year-old classic, *Tso Chuan*.[53] According to Ch'en's summary of ideas

[51] Sun Wei-chen, Cheng Fu-sheng, Li Hsin-t'ien "Ts'ung tui liang-chung ch'iang-tu sheng-yin ts'u-chi ti chien-tan fan-ying k'an ching-shen fen-lieh-cheng huan-che ti ta-nao chi-neng t'e-tien" (Characteristics of the cerebral functions of schizophrenics as shown in simple reactions to sound stimuli), *Hsin-li hsueh-pao*, No. 4 (1964), pp. 381–387.

[52] Ch'en Chung-keng, "Shen-ching shuai-jo ti tzu-chüeh cheng-chuang yü p'i-fu-tien hsien-hsiang" (Psychogalvanic reflex and the subjective states of neurasthenics), *Hsin-li hsueh-pao*, No. 1 (1964), pp. 103–108.

[53] Ch'en Chung-keng, "Tso-chuan chung ti pin-li hsin-li-hsueh ssu-hsiang," *Hsin-li hsueh-pao*, No. 2 (1963), pp. 156–164.

contained in *Tso Chuan*, human emotions were classified into six states (*liu-chih* or *liu-ch'ing*): love, hate, pleasure, anger, sadness, and happiness. Ch'en noted the close connection between psychological and physiological conditions in this document, as well as its emphasis upon psychological factors in explaining somatic and mental diseases. It was believed that the "six natural influences" kept life in equilibrium and that their disturbance caused the "six diseases," including "diseases of the mind and delusions." In the analysis of several cases of emotional disorders contained in *Tso Chuan*, Ch'en noted that mental activities sometimes were indicators of bodily states, and that mental conflict and psychic overstrain often induced or aggravated bodily illness. The book of *Kuo Yü*, a contemporary classic of *Tso Chuan*, further categorized the mentally and physically handicapped into the "eight diseases," with suggestions for "suitable jobs" for each type of sufferer.

Another study of traditional doctrines, published in a psychiatric journal,[54] described concepts that prevailed in psychiatry between the third and tenth centuries. These doctrines constitute the main heritage of Chinese medical knowledge, which had incorporated religious influences from Taoism and Buddhism, including Indian medical theories. This body of knowledge contained fairly elaborate clinical descriptions of both somatic and mental diseases. It recognized, for example, that "madness" (*k'uang*) covered several disease entities with different origins, and that "depression" often took the form of uncontrolled weeping and heavy limbs. While no counterpart to the concept of schizophrenia had been found in these traditional writings, many symptomatic descriptions were recorded that matched up with the modern ones. Another disease entity described was epilepsy, both the adult and childhood variety. Hysteria was recognized, too, and

[54] Hsu Yu-hsin, "Liang-Chin Nan-pei-ch'ao chi Sui-T'ang shih-tai wo-kuo ching-shen-hsueh chien-chieh" (Introduction to psychiatry from Chin to Sui-T'ang Dynasties), *Chung-kuo shen-ching ching-shen k'o tsa-chih*, No. 1 (1959), pp. 14–19.

its mental origins were emphasized. The symptoms of nervous weakness could be found described as well, although, they were not labeled the Chinese equivalent of neurasthenia. Finally, these traditional writings contained accounts of mental defects and stuttering and even some types of mental disturbance in children. Despite empirical observations and efforts at classification, mental disorders during this period were largely attributed to evil spirits. As for treatment, both acupuncture and herb medicine were prescribed.

The revival of interest in traditional theories on emotions and emotional disorders, mainly on the descriptive level, at the time of this study followed two themes. The first was that of nationalistic pride; it seemed to say "Look, Chinese culture offers a considerable body of traditional knowledge about mental illness and mental health!" The second theme was that traditional thought and contemporary Pavlovian theory have in common the unity of mind and body, in contrast to Western dualism.

THE SHAPE OF MEDICAL PSYCHOLOGY IN 1965

By 1965, medical psychology was gradually taking shape as a discipline, although in terms of its self-proclaimed broad objectives only a beginning had been made in research. The psychologists themselves were well aware of their limitations in research designs and methodology. Ts'ao Jih-ch'ang, in particular, emphasized the need for a stronger theoretical orientation in this area. Li Hsin-t'ien pleaded for a higher degree of control over the variables in research design. In neurasthenia research, for example, he proposed studies in which one group received only medicine; a second group, medicine and rational explanations; a third group, both but with the addition of "mass movement techniques to rouse the subjective motivation"; and finally, a fourth group without medicine but with all other techniques. He urged that failures in the speedy synthetic method be investigated and that different treatment procedures be examined for their effectiveness in different kinds of cases.

Other methodological problems of research, such as sampling procedures, coding or classification, or criteria of cure, had not been discussed in psychological publications. On the whole, studies of EEG or PGR employed more sophisticated quantification methods, such as statistical t-tests, while most of the Great Leap surveys and research on the speedy synthetic treatment used simple percentages.

Up to the period of the Great Leap Forward, the new psychology of Communist China had been mainly concerned with building a scientific foundation of Pavlovian conditioned reflex including first and second signal systems) upon a philosophical foundation of Marxism-Leninism, and an ideological foundation of the class nature of at least some aspects of psychological phenomena. Research activities were still largely centered on isolated physiological reactions or learning experiences, while concepts concerning the total person were few and little related to one another. The concept of individuality had been frequently mentioned, but generally in the context of a reaction against the tendency of the physiological psychologists to treat abstract processes of the depersonalized brain. The concept of active consciousness, though occupying a central place in theoretical writings, had not been applied to any significant empirical work. In other words, the theory of behavior during the early years was a static and incomplete one.

The politically instigated Great Leap program in medical psychology and psychiatry not only brought a new area of practical involvement for psychologists but, what is scientifically more important, it advanced the evolution of a psychological theory of behavior. The more articulate statements concerning a theory of behavior, behavior deviations, and corrective measures arising from the work of medical psychology are found in the writings of Li Hsin-t'ien and Kung Yao-hsien. Whatever one may say regarding the research

99

designs or the derived conclusions, these empirically oriented studies did lead psychologists to spell out further a more integrated theory of behavior and of deviation. The following paragraphs summarize this theoretical position.

Based on dialectical materialism, man's psychological activity is entirely the reflection of objective reality, especially of conditions of social life. Objective situations are in constant flux; they can progress from quantitative change to qualitative change. Changes external to the individual constitute the "conditions" of change for him, while changes internal to the individual are the "basis" of change. External causes must "pass through" (*t'ung-kuo*) internal causes to be functional for anyone. Mental disorder results whenever the balance of the excitation and inhibition functions of the nervous system is disturbed, or when the nervous system is rendered incapable of working at its full capacity due to excessive pressures of the environment, physiological disease or impairment, or incorrect attitudes and thoughts. Mental disorders are caused by weakened excitations and/or weakened inhibitions, or a weakening of and obstructions in the nervous process as a whole.

How do unfavorable external influences lead to excessive tension in nervous processes? What are the criteria for favorable or unfavorable influences? External influences are referred to as conditions of "work, *hsueh-hsi*, and living." Because of differing conditions of social life, individuals vary in the activities of their consciousness and in their recognition process. The differences in recognition carry over to attitudes or emotions regarding work and *hsueh-hsi*. Positive, optimistic attitudes can result in heightened capacity for tissue activity and can increase the duration of cell work. Pessimistic, depressed attitudes can produce the opposite effect.

What is the relation between recognition process and other individual characteristics? Elements in individuality other than recognition — such as emotions, interests, needs, and aspirations — are, within broad limits, said to be controlled and changed by the recognition process. Therefore, whether some external influence is favorable or not for a particular individual is largely determined by the correctness of his recognition.

These conclusions about the theory of behavior led Chinese medical psychologists to conclude that neurasthenia was widespread in capitalist countries and difficult to cure. Under the changed, more reasonable conditions of socialist society, neurasthenia would be present only when the individual had mistaken recognition (that is, failure to properly "reflect" the regulations and techniques of work) or when he had faulty responses to a newly awakened sense of responsibility. Under socialism, it was argued, society is more reasonable and problems of neurasthenia are thus greatly lessened and more easily remedied.

The concept of "contradiction," so central in political writing, was not prominent in psychological thinking in China between 1949 and 1965. It was more simply assumed that the citizen of a socialist state could naturally develop the proper kind of active consciousness, if he was guided according to the "process of recognition" toward a correct understanding of himself and his environment. Once this correct understanding was attained, the individual would automatically be motivated to show the correct behavior. Hence, the chief burden for maintaining proper mental health remained with the individual and his recognition process. The family and the socioeconomic environment were relegated to secondary importance as causes of mental illnesses. While the group in its many facets was utilized in the treatment process, the family was largely bypassed in therapeutic thinking.

CHINESE CULTURAL INFLUENCES

Medical psychology evolved partly under the scientific theory of Pavlovianism, along with its philosophical foundation of Marxism-Leninism, and partly under the impingement of the Chinese version of Communism. Since the former was discussed throughout this chapter, it would be appropriate here to summarize and highlight some of the broader cultural factors.

Particularly Chinese elements of medical psychology were noticed in the revival of traditional medicine and techniques in the treatment of mental illness. Yet the influence of traditional medicine seemed to be superficial since traditional Chinese medical thinking about the structure and function of the human psyche was apparently not incorporated or integrated into the main body of modern theoretical thought in medical psychology. A less easily documented or proved kind of cultural influence was the old Confucian emphasis upon the rational aspect of man, the importance of education, and the use of the exemplar, all of which were evident in the practices and discussions in medical psychology just prior to the Cultural Revolution. At least, one could point to a congruence between these traditional elements and aspects of the new.

Several things can be said about political-ideological influences upon medical psychology at that time. First of all, the alternations between an early "scientific" phase, the Great Leap pragmatic-activist phase, and another "scientific" phase were manifestations of the process of accommodation and adjustment between a scientific discipline and national political requirements. More specifically, the very choice of neurasthenia as the mass mental health problem for concerted attack was clearly the outgrowth of ideological rather than scientific considerations; for although not much was known medically about neurasthenia, what could be more urgent politically than a relatively widespread but mildly incapacitating ailment that could affect the productivity of large numbers of people? The treatment program for neurasthenia also embodied the political spirit of activism in Chinese Communism, epitomized in the Great Leap, with its dictum that with enough effort, each individual could, through proper recognition, lift himself out of his problems. The fact that the individual, in the speedy synthetic method of cure, was aided by mobilization lectures, the personal example and testimonials of the medical staff, the mutual support of the *hsiao-tzu* (small group), and the total optimism and dedication of the mass movement reveals the strong influence of political and ideological considerations. These elements, not found in the Soviet precedent of collective therapy, were characteristic of the Chinese elaboration upon a basic idea. Instead of the medical personnel remaining in more or less direct, authoritarian control of the group, as in the Soviet situation, in Communist China the patient small group was self-governing, with its elected leader in charge of discussions. And in addition to the sharing of mutual mental and physical suffering, as in the Soviet collective therapy, the patients in the *hsiao-tzu* were totally involved in one another's struggle toward medical and ideological improvement, much as were ordinary citizens in self-criticism — mutual-criticism groups in the wider society struggle toward ideological improvement. In fact, it is difficult to draw a line between the therapeutic groups in the medical setting and other criticism–self-criticism groups throughout the Chinese society, for the latter also exercised near-therapeutic functions.

Although the influence of politics and ideology on medical psychology was pronounced, the reverse was also true in part; medical psychology had an impact on the national scene. Through the mass attack on neurasthenia, whatever the claimed medical results may have been, a new mass role was created: large numbers were identified as being sick, whereas their behavioral symptoms might otherwise have been defined as willful indolence or ideological deviation. The speedy synthetic program dramatized and popularized the medical, scientific rationale for a syndrome that placed the individual in the borderline region of socially acceptable behavior. It is beyond the limits of this discussion to speculate on the consequences of this, but the public-education aspect of it did provide an innovative and nationally important assignment for the medical psychologists.

The activist, "Chinese" phase of medical psychology gave way to another "scientific" phase during the first half of the sixties, only to be overtaken by the total submersion of the science of psychology to the ideological dictates of the Cultural Revolution. Perhaps the conceptual crystallizations of the activist era will somehow survive as a part of the total scientific tradition in Chinese psychology.

LABOR PSYCHOLOGY

During the first decade and a half of its existence, Communist China sustained a prolonged drive toward increased production, which reached a peak of concerted national effort during the Great Leap. Ideologically, physical labor has been consistently held in the highest esteem, and the masses, or those who "labor," have been considered the most important social entity of the nation.

It is therefore enigmatic that for a society such as Communist China, oriented to production and the role of the masses, labor psychology, or *lao-tung hsin-li-hsueh,* was not more developed among the branches of the new discipline. The accomplishments in psychological research on labor at the time of our study were modest and on a rather narrow range of problems compared to research in other branches. Beginning shortly prior to the Great Leap period, research articles in labor psychology reached a peak of about 20 percent of all journal articles in 1959, but quickly declined to roughly 10 percent during the following three or four years.

Why, then, did not labor psychology reach a larger scope or greater depth relative to other work in psychology? The psychological study of work in the broader sense, for example, might have been a new and appropriate topic for the study of the lives of workers, in or outside the work setting, both as individuals and as organized groups. Furthermore, it is striking that with all the political emphasis on the peasantry, labor psychology hardly touched upon the rural worker except in an incidental way on student participation in rural production. The only study of more import we found was in the area of creativity. It undertook to demonstrate the ideologically derived notion that the working masses were the source of new ideas and new energy for social change.

Can this slow and restricted development in labor psychology be attributed to a late start with respect to the rest of the discipline? Or to a matter of terminology, a narrowness in definition? Or to a lack of knowledge of its potentialities? Or to the shortage of trained personnel equipped with a broad vision and devoted to the task of development?

FROM INDUSTRIAL TO LABOR PSYCHOLOGY

Labor psychology is not a new field for the older Chinese psychologists. The Western tradition of industrial psychology was introduced into China after the First World War, when the Taylor system, or time-motion studies, became known to Chinese psychologists following the translation of F. W. Taylor's *Principles of Scientific Management*. By the thirties, much of the English-language work in this field was available in Chinese, and some indigenous experimentation was begun. For example, the original Institute of Psychological Research under Academia Sinica cooperated with Tsinghua University in 1935 in conducting experimental studies of factory workers.[1] Just before the changeover, Chou Hsien-keng (Siegen Chou) was engaged in a survey on "the psychology of workers," beginning with an experiment on the "suggestion box" system in a railway workshop.[2] In 1958,

[1] Ts'ao Jih-ch'ang, Li Chia-chih, "Chung-kuo lao-tung hsin-li-hsueh kai-k'uang" (Industrial psychology in China), *Hsin-li hsueh-pao*, No. 4 (1959), 204–213.

[2] Chou Hsien-keng and Chen Han-piao, "The rise of industrial psy-

Chou Hsien-keng was a professor of psychology at University of Peking.[3] Contemporary psychologists were thus familiar with the old tradition of industrial psychology and recently published reviews of previous work done in Chinese factories. This phase of the work was known as *kung-yeh hsin-li hsueh* (industrial psychology) or *shih-yeh hsin-li hsueh* (a variation of the same term, meaning "psychology of factory labor").

Preparations for the new *lao-tung hsin-li-hsueh* were started soon after the changeover, since it had been given a place in the original organization plan of the Psychological Research Office of the Academy of Sciences in 1951. Directly following the general retraining for all psychologists in Pavlovian and Soviet theories in the early fifties, research in labor was largely limited to some experiments on the perception of motion. Ts'ao Jih-ch'ang ascribed the slow start to "lack of a clear sense of responsibilities and direction." [4] In February and March of 1958, specific reorientation toward a new viewpoint in labor psychology was provided in a study class for labor psychologists on "the rationalization of work," conducted jointly by the Institute of Psychology, the Psychology Specialty of Peking University, and "other relevant units." Seventy cadres from factories and mining enterprises also attended to learn the "basic contents of labor psychology" and prepare themselves for work in labor research. The class coincided with the establishment of the Labor Psychology Division in the reorganized Institute of Psychology of the Academy and, of course, with the beginning of the Great Leap Forward. Labor psychologists subsequently went down to the factories and mines for concrete research, where they integrated hastily trained nonpsycholo-

---

chology in China," *Tsing-hua hsueh-pao,* Vol. 1 (1936), Joint Publications Research Service No. 3424.

[3] *International Directory of Psychologists* (Washington, D.C.: National Academy of Sciences, National Research Council, Publication 520, 1958).

[4] Ts'ao Jih-ch'ang, Li Chia-chih, "Chung-kuo lao-tung. . . ."

gists in a joint effort. This teamwork resulted in a number of research publications, which will be discussed later in this chapter. The general timetable for the development of labor psychology was thus not very different from that of medical or educational psychology.

Labor psychology probably suffered to some extent from the scarcity of senior men with specific interest in this topic and devoted to its development. Chou Hsien-keng, one of the leading psychologists in industrial work before 1949, was not, possibly for this very reason, part of the new team on labor. Leadership in the Division of Labor Psychology was in the hands of Li Chia-chih, whose predominant strength appeared to lie in general experimental psychology and the highly specialized information theory. (This research could, of course, have been potentially applicable to the industrial setting.) During the Great Leap, he did go down to production sites to do concrete research with other psychologists, and he coauthored some articles on applied issues of labor psychology. But this practical focus was not followed up in the sixties. Other senior men of the labor team remained attracted to other specializations in psychology. Hsu Lien-ts'ang's interest also was in experimental psychology and information theory,[5] and Ch'en Li, who reported on labor psychology in East Germany and directed a study on psychological problems in the training of textile workers, subsequently took up research on color and form abstraction in children. The fact that the review article on the state of labor psychology in 1959 was coauthored by Ts'ao Jih-ch'ang, a general theoretician without specialization in the labor area, suggests that top leadership of this branch retained their original interests. Although we have no information on the disbanding of the research team after 1960, it is at least possible that cooperative efforts in applied labor research gradually disappeared.

The significance the Chinese place on redefining in-

[5] This type of work by Li and Hsu will be discussed in a later context.

dustrial psychology as labor psychology should be stressed. "Labor psychology" is our translation of the new *lao-tung hsin-li-hsueh,* and it seems to us to be closer to the literal meaning as well as to the spirit of the Chinese term, although the English titles and summaries of the official *Journal* render it as "industrial psychology." [6] Contemporary Chinese labor psychologists make a careful terminological distinction in their own writings between the now discarded Western tradition of industrial psychology, known as *kung-yeh hsin-li-hsueh* or *shih-yeh hsin-li-hsueh,* and the new *lao-tung hsin-li-hsueh. Kung-yeh hsin-li-hsueh* (or *shih-yeh hsin-li-hsueh*), in turn, has been denounced as the tool of capitalists for the exploitation of the working class. The Taylor system and pre-Communist experimentation with the suggestion box in Chinese factories have been ridiculed as useless. It was pointed out that the more experienced Chinese workers were not deceived into suggesting more efficient ways of production for the benefit of capitalists. Only a few younger workers were said to have responded at all, and then it was to "demand" improvements in working conditions. All criticism has remained centered on this early phase of Western industrial psychology, with which the Chinese psychologists were directly acquainted. There is very little indication of familiarity or concern with subsequent developments in Western industrial psychology.

Another term sometimes encountered in publications on labor is *hsin-li chi-shu-hsueh,* the Chinese equivalent of psychotechnology, a Soviet designation of Western industrial psychology.

Lao-tung hsin-li-hsueh is also the term used to refer to psychological research on labor in other Communist countries, such as the Soviet Union and East German People's

[6] Peking psychologists may have been motivated by the wish to conform to known international terminology, sacrificing precision. What the Soviet psychologists call their comparable field would be, in English, "psychology of labor."

Republic. In 1957, a delegation of Chinese psychologists headed by Ts'ao Jih-ch'ang was sent on a six-month tour of East Germany to study its accomplishments in psychology. In his report, an entire section was devoted to German labor psychology, stressing its importance in the total development of German psychology in recent years. A Professor Straub, one of two leading labor psychologists there, was quoted as saying, "Labor psychology should not be viewed as an application of psychology but as the very core of psychology itself." [7] The visiting delegation was "very impressed" by the broad program of the German labor psychologists, by their spirit of solving realistic problems in production — "not slighting any aspect of it as being beyond the confines of psychology." It was specifically noted that German labor psychologists regarded even recreation or marriage problems of the workers as relevant because of their potential effects upon production.

Chinese psychologists were also well aware of the work done on labor by Soviet psychologists. Rubinstein's book on labor psychology appeared in Chinese translation, and shorter works by other Soviet specialists on this subject have been referred to in Chinese writings. The 1959 All-Soviet Psychological Congress was reported in the *Chinese Journal of Psychology*. Among the papers noted was one on rural production and the process of mechanization. The Soviet psychologists generally concentrated their research on the role of consciousness in labor. Yet in at least one instance — in discussing sensation and perception during physical activity — they went further to distinguish between the conscious aspect and that part "not reached by consciousness." Another topic reported on was Soviet student participation in rural labor. This report treated a wide range of problems, including motivation for participation, individual differences in learning, and the development of class determination.

[7] Ch'en Li, Ts'ao Jih-ch'ang, "Te-i-chih Ming-chu Kung-ho-kuo ti lao-tung hsin-li hsueh" ("Industrial psychology" in the German Democratic Republic), *Hsin-li hsueh-pao,* No. 2 (1957), 107–116.

The Communist Chinese conception of labor psychology, while not as ambitious as that of Straub, did consider the "entire psychological condition of the individual" as relevant for the productive process. Ts'ao Jih-ch'ang and Li Chia-chih thought the chief concerns of labor psychology lay in three areas. The first or most pressing task was to conduct research on how to speed up the learning processes of new workers and raise the performance of experienced ones. As another psychologist summarized it, the goal was to turn "slow hands" into "fast hands." The second major problem was the relation of production to the social organization of workers. By social organization, Ts'ao and Li were referring to the division of formal work tasks; there was no indication that social organization would involve the study of any informal organization among the workers. The third and broadest concern of labor psychology was defined as the relation between the functioning of an individual during production and his entire psychological condition (*hsin-li chuang-k'uang*). It was pointed out that how a worker grasped production techniques and whether or not he made improvements were regulated by feelings, emotions, and the active consciousness. Ts'ao and Li singled out this third area as the most crucial one for labor psychologists to study. Their reason was that realization of the role of feelings, emotions, and consciousness in production "separates labor psychology from psychotechnology of the West." [8] However, no concrete program for research was proposed, and the two psychologists were careful to disclaim any jurisdiction over "political thought work," which is similarly concerned with emotions and consciousness, but which is acknowledged to be the province of the Party.

Underlying all studies of labor was, again, the Leninist-Pavlovian frame of reference, based on the reflection process. Although the processes of sensation, perception, and motor activity, and the functioning of the higher nervous activities

[8] Ts'ao Jih-ch'ang, Li Chia-chih, "Chung-kuo lao-tung. . . ."

111

are conceptualized as a continuous series of functions, we must arbitrarily divide the work of labor psychologists into psychophysical studies and studies of the active consciousness in production. Somewhere in the middle of the range is the effect of language on sensation, perception and motor activity. For convenience, we have included motor activity in the first area, in which linguistic reinforcement bears directly on behavioral functioning, while we have left more general functions of the active consciousness to the later section, following the outline of Ts'ao and Li mentioned earlier.[9]

EXPERIMENTS

Experiments dealing with the "correct grasp of production tools and techniques" and those aiming at the "rationalization of motor activity" comprise the first category mentioned by Ts'ao and Li — the psychophysical study of the production process. The first kind focuses on processes of sensation and perception. Concretely, the researcher asks these questions: What should the worker see? What is his unit of perception and in what unit of time? And how does he discriminate from broad outlines to details, from the superficial to the essential? An experiment on the visual judgment of flames by steel workers, conducted by the Division of Labor Phychology, attempted to answer some of these questions. It was observed that in operating converters, workers had to make an estimate of the condition of

[9] Since the psychologists in Communist China do not offer a sharp distinction between labor psychology and general or experimental psychology, we shall treat empirical studies as belonging to the field of labor psychology when (1) a direct label is supplied; (2) the setting and target population studied is a production unit; or (3) the major behavior investigated is productive activity. Conversely, a study shall be classified as experimental psychology whenever the focus is conceptual or methodological, even though the workers might be used as experimental subjects. Admittedly, the distinction is arbitrary. Classification is simple when the Division of Labor Psychology of the Institute of Psychology is given as the author of a research publication.

flames inside the furnace, differentiate and coordinate complex stimuli, and make the appropriate responses. The process was broken down and studied in behavioral units, such as visual objects, visual signals, their localization in time and space, and the use of reinforcements, both visual and verbal. On the basis of their findings, the researchers recommended certain methods of training, which were broken down into units of operation.[10]

Another project was done at the Peking Motor Vehicle Factory under the collaborative efforts of the Division of Labor Psychology and the Technical Research Department of the First Machine Industries Ministry.[11] This study moved from localization by means of sensory estimation to the analysis of motor activity, that is, ambidextrous coordination and the elimination of superfluous movements. It was noted that conscious attention to the physical arrangement for work and conscious planning for efficient motion could result in coordination of temporal sequences of motion and of activities of the hands and feet. The eventual goal of studying the conscious coordination of motor activities, said the investigators, was to make them automatic, thereby freeing the higher nervous functions for attention to other matters.[12]

One important ingredient of mental activity accompanying processes of work, as seen by these labor psychologists, is linguistic activity, which can act as reinforcement in learning, in correcting errors, or in raising work capacity. This was the

[10] "Ch'uan-lu lien-kang-kung huo-yen shih-chieh p'an-tuan ti ch'u-pu yen-chiu" (A preliminary study on the visual judgment of flames by steel workers operating the converters), Chung-kuo k'o-hsueh-yuan Hsin-li yen-chiu so Lao-tung hsin-li-tsu (Division of Labor Psychology, Institute of Psychology, Academy of Sciences), *Hsin-li hsueh-pao,* No. 3 (1959), pp. 161–167.

[11] "Kai-chin ch'ung-ya-kung ts'ao-tso fang-fa ti ch'u-pu yen-chiu" (A preliminary study in methods for improving operations on punch), Chung-kuo k'o-hsueh-yuan, Hsin-li yen-chiu so, Lao-tung hsin-li tsu. Division of Labor Psychology, Institute of Psychology, Academy of Sciences), *Hsin-li hsueh-pao,* No. 1 (1959), pp. 51–56.

[12] *Jen-min jih-pao,* Nov. 30, 1956.

justification given to some aspects of training and group meetings. An interesting application of this principle of linguistic reinforcement led to the recommendation by psychologists that workers correct wrong motions by repeating them while saying consciously to themselves that they were wrong. This exercise was then to be followed by correct motion. Thus, it was argued in Pavlovian terms, "inhibition" of the correct motion would be removed and the correct motion itself established with the help of verbal reinforcement. The practice, when tried at some training sessions at the Hangchow Cotton Spinnery, had to be abandoned because of resistance by the workers, trainers, and cadres alike, despite the fact that a trial run with twenty or so workers had brought about "positive results." [13] It seemed that "common sense" finally won out over Pavlovian theory.

A special case study of an advanced textile worker shows most clearly the approach toward the study of efficiency through analysis of behavioral processes and internal linguistic reinforcements. This research was done in 1962 in a Kuangtung spinning and weaving factory, under the direction of Wu Chiang-lin of the Psychology Specialty of Kuangtung Normal College.[14] The researcher spent two months as participant observer beside a model worker and compared her working characteristics with those of an average worker and a poor worker. The conclusions of this research were that the advanced worker showed the following characteristics: (1) proficient and precise operational skill, including the maximum use of her tactile sense, thus freeing vision for attention elsewhere; (2) accurate observation and efficient distribution of attention; and (3) effective

---

[13] Ch'en Li and Chu Tso-jen, "Hsi-sha-kung p'ei-hsun chung ti chi-ko hsin-li-hsueh wen-t'i" (Some psychological problems in the training of fine textile weavers), *Hsin-li hsueh-pao,* No. 1 (1959), 42–50.

[14] Tseng-Ch'eng-jui, "Hsia-sha hsien-chin sheng-ch'an-che ts'ao-tso t'e-tien ti ko-li yen-chiu" (A case study of the characteristics of working of an advanced textile worker), *Hsin-li hsueh-pao,* No. 1 (1963), pp. 75–80.

planning of work. In presenting this last point, in which the mental processes of the advanced worker were analyzed, application of Pavlovian concepts was most explicit. The efficient worker was described as using verbal symbols in anticipatory planning of her operations. Furthermore, it was reported that she "checked her own work and summarized her experiences regularly." Thus, the second signal system was shown to be in full play, affecting the functioning of sensory and motor skills.

The theory of reflection has also been applied in a study of industrial accidents. In 1957, Li Chia-chih and Hsu Lien-ts'ang of the Institute of Psychology studied accident cases in the metallurgical and machine manufacturing industries with the purpose of determining origins of worker errors.[15] The investigators came to the conclusion that the usual classification of errors into worker versus management or physical equipment versus human factors was inadequate. In terms of the new psychology, the proper functioning of the worker's psychological processes — his sensory-motor functions as well as his higher nervous activities — was just as important as the material conditions he "reflected." In this line of reasoning, human and material factors merge. The report concluded that there should be some system of selection of workers for their suitability for specific industrial tasks and then proper training for accident prevention, including the use of mutual verbal reminders in group meetings among workers. A good deal of responsibility was placed on management, who had charge of selection, training, and education programs, as well as the arrangement of "proper techniques of organization for work." Workers were then charged with displaying proper reflection of this work environment. (A concrete recommendation arising out of this study was the shortening of the group meetings (*hsueh-hsi*)

[15] Li Chia-chih, Hsu Lien-ts'ang, "Kung-yeh shih-ku yuan-yin ti ch'u-pu fen-hsi" (Causation of industrial accidents), *Hsin-li hsueh-pao*, No. 1 (1957), pp. 184–193.

before each shift, thus reducing the total working day, including transportation, from ten to eight hours.)

This study unearthed an interesting age-sex difference in accident rate, which was given no explanation or even speculation by the research team. It was merely reported that women under 25 years of age had the highest accident rate of any age-sex group, but that women over 25 contributed almost nothing to the rate. By contrast, men showed no difference in rate by age categories. If these figures had any validity or representativeness at all (no information in the sample was reported for this accident study), the finding should point to a significant social and psychological situation of female labor under 25, at least for this type of industry. That this interesting piece of empirical finding was allowed to slip by without further comment by the labor psychologists is revealing. It is perhaps in part a consequence of the abolition of sociology and social anthropology as academic disciplines, and the lack of development of social psychology as a legitimate branch of psychology. For this sociological "fact" can readily be related to the "psychology of workers" and be subject to analysis within the Leninist-Pavlovian framework.

A study by Lin Chung-hsien in 1963 also reflected an interest in launching a testing and evaluation phase of psychology for the purpose of selecting the persons best suited to a certain kind of job, whether in an occupation or in education. He examined individual differences among aircraft and glider pilots as well as group differences between pilots and other groups such as automobile drivers, basketball players, and research workers. The task was to pursue a moving object by adjusting a rudder and a stick, simulating the flying situation. He noted that individual differences among pilots correlated with their actual flying abilities.[16]

---

[16] Lin Chung-hsien, "Psychological disposition necessary for the study of flying," *Hang-k'ung chih-shih* (Aviation Knowledge), No. 3

Thus, the test could be used for selection and evaluation of pilots. Lin's subsequent work, however, belonged more to pure experimental psychology.

Although theoretical work was given no specific place in the research plan for labor psychology outlined by Ts'ao and Li, some members of the Labor Division — Li Chia-chih and Hsu Lien-ts'ang in particular — turned to such work in the early sixties. Li's publications in 1963 and 1964 dealt with experiments in vision involving manipulation of flashing light signals as stimuli, treated as theoretical topics in coding and semantic noise.[17] He did include some loco-motive engineers in the group he used for testing his hypothe-ses, but the experiment had no direct relevance for labor. Hsu Lien-ts'ang in 1963 described several experiments on aspects of information theory.[18] Beginning with an interest in experimental psychology, Li and Hsu moved into a very modern, highly sophisticated interdisciplinary area involving mathematics and communications engineering as well as psychology. This type of work can be said to belong to the general rubric of what the Soviets call "man and technology" and what the West labels "human engineering." The potential implications of the research for industry are obivous in both terms. While the total output by Li and Hsu was modest thus

---

(Mar. 8, 1960), pp. 24–25, Joint Publications Research Service No. 2973.

[17] Li Chia-chih, "Shan-kuang hsin-hao ti yü-i kan-jao" (Semantic noise in coding flashing lights signal), *Hsin-li hsueh-pao*, No. 3, (1963), pp. 165–174, and "Kuan-yü shan-kuang hsin-hao yü-i kan-jao ti ling-i-hsieh shih-yen yen-chiu" (Further studies on the seman-tic noise in coding flash signals), *Hsin-li hsueh-pao*, Nos. 1–3 (1963), pp. 230–238; 42–47; and 321–329.

[18] "The amount of information as a determinant of reaction-time to complex stimuli," "The role of redundancy in learning signal pat-terns," and "Information transmission of horizontally arranged signal patterns," in Nos. 1, 3, and 4 of *Hsin-li hsueh-pao*; and Hsu, *et al.*, "Stimulus Response Compatibility and Efficiency of Infor-mation Transmission," *Scientia Sinica,* Vol. XIII, No. 6 (June 1964), pp. 1015–1017.

far, it has put them in the stream of pioneering work which in the Soviet Union has shown a sudden spurt of interest in this decade [19] and which in the United States has taken the shape of substantial interdisciplinary research programs since the fifties.

There was very little evidence at the time of the study of accomplishments in or even attention to the second major area of responsibility outlined for labor psychology — social organization and the division of labor in relation to production. The rationalization of production procedures in the sense of efficient division of labor within a work group, or along sequentially arranged work units, is an important problem that can take several forms, with different conceptual approaches, not the least of which is the truly social one of human organization. However, as we found in medical and in educational psychology, the group, in its variety of structures, was not subject to serious scientific study for its bearing on the psychological functioning of the individual. For example, the only report mentioned briefly by these two authors concerned the regulation of work flow along the assembly line in an electronic tube factory.

In a report on a creativity project, there was implicit recognition of the role of the group in raising the individual's creative capacity. This point, however, was not explicitly brought out or given theoretical significance or conceptual formulation as an aspect of the general effect of group membership upon individual psychological functioning. Nor was the group considered in another study, in which students were observed for "psychological characteristics" during participation in rural labor. Only isolated observation was made on the attitude of the "good worker" and the "poor worker" toward fellow students.[20] The typology of "good workers"

---

[19] At the 1963 All-Union Congress of Psychology in Moscow, 16 percent of all papers read (57 papers) were classified as "man and technology," while no such category existed at the 1955 or 1959 meetings.

[20] Li Yi, "Hsiao-hsueh kao-nien-chi hsueh-sheng ts'an-chia nung-yeh

and "poor workers" was in terms of cognitive aspect, on the one hand, and behavioral and attitudinal differences, on the other.[21] The lack of conceptualization on the social organization of labor was in a glaring omission in the development of Chinese labor psychology. Yet precedent for studying the social organization of the work setting was not entirely lacking. The Chinese report on East German labor psychology in 1957 did mention the German study of differential production output between a cooperative shop whose members got along well and one with poorer interpersonal relations. Also, a similar summary of a Soviet study on student participation in rural labor noted that work organization (*lao-tung tsu-chih*) was the variable used to investigate the speed in the formation of desirable moral characteristics.

A most promising idea for research into the effect of social organization upon production appeared in print but was apparently never carried out. The suggestion came from Liu Fan, a psychologist not identified with the labor field. He pointed out that the collective nature of productive labor in the factory could be divided into three types according to work arrangements. In one shop, workers might carry on jobs in parallel fashion, learning from one another or indeed helping one another, but the efforts remained individual in character. A second shop might use the "running water," or assembly line, model, whereby the production of one worker

---

lao-tung chung so piao-hsien ti i-hsieh hsin-li t'e-tien ti ch'u-pu fen-hsi" (An analysis of the psychological characteristics of primary school 5-6th grade students participating in agricultural work), *Hsin-li hsueh-pao*, No. 5 (1959), pp. 293-302.

[21] If motivation remains unprobed, the question of incentives or external inducements, which has occupied the attention of some American industrial psychologists and which turned into the investigation of non-economic, nonrational phenomena such as the setting of group norms or informal production quotas, has not been touched upon in labor psychology. The omission of the incentive question by labor psychologists is not surprising, since private rewards, especially monetary and other material benefits, enjoy no ideological status in a Communist country.

affected the work of the one next in line. A third kind of arrangement would stress the effect of each worker on the production of the entire shop. Members would then be concerned with the work of others and would voluntarily help others. The last type would cultivate the collective spirit most efficiently, Liu hypothesized, and would build a more positive individual consciousness.[22] An example of another aspect of the social organization of work, the management or leadership in the industrial field, was at least known to the Chinese labor psychologists. East German labor psychologists noted that the quality of relationship between the cadre in charge of an industrial unit and the workers under him affected labor turnover in that shop.[23] However, no similar work was found in Chinese labor psychology, except for the brief reference to the responsibility of management for selection of workers and organization of training for accident prevention.[24]

The third major responsibility of labor psychology as conceived by Ts'ao and Li was to understand the relation of the productive process to the entire psychological condition of the individual. This covers a wide area and is indeed a very broad definition of the concerns of labor psychology. On the emotional feelings aspect of productive activity, to use one of their two major categories of psychological conditions, we could not find any published literature. Work on the active consciousness, however, entered into many research discussions, ranging from autolinguistic reinforcement in the learning of specific psychophysical acts, to mutual verbal reminders, and to the mental activities of an advanced worker. Indeed, the active consciousness appeared to be the overriding conceptual preoccupation of the new psychology.

So far, we have only discussed the functioning of the

[22] *Kuang-ming jih-pao,* July 20, 1959.
[23] Ch'en Li, Ts'ao Jih-ch'ang, "Te-i-chih. . . ."
[24] Recent American developments in management and leadership in industrial social psychology were not referred to or criticized in publications of the labor psychologists.

active consciousness as part of simple psychophysical processes. There were several available studies dealing with more complex levels of the functioning of the active consciousness, such as the "awareness of goals," "realization of work norms," or "ability to analyze work demands" and correct one's own errors. These studies were less sophisticated methodologically than those dealing with perceptual processes, undoubtedly a consequence of the nature of leadership in this field.

In one such research project on psychological problems in the training of fine textile workers,[25] two Chekiang Normal College psychologists conducted an experiment in a Hangchou Cotton Spinnery, 1957–1958, to demonstrate that "workers improve most when they understand what is demanded of them." In the language of Western psychologists, this was a test on different feedback of amounts of actual production. Thirty new workers were divided into three training teams of ten each. Team I was tested at the end of each day and told results of the collective training record. Team II was tested every other day and told only the individual percentage of his first day's record. The third (control) team had no knowledge of its own standing, and was tested only at the end of seven days. At that time, the ratio of test results of the three teams was 2.1, 1.9, and 1.1 respectively. The differential results were explained in terms of the influence of goal recognition upon production. "The great activating function of the consciousness of goals is determined by social conditions." In other words, the experiment was said to have demonstrated that when demands of society became incorporated as the individual's demands on himself, production went up.

The low result of team II was cited as proof of two points: that the percentage figure of one's own initial record was "too abstract" and therefore incomprehensible to workers, serving no role in motivating them to increase production; thus, the capitalistic type of individual incentive had "no

[25] Chen Li and Chu Tso-jen, "Hsi-sha-kung. . . ."

121

scientific validity." The latter incentive theory may appear correct, the experimenters cautioned; but because it was based on subjective speculation, it "could not stand the test of actual practice." Team III was not given any progress information and was cited as negative support for the original thesis. The conclusion was drawn that understanding of group norms was essential for the achievement of training efficiency.

Another test in this same textile study, which led the investigators to a similar conclusion on the role of rational understanding, is of particular interest here because it illustrates the possibility of ideological blinders in scientific work. Concerned with cutting down the number of mistakes made by textile workers, the experimentors classified workers according to the "origin" of their mistakes: (1) workers who realized work norms but did not realize their own mistakes, 10%; (2) workers who realized work norms and their own mistakes but still committed them, 70%; (3) workers with imperfect understanding of work norms, 15%; and (4) workers who could not independently analyze work demands and who did not recognize their own errors, 5%. It would seem that the overwhelming majority in category two would demonstrate other than rational understanding of norms as the "cause" of work errors, but the unqualified conclusion was nevertheless drawn by experimenters that workers improved best when they understood what was demanded of them and at the same time could verbalize their own mistakes. The recommendation was that trainers should explain errors in words, so that workers could remind themselves of them.[26]

[26] This experiment was cruder in design than others, perhaps because it was done in a provincial normal college. The test conditions of the three teams were not comparable. Nevertheless, we were more interested in the kind of conclusions drawn from these experiments and the nature of explanations than in passing judgment on their scientific sophistication. It is clear, for example, that these labor psychologists did not take into theoretical account a phenomenon long known in Western industrial psychology as the "Hawthorne effect," namely, that the very existence of the experiment and the extra progress test on Team I (attention of experimenters) can produce

The subject of what Western psychology calls motivation entered much of labor research (as in other psychological research) on a rather global level, almost always in the form of assumptions, with very little direct data or systematic conceptual analysis. In much of research writing on labor, recognition of the socialist goals of the nation was stated as motivating increased production or creativity, but *whether* or *how* that happens was not questioned, nor indeed when it *fails to happen*, as in the case of the 70% who continued to commit work errors. In the textile study, for example, motivation for learning or for cutting down errors was conceived of as automatically following the recognition of goals. Similarly, realization of the socialist goal for technological inventions was said to result in "self forgetting labor," extending the limits of physical capacity for work.

The directions toward which the Chinese labor psychologists seemed to be oriented in studies of the relationship between productivity and the active consciousness were two: the effect of physical labor upon cognitive learning in academic and other spheres, and the influence of productive activity on the growth of individuality. Although research in these two areas was apparently conducted as projects in educational psychology, it does not seem contrary to the broad definition of labor psychology's potential scope to treat them in this context. The effect of participation in labor on the acquisition of theoretical knowledge was dealt with in a project involving Peking middle school students in an electronic equipment factory.[27] The conclusion was drawn that

---

an effect on worker efficiency. Indeed, this effect was observed and recorded by the experimenters in this case, when Team III was said to have requested tests for themselves and was finally granted one. Team I initially fell behind in its record due to the extra "political work." These observations did not seem to lead the experimenters to qualify their results or modify their conclusions.

[27] Liu Fan, Kung Wei-yao, "Yu-kuan chung-hsueh-sheng sheng-ch'an lao-tung shih-chien ho chang-wo li-lun chih-shih ti kan-shi ti ch'u-pu fen-chi" (An analysis of relationship between the practice in pro-

practical work experience deepened the students' knowledge in physics and increased their curiosity toward further theoretical learning. This, in turn, helped the students toward understanding or "correctly reflecting" the conditions of labor, thus raising work efficiency.

In the late fifties, the relationship between productive activity and development in individuality had not yet been the subject of direct research. However, the previously mentioned study of primary school student participation in rural labor alluded to such a relationship.[28] (This was the only reference to any labor study in a rural setting, conducted from the point of view of educational psychology.) The psychological characteristics signaled out for observation and analysis in the "good worker" and the "poor worker" were conceptualized in terms of developmental stages. According to this theory, the child's recognition of his "individual labor activity" was attained first, in the chronological sense, and represented a lower level of development. The differences between the "good worker" and "poor worker" in this phase were said to be not very pronounced. The next level, the recognition of rules and regulations, was achieved to a greater extent by the "good workers" than the "poor workers." Finally, the spirit of collectivism was the stage most pronounced in the "good workers" but difficult to find in the "poor worker." The relationship here was stated in correlational terms, without implying a causal direction either way. However, in the practical recommendations at the end of the article, the writers urged educators to increase efforts at broadening and enriching the recognition function of students, in other words, the correct understanding of the importance of regulations and the spirit of collectivism in labor. Thus, while the role of physical labor was not explicitly stated as a factor in character building, a close association between

---

ductive labor and the acquisition of theoretical knowledge in middle school students), *Hsin-li hsueh-pao,* No. 5 (1959), pp. 279–292.
[28] Li Yi, "Hsiao-hsueh. . . ."

development of individuality and experiences of labor was implied. Soviet psychologists have perhaps proceeded further along this line, for they have investigated work participation from the standpoint of the formation and transformation of individuality, of motivation for joining productive labor, of growth in self-awareness, and of the favorable development of capabilities.[29]

Research on creativity carried out by the Division of Labor Psychology displayed, more than other work of this branch, the characteristic stamp of Chinese Communism in that it embodied some of the "total push" spirit peculiar to the Great Leap period. For this reason, this study will be discussed separately from the three-point division of Ts'ao and Li, which we have utilized for examining the development of this field. In a 1959 article,[30] the labor psychology team of the Institute of Psychology reported on a study of industrial innovation conducted at the Hua-tung Switch Factory at Shanghai. Using the techniques of "concentrated analysis," workers at the switch factory underwent all-night work sessions and "blitz-like attacks," and achieved the creation of "140 sets of automatic and semi-automatic dies." The unit of organization for the task of planned innovation was a vertical one, in accordance with the leveling spirit of those years. It included shop leaders, technical personnel, investigators, and workers in a common task without differentiated functions or status positions. The experience of this group in cooperative innovation was recorded and analyzed in terms of the following psychological principles:

1. "Correct reflections of contradictions in the objective reality, i.e., of production tools and techniques" — in other

[29] Hsu Lien-ts'ang, "Su-lien hsin-li-hsueh. . . ," pp. 276–278.
[30] "Ts'u-chin fa-ming ch'uang-tsao ti ch'ang-shih chin-yen" (Some experiences in attempt at promotion of invention and creation), Chung-kuo k'o-hsueh yuan Hsin-li yen-chiu so Lao-tung hsin-li ts'u (Division of Labor Psychology, Institute of Psychology, Academy of Sciences), *Hsin-li hsueh-pao,* No. 1 (1959), 36–41.

words, rational understanding of the problems. The group approach was then justified on the grounds that because an individual could "reflect" only one aspect of the objective situation, a number of persons were needed to provide a more adequate reflection.

2. Use of prototypes in the solution of contradictions. On the basis of these prototypes, creative thinking was explained on the principle of association of ideas (*lien-hsiang*) and the process of imagination (*hsiang-hsiang*). The prototypes might be modeled after natural objects of technologically created tools or machines. The creation of the prototypes themselves was considered an act of the active consciousness, while in turn the prototype was said to stimulate "active thinking," "rational analysis," and "purposeful activity to meet the demands."

3. Utilization of the chain reaction (*lien-so*) nature of inventions. Building upon past experiences and innovations, successive waves of sudden attacks could proceed from the simple to the complex, from lower to higher levels of invention. Chain reaction was also seen as triggering off related inventions.

On the negative side, psychological explanations were also given for the necessity to overcome obstacles to creativity. Four kinds of psychological obstacles were presented:

1. Overcoming superstition and inferiority feelings. It was pointed out that general mobilization in political thinking alone was insufficient and must be supplemented by specific mobilization through objective analysis, examples, models, and scientific principles.

2. Overcoming the limiting functions of the prototype. This was presented as the opposite of the innovating function of prototypes.

3. Overcoming the confining nature of specialized knowledge. The caution was drawn that although specialized

technical knowledge was necessary for invention, it could, through proliferation of details, ignore simpler solutions accessible to the masses.

4. Overcoming old work habits and methods. The investigators stated that while training workers to follow instructions and diagrams was a good thing, it could also make it difficult for the same workers to exercise creativity.

After analyzing the creative experience of the group, three conclusions were presented: that group creation was possible, using the *hsiao-tsu* or small group as the basic unit; that creativity could be a planned activity under specified conditions; and that invention could result from the sudden-attack method, generating a heightened emotional pitch in the individual and thereby raising the functioning capacity of his brain to a high level.

Two characteristics of this over-all approach to creativity stand out. First is the rationalistic emphasis in the conceptualization of creative activity. In the words of the labor psychologists, the "exercise of intelligence" (*chih-li ti shih-yen*) and the ability to plan one's own work constituted the "main elements in creative activity." Under these conditions, it was explained, "the second signal system takes over the function of directing these activities, thus facilitating the formation of new associations in the brain and activating creative thinking." Nonrational factors were considered only in passing. The heightened emotional pitch of the sudden attack by the group, for example, was mentioned only as "favorable pre-conditions" of creative activity, not as any intrinsic element in it. The second characteristic of this approach was the essentially individualistic conception of group innovation. The members of the group "reflected," thought, and planned mainly in a parallel fashion. Each member of the group was given a specific aspect of the task to accomplish, and each "opened up (*ch'i-fa*) possibilities for the other *without standing in the others' way*" (italics added). Thus, the benefits of the group were largely a composite of individual attributes. Although this theory of group creation was undoubtedly not consciously subscribed to, it does reveal the conceptual underdevelopment of the non-rational and the interactive aspects of the active consciousness.

The labor psychologists contrasted this theory of creativity to what they viewed as the Western approach, which they characterized as one based on "revelation" (*tun-wu*) or "intuition" (*ling-ken*). The contrast, as they saw it, comprised three dichotomies: the Western idea of the sudden flash of insight as against their own of deliberate planning; the Western individual character of creation as against theirs based on the group setting; and the unpredictability of the former as against the feasability of a planned, concerted attack. The authors further charged that industrial psychologists of capitalist nations ignored the intelligence of the worker and neglected his potential for creativity.[31]

To sum up, at the time of this study, labor psychologists favored two areas of research: psychophysical analysis of the productive process (sensation, perception, and motor activity) and study of the role of recognition (rational understanding and correct reflection.) Other aspects of man's psychological condition, such as feelings and emotions, and other parts of the active consciousness besides recognition had been given a place in the total scheme of labor psychology but had barely been touched upon in research.

[31] These criticisms were based on Western psychology of the thirties, a period when the Gestalt school of thought was most influential here. The resulting emphasis upon the total field and sudden insight did lead to the relative neglect of the intellect. More recently, however, increasing stress in the West has been placed on the "think model" for creativity. As for industrial psychology, a greater emphasis upon intelligence as an element in the wider conception of worker goals is potentially present in the current orientation toward human relations in industry. See, for example, Warren G. Bennis, *Changing Organizations* (New York: McGraw-Hill, 1966).

ORIENTATION OF LABOR PSYCHOLOGY

To return to our original problem of appraisal, how, then, do we account for the lack of development in labor psychology in the late fifties? At first glance, we might have expected a concentration of psychological personnel and resources in labor research, making this branch "the very core of psychology itself." Physical labor has been conceived of as an experience with inherent moral and spiritual qualities. In the political area, one finds the periodic use of physical labor as a process of ideological rehabilitation of certain groups or the mass rejuvenation of revolutionary zeal. The value of labor was extolled by medical psychologists in their statement that neurasthenia was more prevalent among "mind workers" than among physical laborers, and by educational psychologists in their finding that labor benefited students in both academic and character development. The Great Leap Forward was the embodiment of the doctrine that every citizen should take part in physical labor to the utmost of his time and ability.

The emphasis placed upon productive labor by the government and Party and the pervasive national concern with work itself seemed to provide rich soil for the growth of a "psychology of physical work," concerned with the over-all conceptualization of the place of work activity in the total functioning of man as a psychological entity. Yet this obviously did not materialize. Some of the reasons for this become clear in a look at the forces restraining such a development, for it is this same national concentration of values and sentiments on labor which is the source of underlying, unspoken inhibitions against the vigorous growth of labor psychology. Work and the readiness to engage in it have been considered unquestionable — it has been unthinkable that there should be unmotivated workers, unless there are corrupting influences external to the system, such as

129

capitalist influences (ruling out biologically determined defects). The basic assumption that labor is good and must be desired by everyone has not been open for study; it has been assumed that behavior would follow directly from this ideologically given value. In a few instances in which data were obtained that appeared to contradict this assumption, no fundamental question was raised or new conclusions drawn challenging the basic value. The empirical discrepancies went conceptually unnoticed. The only problematical aspect that has remained is the level of efficiency, which could be remedied by training and education, and here empirical science was allowed reign.

Second, the technical, scientific potentials for the development of a broader labor psychology were present, at least as much as in the other branches, but not utilized. When labor psychology answered the call for practical research during the Great Leap, it was in a preparatory and rudimentary state similar to the rest of the new psychology. The fact that research workers trained in experimental psychology were available meant that concepts and methods developed in the experimental field were adapted to the study of labor. Broader conceptual notions were available, too, from respectable sources in Soviet psychology and from firsthand observation of the work done in East Germany, but they did not take root. It is true that there was no large pool of trained personnel to draw upon. Nor was there a strong leader present in the branch with broad theoretical interests and with primary devotion to development of the branch in a wider and deeper context. Thus, the potentialities for a new labor psychology as outlined by Ts'ao and Li were far from realized or even seriously tackled.

A third factor had to do with the impingement of labor psychology on other parts of the social structure. During the Great Leap, psychologists were allowed access to factories and other industrial settings for research. In fact, labor psychologists were *urged* along with other specialists to go down to the masses and do cooperative research with representatives from factories and administrative organs. But it remains problematical whether factory managers and party cadres indeed welcomed scientists for other than narrowly defined problems in production. A major hurdle here would be that persons in charge of production would have to recognize the potentialities of a labor psychology and be able to define their own needs in such terms that data of a psychological nature would have relevance or would be helpful in solving their problems. In educational or medical psychology, responsible persons normally in charge of the experimental "subjects" generally have a scientific, experimental outlook toward the groups they work with. Students and patients are already "captive audiences" of the educational and medical professions. They are, by definition, in the process of being socialized or resocialized; therefore, to study their process of socialization would seem natural. The situation does not hold true for labor psychology. The industrial organization does not have a continuous and respectable research tradition in human behavior. Thus, a sudden influx of research workers from outside the production hierarchy might open up issues that are too unsettling or threatening to those persons in positions of responsibility. There was too much at stake to examine the fundamental assumptions about the attributes of the worker. Perhaps this line of argument can be applied to the rural setting to an even greater extent, and if it has any validity, provide us with some clues as to why rural labor was rarely subject to research.

In a wider perspective, the industrial needs of China were quite different from those in the West, where a shrinking labor supply and rising wages require using the smallest number of workers in the most efficient way. In Communist China, the supply of labor was not the main obstacle to increased productivity. Instead, the major problems have been to improve technology and make more efficient use of arable

131

land. Although maximizing the output of each worker was the subject of many emulation campaigns, the reasons have more to do with ideology than technology. That each citizen must produce for the common good is the historically inherited burden. Such broad considerations may not be irrelevant for understanding the special meaning of a new "science" that calls itself *lao-tung hsin-li-hsueh*.

CHAPTER FIVE

EDUCATIONAL PSYCHOLOGY

ORIENTATION AND ORGANIZATION

Educational psychology was the focus of effort in psychology in the sixties just as medical psychology had been toward the end of the fifties. As the nation recovered from the overenthusiasms of the Great Leap, the psychologists turned to research on the learning of curriculum subjects and character training. While the work in these two areas was by no means extensive, it did represent engagement with practical problems of some significance. This was especially true of research on the nature of moral character, which had become a question of national concern in the early sixties and which was potentially a matter of greater and more direct social consequence than the curriculum studies. We shall discuss this work in Chapter Six as part of the broader theoretical question of individuality and individual differences.

As we have seen in the development of the other branches of psychology, educational psychology must be discussed in terms of internal factors and sociopolitical currents. Internal factors refer both to the maturation of a science and to the alignment of personnel and organizational structure. Externally, work in this branch reflects first the Great Leap period of sudden expansion of education, followed by re-

133

trenchment and consolidation of natural and human resources, and then by the new phase of ideological ascendency and consequent restrictions upon scientific inquiry.

The main mission of educational psychology at the beginning of this decade was to find ways to fit itself into educational reform. P'an Shu, President of the Psychological Society and spokesman for the profession, called the task "the work of reforming the instruction in middle and elementary schools." He said in a speech at the Educational Psychology Specialty Conference in 1962 that experimental work was "penetrating in a planned way," and he listed the chief psychological problems that merited investigation: [1]

1. Psychological problems in moral education, or "the training of workers with socialist consciousness and culture." In this moral education, priority was to be given to "love of socialist fatherland, love of the laboring masses, love of the Communist Party, love of the leaders, and love for physical labor, science, and public property." At the same time, there was to be training for "patriotism and international spirit," "willingness to support the leadership of the Party and to serve socialism and the people." Educational psychology was assigned the task of analyzing "the psychological structure of the moral qualities of students, laws governing their grasp of moral concepts, formation of moral sense, moral faith and conduct, development of the will and formation of Communist character, effects of the collectivity on moral qualities, and psychological characteristics of self-discipline.

2. Psychological problems in education for physical labor. Inquiries were to be made into "the psychological characteristics of labor" for students: How does labor promote moral qualities? How do labor

[1] P'an Shu, "Ideas about expanded research in educational psychology," *Kuang-ming jih-pao*, Mar. 13, 1962. Joint Publications Research Service No. 13531.

and knowledge promote each other? How do different forms of labor influence psychological development? How are labor skills formed? And how does labor education adapt itself to individual differences and age differences?

3. Psychological problems in classroom instruction. The broad problems of motivation for learning, mastering of skills, and development of thinking ability were to be attacked as well as a specific problem of how to teach various curriculum subjects.

4. Psychological problems in determining school age. The urgent question was the appropriate age for entering school. A related problem was the coordination between preschool education and school education, and the phases of learning.

5. Individual differences — the need to "discover and develop talents in various fields, and to "analyze the causes of bad behavior and poor learning."

6. Psychological development of the child and pedagogical reform in elementary school.

This statement, of course, concerned general goals and needs and necessarily sounds ambitious for the available trained personnel. But the speech did indicate the direction of attention and the definition of the widened field. Educational psychology had been rather slow in getting started on any scale or in organizing a coherent program until attention focused on it in the sixties. Part of the difficulty lay in definition of boundaries: What distinguished it from the field of education and what was its relationship to general psychology? In late 1961, the Educational Psychology Research Section of the Kuangtung Educational Association held a discussion at its annual meeting on the object of study of the field.[2] Professor Yü Wen-wei proposed that educational

---

[2] "The educational psychology research section of the Kuangtung educational association discussed the problem of the object of study of

psychology should ascertain the developmental laws concerning the acquisition of Communist consciousness and moral qualities in the student, and psychological laws concerning his mastery of knowledge and techniques. Participants in the meeting raised the problem that if the object of educational psychology were determined by requirements of socialist educational practices, it would be indistinguishable from the object of education. Other psychologists pointed out that since the development of the child's mind was involved in the process of education and instruction, the content of educational psychology overlapped with that of child psychology. Another commentator on Yü's proposal wanted to add the development of the students' individual capacities and characters. Still others mentioned the inclusion of the psychology of school guidance work and of problems in adult education.

Part of the confusion of boundaries could be explained by the fact that, numerically speaking, the vast majority of the nation's psychologists were engaged in teaching in various normal institutions (90% of the 585 members of the Chinese Psychological Society in 1958).[3] A high proportion of the Western-trained Chinese psychologists had come out of teachers' colleges and schools of education in the United States. Indications are that the increase in gross numbers after 1958 came almost entirely from those in education. Although they were identified with teacher-training programs, only a few were specialists in the psychology of education. Under Soviet influence after 1949, more approaches to educational psychology were introduced, for much Soviet

---

educational psychology," *Kuang-ming jih-pao,* Jan. 29, 1962, p. 2. Joint Publications Research No. 13039.

[3] P'an Shu, "Mien-tui keng-ta ti yueh-chin hsing-shih, p'an-teng hsin-li-hsueh ti kao-feng" (Responding to the Big Leap, scaling the peaks of psychological science), *Hsin-li hsueh-pao,* No. 2 (1960), pp. 63–66.

psychological research in general was conducted in institutes of pedagogy.

The overlap of educational psychology with general and experimental psychology on the one hand and with social and moral questions on the other continued, since the main expansion of work by the psychologists was called the psychology of education in the broad sense. Organizationally, there had been, until 1966, a split in the training program between the numerically strong normal institutions, with their more practical, more political concerns, and the scientifically oriented in-service training at the Institute of Psychology. Under these conditions, overlap and fluctuations in interest as well as jurisdictional arguments as to the "proper" subject matter for psychological research was inevitable. As political pressures and ideological campaigns wax and wane, educational psychology turned to one or the other arm of its research interests.

The dual orientation of personnel and intellectual tradition was paralleled by overlapping organizational jurisdiction. The Ministry of Education announced the creation of the Educational Science Research Institute in 1957, as we have noted earlier.[4]

When the Institute of Psychology of the Academy established its Division of Educational Psychology to engage in team research on concrete problems, many Academy psychologists with specialized interests such as sensation and perception, memory, and other topics in experimental psychology seemed to have chosen educational psychology. This organizational measure resulted in some broadening of the theoretical and methodological base of educational psychology and perhaps introduced a more scientific slant to basically educational research. It is not clear how long this team division remained after the Great Leap.

[4] "Hsin-li-hsueh li-lun lien-hsi shih-chi shou-ch'eng-hsiao" (Unification of theory and practice in psychology brings results). *Wen-hui pao* (Shanghai), Dec. 21, 1959.

The big expansion and consolidation of educational psychology began to be evident at the 1960 Second Congress of the Psychological Society. At its First Congress in 1955, no mention was made of any psychological study of the educational process. Even the 1960 meeting did not group all research having to do with education into a major area of interest, although the Educational Psychology Division of the Psychology Institute did report work in progress on (1) a comparison of 6- and 7-year-olds; (2) psychological principles in the teaching of curriculum subjects, such as the acceleration in arithmetic teaching and work analysis, or effects on physics learning through labor (*lao-tung*); and (3) labor education, that is, psychology and the teaching of production methods. The other institutions of higher education, including normal colleges and universities, presented smaller scale research at that meeting along lines parallel to those of the Division. Several of the latter kind of research projects — in fact, 5 out of 6 "local reports" — were already focused on the educational process, but were not so classified. Hangchow University reported a study on the role of language in picture recognition. Hunan Normal College studied the ability of 6- and 7-year-olds to comprehend language, arithmetic, rules of conduct, and moral ideas. Southwest Normal College made a survey of the "weekly diaries" (*chou-chi*) of sixth- and seventh-grade children for manifestations of their concern with school affairs. Kueiyang Normal College studied motivation for entering middle school. Finally, Harbin Medical College reported work on age characteristics of middle-school students.[5]

In February 1962, the Committee on Educational Psychology called a meeting of representatives from provincial, municipal, and autonomous regional units. The central topic of discussion was the psychological age of school children.

[5] Ch'en Ta-jou, "Chung-kuo Hsin-li-hsueh Hui ti-erh-tz'u tai-piao hui-i" (Second congress of the Chinese Psychological Society), *Hsin-li hsueh-pao*, No. 2 (1960), pp. 128–131.

Plans called for a five-year concentration of study on the 3 to 7 preschool group and the 7 to 12 early school years, with particular attention on their acquisition of knowledge and character training. The process of knowledge acquisition was to be approached through the conventional subfields in psychology: feeling, language, thought, attention, and memory; while character training studies were to be subdivided into interest, motivation, ability, and character. In discussing the work of psychologists abroad on growth studies, the only Western work cited was that of Piaget, along with Soviet psychologists. Opinion was divided on the desirability of quantification as a research method. We can see here a slight relaxation of earlier prejudice against Western psychology and the statistical treatment, although psychological testing remained a taboo method because of its association with a theory of native intelligence attributed to Western psychology. The submitted papers included psychological principles of learning language and arithmetic, EEG (electroencephalogram) measures of brain development from infancy to old age, and children's motivation for learning. There were also reports introducing the work of foreign psychologists. Finally, some arguments were presented on both sides on the use of quantitative studies and on psychological testing. These arguments on hitherto avoided subjects suggested an opening of scientific doors to the wider spectrum represented by international psychology.

This conference also announced the undertaking of educational research by the seven districts or regions for psychology. Evidence of heightened local activities can be found in reported gatherings of various joint conferences in the provinces. The result was that at the local level educational psychology tended to dominate the field of psychology. For example, besides the 1961 annual meeting in Kuangtung just referred to, early in 1963 there was the first meeting in Canton of the south-central five-province district on psychological and educational research. Present at this regional meeting were representatives from 12 higher normal institutions and related institutions. The 50 or so delegates discussed methods of doing cooperative research, and resolved to push toward popularization of the joint field.[6] The Tientsin branch of the Psychological Society in August 1962 also held a joint meeting with Hopei University's Psychology and Education Research Center under the auspices of the Education Department. Assistant professor Chang Shu-tsu presented a paper on "the relationship between perception and concept under strong increase of stimulation." [7] Again in T'ai-yuan there was a joint meeting in December of 1961 between the Shansi provincial branch of the Psychological Society and the Education Department of Shansi University. A professor of psychology, Professor Chou, introduced a "new" topic of research, "the communication of thought," and discussed his opinion of two current approaches to psychological phenomena and matter.[8]

By the end of 1963 when the Psychological Society had its "annual academic discussion meetings," the majority of the research reports came to be grouped under educational and child psychology, including work done on individuality and moral education. In spite of this new focus of attention, Ts'ao complained that certain important questions remained untouched or too little studied, and he suggested character development as the greatest need. He pointed to the necessity of linking concrete research with theory, as he had throughout the controversy of theory versus reality during the debates of 1958–1959; and he pleaded for the adoption or creation of new research methods while continuing the general Pavlovian tradition.[9] At this national meeting, psychology

[6] *Kuang-ming jih-pao,* Feb. 1, 1963.
[7] *Kuang-ming jih-pao,* Aug. 4, 1962.
[8] *Kuang-ming jih-pao,* Dec. 25, 1961.
[9] Ts'ao Jih-ch'ang, "Kuan-chi li-lun lien-hsi shih-chi, k'o-hsueh yen-chiu wei she-hui chu-i chien-she fu-wu ti fang-chen, t'i-kao hsin-li-hsueh kung-tso ti shui-p'ing" (Raising the scientific level of psychological research: address to the 1963 annual meeting of the Chinese Psychological Society), *Hsin-li hsueh pao,* No. 1 (196).

of teaching and psychology of moral education were also discussed, as well as memory and thought in relation to children.[10]

The Party and the government were both represented at this meeting. Chang P'an-shih, Deputy Director of the Party's Propaganda Section, again attended; and he was joined by Deputy Education Minister Liu Ch'i-p'ing. Both spoke to the assembly.[11] Educational Psychology had come to full bloom. Recognition of its status had been achieved on both the local and national scene.

RESEARCH ON CURRICULUM SUBJECTS

With the expansion of educational psychology, we found a plethora of empirical studies on various aspects of teaching material, procedures, and technologies. The more descriptive classroom studies in specific fields of arithmetic and language were usually published in education journals or regional normal school journals. In works by psychologists, there was a deliberate attempt to fit procedures of learning mathematics, arithmetic, language, and so forth, into the general psychological principles of attention, recognition, memory, and thinking. Instead of systematic attempts to advance theories and test derived hypotheses, much of the psychological research on education applied and illustrated the principles, and sometimes arrived at inductive generalizations without systematizing them. Leading psychologists were themselves aware of this shortcoming. In the December 1963 annual meeting of the Psychological Society held in Peking, Ch'en Yuan-hui stated in one of the "special reports" that, henceforth, research on thinking should proceed from child development, language, and logic to the use of quantitative methods and recent scientific techniques, especially information and control theory, and that it ought to employ a

[10] *Ibid.*
[11] Ch'en Ta-jou, "Chung-kuo Hsin-li-hsueh hui 1963 nien hsueh-shu nien-hui" (Annual academic meeting of the Chinese Psychological Society), *Hsin-li hsueh-pao,* No. 1 (1964), pp. 109–112.

stimulus-response (S-R) approach whereby one can "grasp two ends and aim toward the middle." [12] He was graphically saying that the researcher should specify the stimulus and the response conditions. Between these two ends, the psychological characteristics of the organism could be "grasped" or inferred through the relations between the stimulus (S) and the resulting behavior (R). It would seem that Ch'en's statement may well point to a trend toward lifting educational psychology to a higher level of systematic treatment and theoretical integration. Of course, it must be noted that in the United States, such integration has not been successfully achieved either. One of the bridges in the U.S. has been programmed learning, popularly known as teaching machines.

Teaching machines did come in for brief attention by Communist China's psychologists at the 1962 meeting. In introducing "new directions in contemporary psychology," Ch'en Li (Ph.D., 1933, from London University [13]), President and Professor of Psychology at Hangchow Pedagogical Institute, said that research abroad on "the psychological problems in teaching programs" (teaching machines) has "achieved certain results" but that "there are still controversies." [14] He pointed to the disagreements on arrangement of teaching materials, big or small units or steps, procedure formats, and problems in the reinforcement of learning. It is not known if interest progressed any further than a mere notice of the matter. At least the general tone of Ch'en's report was positive — he raised no criticisms against it. In the Soviet Union, an observer at the 1963 Leningrad Congress of Soviet Psychology noted that programmed learning was covered in the section on "Psychology Abroad," and that the topic received serious attention.[15]

[12] Reported by Ch'en Ta-jou, *ibid.*

[13] *International Directory of Psychologists.* (Washington, D.C.: National Academy of Sciences, National Research Council, Publication No. 520, 1958), p. 95.

[14] In Ch'en Ta-jou, "Chung-kuo Hsin-li-hsueh hui 1963 nien. . . ."

[15] Joseph Brozek, "Contemporary Soviet Psychology," in *Transactions*

We shall treat the material on subject-matter learning under two headings: mathematics-arithmetic and language, with emphasis on the more recent literature on these topics and on any discernible continuity of approach on the part of major psychologists or leading research organizations.

Research on Classroom Teaching and Learning of Mathematics

Beginning in 1960, there was a sudden outpouring of research reports on the teaching of arithmetic and mathematics. Some of these reports represented the fruit of projects carried on during the three previous Great Leap years. A total of 33 studies were done during that period,[16] a considerable number in light of the total scope of psychology. In these studies, as well as throughout subsequent articles in the journal, there was a coherent point of view: the effect of ideas and thought processes on the learning of arithmetic or mathematics problems. The emphasis, at least on the part of the psychologists, was not on the sheer speed or amount of retention. Interest was centered on what was summarized at a conference as the "formation of number concepts, the development of logical thinking and problem solving." [17] These goals, apparent in varying degrees in the experimental designs and conclusions, brought about the re-evaluation of some old teaching materials and preparation of new experimental materials, as in the following case of an algebra-learning experiment.

The first research on the teaching of mathematics

---

of the New York Academy of Sciences, Vol. 27, No. 4 (Feb. 1965), pp. 422–438.

[16] Lu Chung-heng, Hao Yü-yen, Ying Yü-yeh, Ma Chieh-wei, Chang Mei-ling, "Chiao-hsueh kai-ke chung ch'u-chin hsueh-sheng chang-wo shu-hsueh chih-shih ti i-hsieh hsin-li yin-su" (Some psychological factors in promoting the students' grasp of arithmetical knowledge, as found in recent educational reforms), *Hsin-li hsueh-pao,* No. 3 (1961), pp. 190–201.

[17] *Kuang-ming jih-pao,* Mar. 9, 1962.

conducted during the Great Leap was done on 87 fifth-grade children in Peking. Liu Ching-ho of the Institute of Psychology, who wrote about this study, stated her problem in this way: "On the hypothesis that abstract ideas can be better grasped through abstract symbols than numerals, an experiment was done to see whether algebra could be taught to children earlier than is customary." [18] The results were considered highly satisfactory, both in the amount of advanced material successfully covered, and also in test scores on the regular term-end municipal examination in arithmetic. Liu concluded that "tests in the grasp and use of formulae showed an appreciable level of understanding not based on mechanical memory." [19] She recommended that algebra might be introduced as a method of solving arithmetic problems. After the experiment, psychologists "took the initiative" in preparing teaching material on fundamental algebra "based on the nature of thought processes, breaking the previous pattern of primary school teaching system." [20] The actual implementation of test results, at least in this experimental situation, and the writing of new teaching material by psychologists indicate that their recommendations were given serious consideration in educational reform. The extent of implementation is difficult to estimate and lies beyond the primary concern of this study.

Concerning the teaching of geometry, Lu Chung-heng led a team in presenting a series of three or more reports on the relationship between the perception of geometric shapes and thought processes. Some idea of their approach can be gained from the titles of some articles: "An experimental study of the effects of different methods of teaching on the

---

[18] Liu Ching-ho, "Tsai hsiao-hsueh shih-chiao tai-shu ti shih-yen yen-chiu" (A psychological study on experimental teaching of algebra to primary school children), *Hsin-li hsueh-pao,* No. 1 (1960), pp. 13–27.

[19] *Ibid.*

[20] Ch'en Ta-jou, "Hsin-li hsueh tsen-yang wei she-hui chu-i chien-she fu-wu ti" (How psychology serves socialist construction), *Hsin-li hsueh-pao,* No. 3 (1959), pp. 142–145.

formation of fundamental geometrical concepts," "The negative effects of crossing of geometrical figures on the perceptual and thought processes," and "The effect of outer shape on the perceptive structure of geometric figures and thought processes." In the last experiment,[21] for instance, children of an experimental school in Liaoning were asked to draw certain geometric shapes and simultaneously to talk aloud of what they were thinking. The experimenters were interested in how perception of the outer shape could influence the perception of the internal relationship of lines forming smaller geometric figures. In all this work on learning mathematics, psychologists like Lu were heavily influenced by Soviet scientists in this field, particularly by the works of Rubenstein on thought processes, which had been translated into Chinese in 1963. Studies on the teaching of arithmetic also stressed thought processes and their effect on the handling of numbers. Ch'en Li of Hangchow Pedagogical Institute directed two studies on arithmetic teaching in primary schools. The first was concerned with the process of abstraction and development of the "active nature" of thought in children when they were learning the concepts of greater and less.[22] The second study compared the "contrast method" of teaching (reverse operation of a problem) with the "successive method" (only one-way operation). After one year of observation, it was shown that the contrast method was not only "superior in problem solving" but also superior in achieving "flexibility of thinking." [23]

[21] Lu Chung-heng, Chu Hsin-ming, "Wai-chou hsien-tuan tui t'u-hsing chih-chueh chieh-kou ho ssu-hsiang kuo-ch'eng ti ying-hsiang (III)" (The effect of outer shape on the perceptive structure of geometric figures and thought processes), *Hsin-li hsueh-pao,* No. 3 (1964), pp. 248–257.

[22] Lü Ching, Wang Wen-chun, "Ti nien-chi erh-t'ung chang-wo ying-yung-t'i kai-nien ti ssu-wei ling-huo-hsing. (The thinking processes in arithmetical operation in lower-grade school children), *Hsin-li hsueh-pao,* No. 2 (1960), pp. 121–135.

[23] Lü Ching, Wang Wen-chün, Cheng Yü-tan, "Hsiao-hsueh ti-nien-chi erh-t'ung chang-wo suan-shu k'o-ni t'ui-li yü ssu-wei ti ling-huo hsing" (The mastery of reverse operation and flexibility of thinking

Other arithmetic investigations were concerned with the comprehension of problems and source of errors. In teaching addition and subtraction by the contrast method, it was found that presenting the two operations simultaneously rather than sequentially facilitated learning. This possibility was recommended to teachers.[24] In a preliminary write-up on the "psychological factors affecting the nature and causes of difficulty" in solving complex verbal arithmetic problems, an experiment done at Hsi-nan (Southwest) Normal College, emphasis was placed entirely on components of the verbal problems and their unfamiliarity or unusual sequential arrangement.[25] Children were interviewed for an introspective account of difficulties in comprehension, but among psychological factors only that of rational understanding was analyzed, leaving emotional factors unprobed. This emphasis on rational understanding followed the general trend of development in mainland Chinese psychology.

An experiment on the abacus, conducted in Shanghai at Hua-tung (East China) Normal University by Ch'iu Hsueh-hua,[26] linked physiological movement of fingers with the subjects' overt or silent verbal behavior, again emphasizing thought processes in manipulative learning. Ch'iu observed that in acquiring digital mastery of the difficult middle finger by third grade children, there were stages and plateaus in learning. At the first stage the children used verbal signals aloud to themselves. In the second stage the silent verbal

in arithmetic in school children), *Hsin-li hsueh-pao,* No. 3 (1964), pp. 237–247.

[24] Chang Tseng-chieh, Wang Pan-hsia, "Ying-hsiang erh-t'ung kan-chih suan-shih ti liang-ko yu-kuan yin-ssu ti shih-yen (An experimental study of the factors influencing the comprehension of arithmetical problems), *Hsin-li hsueh-pao,* No. 4 (1963), pp. 304–311.

[25] Mao Yü–yen, Kung Wei-yao, Ch'en P'ei-lin, "Fu-ho ying-yung-t'i chieh-ko ch'u-pu t'o-t'ao", (Preliminary study on the structure of complex arithmetic problems), *Hsin-li hsueh-pao,* No. 1 (1964), pp. 57–71.

[26] Ch'iu Hsueh-hua, "Erh-t'ung hsing-ch'eng chu-suan yun-suan hsu-lien ti yen-chiu" (A study of the skill of calculation with abacus in school children), *Hsin-li hsueh-pao,* No. 2 (1963), pp. 107–112.

calculations took over except when difficulties were encountered, at which time there was a return to overt verbal direction of finger movements. In the third stage, the finger movements became automatic. While his orientation and conclusions can be fitted into the second signal system of Pavlov, Ch'iu curiously did not mention Pavlov or his theories.

Instead, there were two references to the early work of Ts'ao Jih-ch'ang, the leading experimental psychologist at the time of our study. Ts'ao wrote the first article on the abacus in the Tientsin *Ta-kung Pao* in 1934, and another article reviewing 20 years of abacus research in *Chung-hua chao-yü* (*Chinese Educational World* of 1935). These references indicated something of the reputation of Ts'ao: his firm, long academic standing to add to his strong leadership until at least 1965.

There was only one study that could be considered to have used class background as an implicit variable, although the author, Liu Ching-ho, did not explicitly use the "class" factor in discussing her study. She described a project comparing numerical concepts of peddlers' children with children of professors and office workers. Children of peddlers were found to have better conceptual grasp of numbers. Liu attributed the result to the superior "past experience" of the peddlers' children and made the recommendation that teachers should "reform past experience" in the process of teaching, especially in such a way as to form new ideas of a higher level in children — for example, ideas of right and wrong.[27] One might bear this experiment in mind when considering the developmental approach and theories of individuality in later pages.

Research in Language Learning

Psychological studies on language learning and the role of language in other learning also did not gain momentum

[27] Liu Ching-ho, "A preliminary discussion on some of the problems regarding the learning process of children," *Jen-min jih-pao,* Mar. 26, 1961. Joint Publications Research Service No. 9398.

till the end of the Great Leap period. One or two earlier experiments were close follow-ups of Soviet examples, such as the 1955 experiment by Hsu Shu-lien and K'uang P'ei-tzu that replicated the work of Ivanov-Smolenskii on conditioned reflex. Hsu and K'uang demonstrated the coupling of higher nervous activity by 43 first- and second-grade children by means of a verbally reinforced motor conditioning method.[28] Another early study was on the effect of words on children's generalized cognition.[29] Indigenous interest in the psychological study of language came after 1960. In 1962 alone, 12 articles appeared on this subject, of which 9 were on word recognition.[30]

Language research was carried on by two groups of psychologists at the Institute: Ts'ao Chuan-yung and Shen Yeh on word recognition and Ts'ao Jih-ch'ang and his colleagues on memory. Both groups represented the relatively rigorous, scientific side of Communist Chinese psychology, and although their research on language had immediate empirical importance, they drew no conclusions for the educators. Their methods and design were strictly psychological and comparatively sophisticated. Both cited predominantly Western, especially American, psychological work in this language area.

Ts'ao Chuan-yung attributed the origin of his series of

[28] Hsu Shu-lien, K'uang P'ei-tzu, "Yung yen-yü ch'iang-hua ti yun-tung t'iao-chien fen-she fang-fa yen-chiu 8–10 sui erh-t'ung chieh-t'ung chi-neng lei-tien t'e-hsing ti i-tien chin-yen." (Note on types characterized by the coupling of the highest nervous activity in children by means of verbally reinforced motor conditioning method), *Hsin-li hsueh-pao,* No. 1 (1958), pp. 53–64.

[29] Chang Shu-tsu, Chan Lung-tze, Shen Te-li, "Tz'u tsai erh-t'ung kai-kua jen-shih chung ti tso-yung" (The effect of words in children's generalized cognition), *Hsin-li hsueh-pao,* No. 1 (1957).

[30] Ts'ao Chuan-yung, Shen Yeh, "Tsai su-shih t'iao-chien hsia erh-t'ung pien-jen han-tzu tzu-hsing ti shih-t'an yen-chiu" I. (The recognition of Chinese characters under tachistoscopic conditions in primary school children I.) *Hsin-li hsueh-pao,* No. 3 (1963), p. 203. (Footnote quoting from "Hsin-li hsueh tung-t'ai" [activities in psychology] compiled by the Psychological Society of Fukien.)

studies on word recognition to P'an Shu, whom Ts'ao assisted in a perception project.[31] Shen Yeh had done some previous work on the ability of primary school children to recognize Chinese characters.[32] The theoretical purpose of their joint project was "to examine characteristics of the intake of language signals as a preliminary step to the study of language mechanisms in thought." [33] This was seen as a part of the larger topic of the psychology of the recognition process. The authors placed their work in the mainstream of international development of the past decade on the "psychology of language," especially in the scientific spearhead on the input, storage, transformation, and reorganization of language signals within the organism and the final output of information. Although the framework was modern control theory and information theory, the experimental design was that of traditional experimental psychology. Particular reference was made to the work of Woodworth, dean of American experimental psychology, whose contribution the authors described as "solidly established" in perception and attention. On the practical side, they acknowledged the urgent needs for educational reform in the teaching of language.

Ts'ao Chuan-yung and Shen Yen's program on recognition of characters was reported in four articles. Ts'ao and Shen constructed their own tachistoscope (an electronic apparatus for very brief and precisely measured time exposures) to test the recognition of single characters or phrases and sentences.[34] The thoroughness of this research program as compared to many others was indicated by the fact that work on the apparatus itself took place from 1959 to 1960, and experimentation lasted from then until May 1963, when the

---

[31] In a footnote to report I, *ibid.*

[32] Published in *Hsin-li hsueh-pao*, No. 46 (1959), an unavailable number.

[33] *Ibid.*, p. 202.

[34] Ts'ao Chuan-yung, "I-ko tien-tzu tien-lu k'ung-chih ti ch'eng-shih ch'i" (An electronic tachistoscope), *Hsin-li hsueh-pao*, No. 3 (1963), pp. 247–250.

first report was submitted to the journal. Furthermore, an entire article was devoted to reporting on methodology and standardization of some of the variables, such as familiarity, single versus multiple words, whole coherent phrases as compared to scrambled phrases, size of characters, amount of illumination, and duration of exposure before recognition is achieved. The statistical procedure in this series of studies was also sophisticated relative to general practice in Communist Chinese psychology: They used a three-way analysis of variance, and reported on statistically significant results with F ratios of .01 to .001.

The experiments were conducted on groups of primary school grades one, two, and five. The first research report [35] was on experiments in method: the relationship between visual duration threshold (VDT) and the size and brightness of stimulus; and the VDT of words, phrases, and disconnected word groups under different procedures. Report II dealt with the effect of the structure of characters on recognition: how the degree of similarity in structure influenced recognition, how characters with the same contour and different contents presented difficulties in identification, and how familiar "radicals" (word roots) played an important role in the reproduction of unfamiliar "radicals." [36] In Report III,[37] familiar and unfamiliar phrases were adopted, with the additional variable of scrambled word order. (One of the familiar phrases used was "T'ing Mao-chu-hsi ti hua," or "Heed the words of Chairman Mao," which when scrambled became "Hsi t'ing Mao hua ti chu"!) In explaining the result that recognition time for scrambled familiar phrases was significantly longer than for scrambled unfamiliar phrases, the authors suggested that "central effects" of the nervous system may have influenced recognition in two ways, "facilitating and interfering."

[35] Ts'ao Chuan-yung, Shen Yeh, "Tsai su-shih. . . ."
[36] Ts'ao Chuan-yung, Shen Yeh, "Tsai su-shih . . ." II. *Hsin-li hsueh-pao*, No. 4 (1963), pp. 271–279.
[37] Ts'ao Chuan-yung, Shen Yeh, "Tsai su-shih . . ." III. *Hsin-li hsueh-pao*, No. 4 (1963), pp. 280–286.

These interpretations were then examined within the larger problem of "storage system of language in human brains."

In this series of studies, Ts'ao and Shen cited many works. Only one reference was to a Soviet source, that of Luria on language, published in 1962 (in *Soviet Psychological Science,* Vol. I). The majority of the references were in English, to Western writers, with a few to Chinese psychologists. Specifically, the authors quoted some of the American psychologists who were doing research in the Gestalt tradition. Some of the results obtained by Ts'ao and Shen—and also their concepts—seemed similar to those of Gestalt works on perception.

A much less elaborate study on word recognition on short exposure was reported by Li Chen of Hofei Normal College, Anhuei. In an article entitled "A preliminary study," Li wrote about the effect of the external shape of characters on recognition. He discussed similarities between his own work and that of Lu Chung-heng on recognition of geometric shapes, thus providing a bridge between the two lines of research on recognition, language and geometric symbols. Li, however, referred much less extensively to Soviet sources than Lu did.

In 1965, Ts'ao Chuan-yung and Shen Yeh started a new series [38] on recognition of Chinese characters, with a new, developmental orientation. Their plan was to study the stages by which the child acquired knowledge of characters. They studied the typical learning curves, which they called developmental curves, and found the typical negatively accelerated curve for familiar Chinese characters, positive accelerated curves for unfamiliar Chinese characters, and a simple accelerated curve for foreign (Korean) characters.

[38] Ts'ao Chuan-yung, Shen Yeh, "Hsiao-hsueh erh-t'ung fen-hsi, kai-k'uo ho pien-jen han-tzu tzu-hsing neng-li ti fa-chan yen-chiu" (Developmental studies on the recognition and generalization of Chinese characters in primary school children I. (Development of recognition under tachistoscopic conditions), *Hsin-li hsueh-pao,* No. 1 (1965), pp. 1–9.

They suggested that the two important points of acceleration in the learning of characters by children were immediately after the first month of learning Chinese characters and between the first and second grades. In this report, three of the four references were to Chinese works and the other referred to the standard American statistical text of A. Edwards.

Another focus of interest in the learning of language was memorization. Ts'ao Jih-ch'ang, in collaboration with less known, presumably younger psychologists, conducted a series of three experiments on the process of memorization by school children. In the first article, coauthored with Chao Li-ju,[39] an investigation was made into the methods of memorization used by first-year junior middle-school pupils of 20 four-word phrases. The phrases could be treated by the subjects as separate entities with independent meaning, grouped by meaning into a number of categories, or made into rhyming units. The purpose of this first, inductive, study was to find out the different methods of memorization actually used by children, as groundwork for the more intensive analysis of processes of memorizing complex prose arrangements. The results, in the words of the authors, unearthed some methods of memorization seldom reported on in previous works on Chinese language learning. Aside from the usual method of remembering by grouping passages by meaning, an accomplishment not yet widely attained by this age group, pupils also used the first word of each phrase or section for a clue or relied on the physical arrangement of the written material. Also, as the experimenters reported with some horror, some children memorized the sentences one by one! The third article on the memorization series [40] compared the learning

---

[39] Chao Li-ju, Ts'ao Jih-ch'ang, "Ch'u-chung hsueh-sheng ti shih-chi fang-fa I. tui ssu-tzu tuan-chü ti chi-i fang-fa" (Studies on the methods of memorization used by junior middle school pupils I. Methods for memorizing 4-word sentences), *Hsin-li hsueh-pao*, No. 4 (1963), pp. 312–320.

[40] Tuan Hui-fen, Ts'ao Jih-ch'ang, "Ch'u-chung hsueh-sheng ti chi-i fang-fa III. Wen-yen wen ho pai-hua wen ti chi-i fang-fa yü kuo-

of *wen-yen,* or classical prose, with *pai-hua,* modern prose, by 30 junior middle-school girls. (The second study on the learning of *wen-yen* is not available.) It was found that *wen-yen* tended to be learned by sequential memory, while *pai-hua* was more often learned by organizing the material schematically according to the essential points and memorizing the details as part of a total structure. The authors explained the difference in terms of the greater ease of understanding modern prose.

While the immediate results of this experiment may have had practical importance for education, of greater significance in terms of psychological theory was the author's conclusion that there were individual differences in the method and capacities for memory: differences in earnestness, or volition factors in *hsueh-hsi* (that is, motivation for study), differences in the level of understanding achieved from the past, and differences in "capacity for memory" (*chi-i neng-liang*). It will be recalled that in the fifties attention in educational circles was on the similarity of learning capacity among pupils; it had been stressed that with skill and effort on the part of teachers, entire classes of pupils could be raised to a high level of achievement. No mention was then found of the term "individual differences." While the two statements are not mutually exclusive in principle, they do manifest different prevailing ideological sentiments of the times. Increasingly, emphasis by psychologists, undoubtedly related to wider opinions, was turned to *differences* among children rather than *sameness,* as our later section on individuality will attempt to demonstrate. The authors quoted and approved of Binet's position that the achievement levels of individuals could be raised through special methods of study and through improved teaching procedures.

---

ch'eng" (Studies on the methods of memorization used by junior middle school pupils III. Methods and courses of memorizing classical and modern prose), *Hsin-li hsueh-pao,* No. 1 (1965), pp. 10–27.

These experiments on memorization, led by Ts'ao Jih-ch'ang, showed comparatively light Soviet influence. The 1963 article had seven references, only two of which were in Russian (including Smirnoff on the development of memory); one was Chinese and four were in English. A Cambridge University professor, F. C. Bartlett, was cited for his writing on remembering, and American authors were cited for recent work on information processing and information "chunking" (G. A. Miller, and M. S. Mayzner and M. Gabriel). The 1965 article had no Russian references at all: five of the six were Western sources.

Although at the time of this study there was an increasing trend in technical psychological publications to cite Western works and a corresponding decline in the use of Soviet publications, especially in certain subjects such as memorization or the learning of numbers, the influence of Pavlovianism was still discernible. In another experiment on memory, by Yeh Hsuan and Ts'ao Jih-ch'ang,[41] on the cross modality of eye and ear memorization, the explanation was couched entirely in Pavlovian terms. Yeh and Ts'ao had asked 24 staff members of the Institute of Psychology (!) to memorize two different lists of words that were presented simultaneously, one list sounding on a tape recorder and a different list projected synchronously on a screen. The resulting decline of efficiency in learning—in recall time, in reaction time, in error making—was accounted for by the authors in terms of excitation and inhibition in the brain, strictly Pavlovian concepts: "The two centers in the brain inhibit each other so that the general efficiency of memorization is low and there may be a temporary dominance of one center over the other."

An empirical study [42] done at a primary school in Yun-

[41] Yeh Hsuan, Ts'ao Jih-ch'ang, "Shih, t'ing yü-wen ts'ai-liao t'ung shih shih-chi ti kan-jao yü hsiang-tui yu-shih" (Interference and dominance in simultaneous memorization of different visual and aurally presented materials), *Hsin-li hsueh-pao*, No. 2 (1964), pp. 131–142.

[42] Chiang Ch'i-pin, "Cheng-mien yao-ch'iu yü kai-ts'o tui hsueh-sheng

yang Hsien, Szechuan, might also have arisen from the Pavlovian notion of inhibitions in the higher nervous system. Students in fifth and sixth grades were asked to learn Chinese characters and arithmetic exercises by reproducing correct information and by making corrections on erroneous statements. It was found that the reproduction method was superior, while "errors put in the exercises caused confusion."

Other studies on word learning briefly referred to in the 1961 Conference on Educational Psychology included tracing strokes of characters, analysis of characters, comparing right and wrong characters, and studies of memorization.[43]

Relative to the amount of other language studies, little research attention was paid to the two major language reforms under the Communist regime: the renewed effort in romanizing the written language, and the systematic application of the simplified written character.

The question of memory in connection with age brought forth two opposing views. It might be noted in passing that this was a rare instance in which the work of one mainland psychologist was directly discussed by name and criticized by another. Kan Feng had written, "childhood is the golden age for memory power, surpassing adults. Much knowledge can be fed to children through memory; provided they understand the material. Deeper explanations can follow. Exercise of memory on a wide range of knowledge increases the power of understanding, which in turn stimulates memory." [44] Ts'ao Jih-ch'ang, in a direct rebuttal against Kan Feng and another psychologist with a similar opinion, Shan Yu, cited three studies as evidence of conclusions to the contrary. Ts'ao presented the resulting scores of three of his own experiments

tso-yeh hsiao-kuo ti ying-hsiang" (The effects of reproduction and correction in the exercise on achievements), *Hsin-li hsueh-pao,* No. 1 (1965), pp. 57–62.

[43] *Kuang-ming jih-pao,* Mar. 9, 1962.

[44] Kan Feng, "T'an-t'an chi-i ho li-chieh ti pien-cheng kuan-hsi" (On the controversial relationship between memory and understanding), *Kuang-ming jih-pao,* Sept. 25, 1963.

155

— one on memory of disconnected numbers, a second one on the learning of English phonemes, and a third on recall of motion picture content by 765 subjects — to prove that memory power was highest between 20 and 30 years of age and that this high level was maintained until about age 45, after which it began to decline. He again argued for theoretical explanation of memory in terms of brain activity, although he thought that in order to improve memory, one should teach students "methods of memorizing and systematic review of material." [45]

AGE LEVELS AND DEVELOPMENT

The problem of age levels and psychological stages was approached by educational psychologists in the earlier sixties in terms of the learning process rather than intellectual achievement. Beginning with the Great Leap drive to accelerate and improve education, the interest of psychologists was focused on bettering the teaching of specific subject matter, such as mathematics and language, and also on investigating phases of learning and development. Within the area of development, emphasis was on psychological stages related to but not identical with or determined by chronological age. In fact, no mention was found at all of any measurement studies of scholastic achievement and age grading in schools. Research rather was directed toward readiness for school, stages of learning, differences in capacity for learning, and character development.

On the specific question of lowering the entrance age for formal schooling from 7 to 6, the Institute of Psychology reported on an experiment with the avowed intention of providing data for "reforming the school system." [46] Schools in Shanghai, Peking, Tientsin, Changsha, Kueilin, and Lanchow

[45] Ts'ao Jih-ch'ang, "Chi-i ti fa-chan ho shih-chi hsiao-lu" (Memory and efficient recognition), *Kuang-ming jih-pao,* Apr. 4, 1964.

[46] "Hsin-li hsueh li-lun lien-hsi shih-chi shou-ch'eng-hsiao" (The linking of theory with reality in psychology reaps results), *Wen-hui pao,* Dec. 21, 1959.

set up experimental first grades for six-year-olds for purposes of comparison with the regular classes of seven-year-olds. Local psychologists, in cooperation with the education departments in these cities, studied the results in the learning of Chinese characters, sentence construction, ability to adjust to school environment, building of moral character, and so forth. There was also some concern about raising the achievement of students with poor records. Details of the experimental design or method are not available, but after one year of study the preliminary recommendation was that six-year-olds could be successfully placed in first grade, given proper teaching methods; in the first part of the year, however, the six-year-olds were found to be not up to the level of the seven-year-olds in grasp of knowledge. The report concluded that final choice rested with the Education Ministry, if the Ministry would give special attention to "providing for preschool education, modifying teaching material, improving school arrangements, etc." [47]

This experiment indicated that, within alternative ideas and theories of child development open to these educational psychologists, the emphasis was clearly on the *flexibility* of developmental stages rather than rigid, chronological age grading.

One of the specialists in educational psychology, Liu Ching-ho, a Columbia University Teachers College Ph.D. and member of the Institute of Psychology, saw individual differences in children's mental development as closely related to rational understanding and "positive spirit." These were the same elements of rationality prominent in the medical psychologists' treatment of neurasthenia, to a lesser degree in labor psychology, and, as we shall see, again in moral education. Liu wrote [48] that children's learning could be described by two processes: from sense knowledge to rational knowledge to practical knowledge. Mental development, ac-

---

[47] *Ibid.*
[48] Liu Ch'ing-ho, "A preliminary discussion. . . ."

cording to her, must be seen against the different age levels and individual characteristics of the child. Since the child progresses from concrete learning to abstract learning, teaching materials should be designed to suit the changing need. Furthermore, she stated, "Experiments show that the quantity and quality of learning achieved by children are different according to positive mental activities." This she called "an indispensable factor." Admitting that not much was known about how to mobilize this positive spirit or how to observe its beginning in a child, Liu went on to describe some of the favorable conditions under which this positive spirit may best function. Children's positive spirit could be mobilized:

1. if they clearly understood the social significance of what they learn;
2. if their task of learning was clearly assigned to them;
3. if teaching materials and methods were suitable and could develop their ability to understand, and also if they were taught regulations and took part in question and answer.[49]

Liu Ching-ho regarded the learning experience as a discontinuous curve and presented some ideas on "crucial age levels" or "turning points in the process of learning." The crucial ages she proposed were socially derived, as compared to physiologically based discontinuities, described by other psychologists (as discussed in following pages). The crucial ages suggested by Liu were the following: about 2 (the child begins to talk), 6 to 7 (enters school), about 9 (is able to join teams and officially take part in productive activities), and 11 to 12 (begins to enter adolescence). Liu proposed studies on these turning points as transitions from learning nonethical concepts to learning ethical ones and from understanding concepts to applying them to the solution of practical problems.[50]

[49] *Ibid.*
[50] *Ibid.*

Another strand in the developmental area, which had not yet reached a programmatic statement on research but which apparently revived some old controversial issues, was that of differences in levels of development in school and the factors leading to these differences. The controversial aspect of this problem harks back to the debate question on the province of psychology as a science and its independence from other social sciences. Ts'ao Jih-ch'ang, in a short review of the current state of psychological work, placed this new concern of developmental psychology explicitly in this context. Ts'ao wrote: [51]

> Development of children's thinking ability on abstract things is mainly determined by their education, teaching methods, and teaching progress. The more you raise the teaching standard and progress of the class, the bigger the difference between slow and fast students. The former problem involves levels of psychological development, the latter the problem of differences between individuals. . . . We could consider development of children's minds to be a matter of education and effect of teaching. We could consider differences in students' learning ability to be the result of their learning attitude. . . . Then we could try to judge the effects on students' mental development and learning attitude under different educational environments . . . these belong to the method of social science. It is also possible to consider mental development to be a natural process so that differences of talent and sensitivity are determined by psychological characteristics — this method treats psychology as natural science. To understand children's mental development, we must study both educational conditions and maturity of the brain.

Ts'ao pointed out that the old arguments on whether psychology belonged to natural or social science did not reach any conclusion. He labeled as unsatisfactory some people's view that human mental activity was a predominantly social

---

[51] Ts'ao Jih-ch'ang, "Why should we discuss the nature of psychology?" *Kuang-ming jih-pao,* June 2, 1961, p. 2. Joint Publications Research Service No. 4937.

phenomenon, but declared that "the reacting activity of the human brain is still the activity of the brain for the development of higher functions." [52]

We might have expected more future discussion on developmental stages in school children to be tied back to the question of natural versus social science, an issue that remained a central and recurrent problem among these psychologists. For the moment, Ts'ao who acted as leader of the natural science group among psychologists, reiterated his position of a specifically psychological approach as opposed to a social or class approach to the expanding field of development in children.

The measurement of changes in physical characteristics was not entirely neglected, although this topic did not receive the same professional attention as other aspects of growth. In 1951, about 6,000 children between the ages of 5 and 18 in Chekiang, mostly from Hangchow, were measured for their grip strength on a dynamometer. It was found that the growth curve of grip strength was similar to other growth curves and that the rate of growth showed a tendency to decrease with age. Male and female growth curves were found to be very similar, with the female measurements lower at ages 5 to 8 and 15 to 18. In fact, the absolute grip strength for the girls aged 11 to 12 was above that of boys at the same age.[53] The same project also measured stature, body weight, span, sitting height, trunk height, and three chest circumferences. The data showed that the period of rapid growth occurred during the periods of 11 to 16 years of age in the male and 10 to 15 in the female.[54] Although the report of this physical measurement study appeared in the psychological journal,

[52] *Ibid.*

[53] Wang Pai-yang, "Che-chiang erh-t'ung ti wo-li ti fa-chan" (Growth of grip strength of Chekiang children), *Hsin-li hsueh-pao,* No. 3 (1963), pp. 239–246.

[54] Wang Pai-yang, "Che-chiang erh-t'ung sheng-t'i fa-yü ti i-hsieh kuei-li" (Physical development of Chekiang children), *Hsin-li hsueh-pao,* No. 4 (1963), pp. 336–346.

the references cited by the author were, with one exception, from applied physiology and biology. Other studies may have been published in physiology or biology journals. This article established one extreme in the continuum of psychological interest in man. The fact that such an early study was resurrected for publication twelve years later, in 1963, may also have reflected an editorial policy of Ts'ao Jih-ch'ang to encourage integration of physiological factors with mental development studies.

These early thrusts in the area of developmental stages should be considered against the organizational framework of the 1962 Conference of Educational Psychology. At that conference, it is recalled, plans were laid for studying the "psychological age characteristics of the child." The proposed research on the early years (3 to 7 and 7 to 12 age groups) was to last five years, covering cognitive processes and characteristics of the individual. The latter category, including interest, motivation, ability, temperament, and so forth, represented a fresh new direction in Communist Chinese psychology. In the fifties, psychological study of the individual dealt largely with segments of psychological processes. But during and after the Great Leap era, interest shifted to the whole individual: his learning ability and rate, his developmental phases, and his moral character; and differences between him as a concrete individual and others in his age group or school class. The new direction was articulated at the 1962 Conference and implicit in subsequent research programs and discussions. By the following year, local groups had picked up the same theme, as, for example, the Canton meeting of the south-central five-province district for psychological and educational research. That group laid out its own five-year cooperative research program on the "inner contradictions in psychological development." [55]

Besides classroom research, the new developmental interest was also evident in the laboratory experiments reported

[55] *Kuang-ming jih-pao,* Feb. 1, 1963.

at this Conference.[56] An EEG survey of 1,700 people of all ages, including normal, pathological, and handicapped people, was made with the purpose of studying the regularity in the maturation process of the cerebrum. The EEG recordings showed "two leaps of discontinuity, one at the 5- to 6-year-old level and the other at the 13 to 14 age level." Such findings fit neatly into the age groupings of Liu Ching-ho, it may be recalled. The account interpreted the findings as providing "the material foundation for psychological development and age characteristics."

What, then, was meant by the psychological characteristics of a child at a given stage of development? What "dimensions" of development were relevant to these educational psychologists, and how were such dimensions manifested and how were they measured or at least observed? Until psychologists conducted actual experiments on the nature and formation of moral judgment and moral character (see next chapter), what was understood as psychological characteristics remained mechanistic and common-sense-descriptive. For example, a teacher-training manual [57] outlined the items to be observed in case studies on psychological characteristics of children as follows: (1) general environment, (2) higher-nervous-activity model, (3) interests and abilities, and (4) character. Into the category of general environment was lumped all of one's past history, such as family conditions, childhood experiences, school and group life, record of learning, and health, as if these were to be noted in passing before getting to the business at hand — character. Under character, then, were listed attitudes toward society, toward group activities, toward people, and toward self. The attitudes were phrased in moralistic terms: "stable or wavering,"

---

[56] *Kuang-ming jih-pao,* Mar. 9, 1962.

[57] Chu Man-shu, Shao Jui-cheng, "Hsin-li chiao-hsueh ti chi-ko wen-t'i" (Some problems in the teaching of psychology), ed. by the Shanghai Branch of the Psychological Society (Shanghai: *Hsin-chih-shih* Publishing Company, 1958), pp. 70–79.

"diligent or lazy," and so forth, toward group activities; "courteous or rude," "selfish or sociable," and so forth, toward people; and "modest or conceited," "truthful or deceiving," and so forth, toward self. Character traits were apparently considered statically, almost divorced from life history, a view hardly developmental in conception. The other items to be observed, higher-nervous-activity model and interests and abilities, were likewise not integrated. Recent Soviet work had connected modified versions of the Pavlovian typology of nervous activities with abilities and learning style,[58] but a comparable theoretical sophistication had not been reached by the educational psychologists in Communist China. Thus, while the developmental approach was claimed, adequate conceptual tools for a dynamic treatment of the individual child had not yet been formed. The notion of class conditioning of mental characteristics was seen to be too global and too far removed from concrete characteristics. The manual thus warned trainees to avoid too general characterizations such as "politically backward," "self-centered," or "bourgeois in attitudes."

Concurrent with preoccupation with developmental phases on the local scene was renewed interest in the work of foreign psychologists. Piaget's pioneer work on the cognitive development of children, still a classic in Western psychology, was reviewed at the 1962 Conference in addition to "current Soviet studies." On the subject of personality development, Nesmeyanov, president of the Soviet Academy of Science, was quoted as saying: "Early self-determination is the guarantee of a life-time's achievements; it is the guarantee of genius. Besides, this is genius itself." Another Soviet psychologist, Ushinskii, was supposed to have said, "A human being's personality traits formed in these early years

---

[58] B. M. Teplov and V. D. Nebylitzyn, "The study of the basic properties of the nervous system and their significance for the psychology of individual differences," tr. in *Soviet Psychology and Psychiatry,* Vol. IV., No. 3–4 (Spring–Summer 1966), pp. 80–85.

hold fast and remain firm. They become the second nature of man." Shan Yu, who introduced these Soviet views, added that "formation of personality characteristics, especially during childhood years, should definitely be studied. If this could be done with psychological age, it would be wonderful." [59] Summarizing foreign psychologists on this problem, it was concluded that "psychological development is not linear, nor is it of constant speed." Thus, Communist China's psychologists saw themselves as following the Soviet lead in uniting the materialist approach of Marxist ideology with at least part of the Western tradition in developmental psychology.

[59] Shan Yu, "Feng-wei chih-kuo k'o yü-ch'i Chung-kuo Hsin-li-hsueh Hui Chiao-yü Hsin-li Chuan-yeh hui-i tsui-kan" (Fruitful results can be predicted — impressions of the Educational Psychology Specialty Conference of the Chinese Psychological Society), *Kuang-ming jih-pao,* Mar. 14, 1962.

CHAPTER SIX

MORAL CHARACTER
AND INDIVIDUALITY

Having begun to look at the whole child through the study of age levels and developmental stages, the educational psychologist came directly up against the thorny problem of individuality and individual differences. For there are two fundamental questions that must be answered by any adequate conceptual scheme dealing with psychological processes leading to social behavior: How do past experiences of the individual affect present processes? And how does one conceptually organize the processes with the individual as the unit of analysis? Nowhere is this problem more dramatically encountered than in the area of moral character.

The mechanistic model of explaining human behavior — the early "environmental determinist" school that enjoyed brief vogue in Soviet psychology in the twenties — never took root in Communist China. Instead, the emphasis upon the active consciousness of man meant that Communist Chinese psychology always placed moral responsibility upon the individual, as an active agent in the transmission belt between social "reality" — psychological processes — and behavioral output. The question then becomes: What accounts for the similarities and differences among individuals? What are the universals, the mechanisms governing the processes, and what are the particulars, the forces that go toward the shaping of each unique individual? The closer the researcher comes into contact with the whole person, whether it be the school child, the worker, or the neurasthenic, the more necessary it becomes to study and explain individuality, individual differences as well as group differences.

Within the broad framework of a Communist theory of behavior, as differentiated from a mechanistic-deterministic theory, variations in behavior were viewed and analyzed by mainland Chinese psychologists in terms of two different kinds of variables: nonclass variables, such as age, sex, intelligence, academic achievement, developmental phases; and class variables, in the sense that class background determines either primarily or exclusively one's active consciousness, which in turn determines behavior. During the fifties, the politically oriented psychologists periodically criticized the use of nonclass variables in the treatment of any psychological data and proposed the use of class analysis for all problems. Despite ideological pressures, psychologists had been, until the cultural revolution of 1965, more or less successful in carrying on self-learning and research based on nonclass variables, while acknowledging on the whole the ultimate supremacy of the role of active consciousness and its class foundation in explaining behavior.

RESEARCH ON MORAL CHARACTER

During the fifties, even the term moral education, or *tao-te chiao-yü,* was seldom found in the available psychological literature. Interest had indeed been scant and schematic on the questions of the formation of the individual's moral sense, motivation for moral or antimoral behavior, or the role of the group in individual behavior. Early attention on this general area was almost entirely in the nature of arguments for the class standpoint and arose in connection with the debate on the nature of human consciousness. The "natural science" faction of psychology represented by the Institute emphasized that all psychological studies of the consciousness must be seen through the intervention of brain processes, while the "social science" faction insisted that the analysis of psychological processes include the "class viewpoint" or concentrate on the social content of consciousness. Both sides rested with their assertions, without empirical studies or data to back them up. At a debate meeting at Shanghai Normal College when Li Po-shu alone reported an empirical study he had conducted on the "psychological activities of 7- and 8-year-old school children," it "aroused much interest and stimulated resolutions to do more concrete research." [1]

The little work that was done in that period on the moral makeup of the individual was largely aimed toward answering the question of *whether or not* children had class consciousness. Ch'en Yuan-hui, of the Educational Science Research Institute, declared that class analysis was not appropriate in the study of child psychology.[2] Chu Chih-hsien, of Peking Normal University and member of the Educational Psychology Committee of the Society, stated: "Children's psychological development follows racial history: first simple sensations, then conscious thought, emotions, and will." A child's acquisition of class consciousness, he continued, took two routes: from early age, "he hears this is mine and that is yours," manifestations of adult class consciousness. In propertyless classes, children learn to love labor, help others, and so on. After systematic education, which Chu said came after the primary grades, children begin to acquire "stable class consciousness tendencies such as needs, motives, imagination, beliefs, and world views." [3] The implication was that

---

[1] "Shang-hai hsin-li-hsueh chieh chan-k'ai cheng-lun" (Shanghai psychologists open debate meetings), *Wen-hui pao,* Apr. 14, 1959.
[2] *Kuang-ming jih-pao,* Apr. 7, 1959.
[3] Chu Chih-hsien, "Kuan-yü jen-ti hsien-li ti chieh-chi-hsing wen-t'i" (On the question of the class nature of human psychology), *Kuang-ming jih-pao,* June 23, 1959.

class consciousness was first learned via simple imitation, and that, later, class ideas were acquired via a seemingly separate process from the day-to-day activities of children.

An example of the class concept being used as the simple determinant of the social content of consciousness during that early period was a survey aimed at finding out manifestations of "class struggle and contradictions" in ninth-grade children.[4] Children were asked to discuss the topic of "opening the doors of schools to children of workers and peasants." It was found that "children of workers and peasants are full of gratitude for this educational opportunity. Children of exploiting classes feel the Party discriminates in favor of workers and peasant children, who should really compete on the basis of merit. Children of petty bourgeois and intellectuals care only for their own future, or express the desire for moderation on the class question."

Another study on the same theme of class influence on "children's character" was conducted by a group of Kuang-tung teachers of psychology on second- and third-grade children, with classroom teachers as research assistants.[5] The intensive analysis of three kinds of children's activities — *lao-tung* (physical labor), class work, and group activities — brought the conclusion that "remaining class contradictions affect psychological development of children. Young people living in contemporary society show waves in the course of psychological development, thus providing a challenge to the teachers."

The only known study toward the end of the fifties that displayed concern with nonpolitical, what Western psychologists would call personality, characteristics of social types was

[4] Reported in Yang Ch'eng-chang, "Shih-lun jen-ti hsin-li ti mao-tun ti t'e shu-shing" (Some considerations on the specificity of contradictions of mental activity), *Hsin-li hsueh-pao,* No. 3 (1961).

[5] Kuang-tung hsin-li-hsueh chiao-shih hsia-hsiang hsia-ch'ang tiao-ch'a yen-chiu" (Kuangtung teachers of psychology go down to villages and factories for investigation and research), *Kuang-ming jih-pao,* June 12, 1959.

that of Li Yi on psychological characteristics of the attitude structure of "good workers" and "poor workers" among fifth- and sixth-grade pupils participating in agricultural work.[6] Li, a member of the Institute of Psychology, observed and interviewed two groups of eight children each who had been recommended by their teachers as "good workers" and "poor workers" in the *lao-tung* or work situation. The subjects were asked to describe (1) what they considered characteristics of "good workers" and "poor workers"; (2) what their own good points and bad points were while doing *lao-tung*; and (3) what the good points and bad points of X (a specific good worker) and of Y (a specific poor worker) were. What Li found distinguished a good worker from a poor one was not surprising: a positive attitude toward work, rest period, tools, schedules, and so forth; a sense of responsibility toward output, common property, and fruit of the labor of others; a positive attitude toward rules; and a good relation to others in work. The last point was of some intrinsic interest to the psychologist of personality, a good worker not only voluntarily helped others but also made demands upon others. Li further pointed out that good and poor workers differed most in collective spirit, next in obedience toward rules, and least in individual work schedules.

The children's own opinion of what they considered to be features of good and poor workers turned out to be Li's greater contribution toward a beginning in the psychology of personality characteristics. The group of good workers, as chosen by the teachers, saw both good and bad points in the poor worker, Y. The group of teacher-selected poor workers saw only good points in the model student and only bad points in the other. In short, a tendency toward realistic, full-

[6] Li Yi, "Hsiao-hsueh kao-nien-chi hsueh-sheng ts'an-chia nung-yeh lao-tung chung so piao-hsien ti i-hsieh hsin-li t'e-tien ti ch'u-pu fen-hsi" (An analysis of the psychological characteristics of primary school 5–6th grade students participating in agricultural work," *Hsin-li hsueh-pao*, No. 5 (1959), pp. 293–302.

rounded appraisal of fellow students was displayed by the exemplars among the children and a tendency toward stereotyping was noted among those who did not live up to expectations. (The criteria used by the teachers in designating good and bad were not given in this study, so the independence of teacher and student ratings could not be assumed.) This study could have fitted neatly into the development of systematic knowledge on perceptual and cognitive processes of the desired type of personality—ever critical, seeing contradictions and faults, high conscious awareness, and still a good worker. But the potential leads were not crystallized; neither were they exploited in any further study so far uncovered.

It was toward the end of the recovery period from the Great Leap Forward, when the class question had temporarily receded from psychological circles and doors were opened to the broad examination of character training, that truly psychological variables rather than political ones were used to study observable aspects of normative behavior, formation of moral judgment, and motivations for moral behavior.

In the early sixties, moral education had come to be explicitly spoken of by top leaders in psychology as the most important topic of research to be developed. P'an Shu, in a statement to the press,[7] specifically named psychological problems in moral education as the priority psychological problem meriting investigation. With the objective of training "workers with socialist consciousness and culture," the educational psychologist was to "analyze the psychological structure of the moral qualities of students, laws governing their grasp of moral concepts, formation of moral sense, moral faith, and conduct, development of the will and formation of Communist character, effects of the collectivity on moral

---

[7] P'an Shu, "Iideas about expanded research in educational psychology," *Kuang-ming jih-pao*, Mar. 13, 1962. Joint Publications Research Service No. 13531.

qualities, and psychological characteristics of self-discipline."
P'an added that, up to then, they had made only general surveys and a mere beginning in experimental studies.

Ts'ao Jih-ch'ang delivered substantially the same message in his address to the 1963 Annual Discussion Meeting
of the Psychological Society.[8] He said that "character education" was one of the important questions "either untouched
or too little studied." Actually, 18 percent of the 206 papers
submitted to Ts'ao for that meeting already belonged to
moral education, not an unimpressive beginning. But when
he compared psychology with education, where "attention
has always been paid to political and moral education," psychological research on moral education was "a blank."
"While the nation's attention was focused on class education
for children and youth," he continued, "there are many psychological problems to be studied. For example, the formation and development of young people's class attitudes and
class feeling, training of children's will (*i-chih*), how to suit
the content and form of class education to different age levels
and different levels of intellectual development of children,
etc."

Studies in the psychology of moral education highlighted
the 1963 Annual Meeting. Ch'en Ta-jou, rapporteur for recent major meetings and then a rising psychologist, said in
describing the psychology of moral education that "because
it is a new subject, papers are not many, but the contents
covered are broad." [9] He went on to give a separate listing
of titles of the ten papers on moral education. Since only
three of the ten papers are available for examination, it is

---

[8] Ts'ao Jih-ch'ang, "Kuan-ch'e li-lun lien-hsi shih-chi, k'o-hsueh yen-
chiu wei she-hui chu-i chien-she fu-wu ti fang-chen, t'i-kao hsin-li-
hsueh kung-tso ti shui-p'ing" (Raising the scientific level of psychological research: address to the 1963 meeting of the Chinese
Psychological Society), *Hsin-li hsueh pao*, No. 1 (1964), pp. 1–18.
[9] Ch'en Ta-jou, "Chung-kuo hsin-li-hsueh hui 1963 nien hsueh-shu
nien-hui (The 1963 annual academic meeting of the Chinese Psychological Society), *Hsin-li hsueh-pao*, No. 1 (1964), pp. 109–112.

worth repeating the other titles here in order to give an impression of the nature and direction of work on this topic:

1. "Children's classroom discipline" — Li P'ing-hsi
2. "Goal formation in *hsueh-hsi* (learning)" — Wuhan Normal College Education Department
3. "Development of imagination in children" — Wu Chan-yuan
4. "Exemplar education" — Tseng Hsin-jan
5. "Problems of organization for *hsueh-hsi* — Ho Tsung-ting
6. "Character education" — Liu Chao-chi
7. "Children's perception of time" — Chang Tseng-chieh

It is no accident that this new branch of psychology should have been pushed just when the Party was concerned with rousing the revolutionary zeal of youth during the recovery years after the Great Leap. As our discussion of the growth of medical psychology, and to some extent of labor psychology, pointed out, there had been a curious lack of explicit research attention on the effect of the group on individual behavior, or on the role of the group in the acquisition of the "active consciousness." Then, in the sixties, psychologists were at last taking a direct look at the origin and development of morally oriented behavior.

The subject of moral education revived the old debate issue of social science versus natural science once again. A Japanese edition of the *Jen-min Chung-kuo* (*People's China*),[10] in covering the 1963 meeting, reported the following: "Some think that psychology of morality belongs to social science, and not to an in-between science. Others feel that even though people's moral behavior is social phenomenon, because it passes through the human brain, it cannot be separated from the natural science study of the physiological

[10] *Jen-min Chung-kuo* (People's China), Japanese edition, No. 3 (1964), pp. 65–66.

organ." Someone at the meeting proposed a compromise of principles to follow in pursuing the pyschology of moral education: [11]

1. It must follow class analysis.
2. It must respect educational principles.
3. It must maintain our objective viewpoint.

Yet the resulting work did not represent either of the extremes, as the discussion of the following three studies will show.

Chuang Chih-k'uang of Peking Normal University collaborated with Chu Wen-ping on a small-scale but intensive study of 14 fifth-grade children from the experimental school attached to the university on the formation of a sense of responsibility toward homework.[12] Their methods combined experimentation, observation, questionnaire, analysis of homework, and case investigation. The 14 children were divided into matched halves: experimental and control groups. Both groups heard "mobilization lectures" on the meaning and standards of good homework in arithmetic. The experimental group was retained after school hours for three days to carry out recommended practice under supervision. Thereafter, this group went home as usual and their parents were asked to supervise homework. Children of the experimental group were further told to remind one another and to talk over their experiences together, analyzing reasons for their own improvements and methods to conquer difficulties. The experimenter made frequent checks of their progress, giving praise or criticism. Each student also kept a diary. The control group did not receive any such guidance after the initial lectures. At the end of seven weeks, tests were made of the students' attitudes toward homework responsibility, conditions

[11] Ch'en Ta-jou, "Chung-kuo hsin-li-hsueh hui 1963. . . ."
[12] Chang Chih-kuang, Chu Wen-pin, "Hsiao-hsueh-sheng k'o-yeh tse-jen-hsin hsing-ch'eng ti shih-yen yen-chiu" (Research on the formation of primary school students' sense of responsibility toward homework), *Hsin-li hsueh-pao,* No. 2 (1964), pp. 194–202.

for the formation of a sense of responsibility, and changes in homework records. Two criteria were used for the successful formation of a sense of responsibility: (1) behavior in completing homework—did he complete it according to schedule after school hours, did he go over the answers, did he correct errors in the last assignment?—and (2) the amount of careless mistakes.

This experiment showed that as a consequence of the experiment both groups changed their attitudes toward homework, raised their grades, and improved their work habits, although changes in the experimental group were a little more marked. In making corrections or in doing work on schedule, there was not much difference between the two groups, although careless mistakes in work decreased more with the experimental group. Grades also became more consistent within the experimental group. Although immediate differences were not very great, tests a month later showed a widened difference between the two groups. A generalizing effect was also noted: it was observed that in a "natural experiment" sometime later in copying compositions for an exhibit, the experimental group completed the task before the control group did.

The results of this experiment are hardly surprising considering the loading of all factors in favor of the experimental group. Of greater significance is the discussion of the results in the article. The experimenters pointed out that mere comprehension of the tasks demanded of the children was not enough to bring about a sense of responsibility: "adults must give concrete guidance in the steps to be taken in achieving it." It should be recalled that medical psychologists, in demonstrating the effectiveness of psychotherapy a few years before, had at first argued solely for the role of recognition and later had begun to point to the importance of the doctor-patient relationship. The authority figure of the teacher in making the demands and in "showing students seriousness of his concern" was here given a place in the conceptual thinking regarding motivation leading to a change in behavior. However, rational explanation was still given primary importance because "it can act as temporary motivation for carrying out teachers' demands, and can be self-reinforcing via language." Group practice was also mentioned as "shortening trial and error procedures and providing the teacher a setting to observe problems and render help." No theoretical analysis was offered on the group as a social system of peers and its role in affecting behavior. Instead, the experimenters stressed specific practices for inculcating the sense of responsibility in children: placing immediate work on their consciousness and banishing temptations for play and encouraging them to inspect their work and summarize their experiences. It is evident that the role of consciousness continued to play a major part in the theoretical thinking of psychologists. "Training in this responsibility not only makes learning positive but also develops will and raises intellectual capacity."

The authors proposed this theory in opposition to two supposedly Western theories of character formation singled out for criticism: the "intelligence theory" of W. W. Charters, and the "habit theory" of K. Dunlap. According to Chuang and Chu, Charters maintained that character depended upon native intelligence and moral knowledge, while Dunlap made character the result of the "systematization of superior habits." Western approaches to this broad problem were thus dismissed in these brief and greatly simplified representations as foil for the theory of active consciousness.

Up to the time of the cultural revolution, motivation was a little studied concept and only an occasionally encountered term in Communist Chinese psychology. This situation makes the following 1964 article dealing with "motivation for moral behavior" in children important because for them it pioneered a new direction. The study by Li Po-shu and Chou Kwan-sheng, based on a questionnaire administered to 297 pupils between 9 and 16 years of age, investigated characteristics of moral motivation under hypothetical and realistic situations.[13] The former was called "recognition motivation" (*jen-shih-hsing tung-chi*) and the latter "reality motivation" (*shih-chi tung-chi*). A pretest in a Shanghai middle school asked children to write down one or two personal incidents of moral and antimoral behavior. These personal accounts were then used as a basis to construct a questionnaire with three hypothetical stories of antimoral behavior, administered to a different group of 142 middle-school students. Subjects were requested to reply how they would act in each situation, giving reasons for doing so and noting down thoughts about it. This procedure hoped to tap characteristics of "recognition motivation." A month later, a study of "realistic motivation" was done on the same 142 students by asking them to relate one or two moral and antimoral personal events, again giving reasons and thoughts. The double questionnaire was repeated on 153 primary school students in Shanghai. The experimenters classified 93 percent of children's ideas of moral behavior arising out of their daily lives as being concerned with "helping others," "for the good of the public," or "honesty," while 70 percent of the antimoral behavior was "harming others," "harming the public," or "dishonesty." Concerning the nature of moral motivations, the *hypothetical* situations presented to the children elicited varying reasons for behaving in a moral or antimoral manner. The primary school children were found to be mainly following rules of behavior provided them by parents or teachers, while middle-school students showed an increasing tendency to make the reasons given by others their own subjective moral standards. In considering consequences of antimoral behavior, younger children thought of concrete, objective results, such as, "This kind of behavior

---

[13] Li Po-shu, Chou Kuan-sheng, "Shao-nien erh-t'ung tao-te hsing-wei tung-chi t'e-cheng ti hsin-li fen-hsi" (Motivational characteristics of moral behavior in children), *Hsin-li hsueh-pao*, No. 1 (1964), pp. 25–32.

means others cannot read the book," or "seller will lose out." The older ones named abstract, internal effects upon their own thought level or moral growth, such as, "This behavior will not help my thought level even a little bit," or "If I take money that doesn't belong to me, it will stain my entire life." Thus far, the educational psychologists were merely talking about the well-known process of internalization of norms in children without using the Western conceptual term. It is as if these psychologists were discovering the process afresh and inductively from this study.

When the authors began to examine motivation in *realistic* situations — that is, when the children described out of their own experiences some moral or antimoral behavior — they came face-to-face with psychological phenomena hitherto completely overlooked in the growing field. Instead of discussing competing ideologies, such as capitalistic thought or bourgeois habits, that might prevent the realization of socialistic norms for behavior, psychologists wrote of complex motivational conflicts, which they labeled "temptation, excitement, bad habit, love of fun, etc." or "bad thinking such as jealousy, greed, vengefulness, blaming others, taking from others to replace own loss, etc." In other words, the antimoral motivation in realistic situations came from within the socialistic social system, not from without. There were psychological processes intervening between rational understanding of moral norms and acting them out in moral behavior, processes that revealed permanent weakness of human beings in social life.

Another empirical finding of this experiment was that standards for their own moral behavior were not absolute in the children's minds but could be flexibly interpreted to allow for less-than-moral conduct, including the taking of money. For example, children wrote in describing their own behavior: "Picking just a handful of beans from the public farm would not do any harm," or "Taking 20 *yuan* from the seller does not amount to much," or, in making fun of a fellow student by a nickname, "It was just for fun — it is of no importance." The experimenters pointed out that the same situations, if posed in hypothetical questions, would have elicited remarks such as these: "Even 20 *yuan* belongs to the nation," "One must not take from public property," or using a nickname would "harm his self-respect."

Although educational psychologists were studying concrete moral behavior in children and unearthing complexities in motivation that might lead to a breakthrough within the Communist theory of behavior, the central concept used remained that of active consciousness. No explicit conceptual differentiations emerged from this study, a fact that hampered concise analysis and theoretical advance in the field. There was still the tendency to treat rational knowledge of the proper goals as ultimately and almost automatically producing socially desirable behavior, blurring a more complex process revealed by their own empirical data. For in concluding this article, the authors wrote: "Struggles show that the recognition motivation acts to constrain antimoral behavior in real situations. But this control function does not work uniformly: it becomes stronger in older children." Lost were the lessons that might have been pointed out in the psychological meaning of moral or antimoral behavior, in the mental processes that accompany the application of abstract norms in concrete behavior. Preconceived concepts were again blinders limiting scientific advances from empirical findings.

The ability of young people to make moral judgments was the subject of a third pioneering study (for mainland psychology) on moral character, conducted by Hsieh Ch'ien-ch'iu with 281 middle-school students in five Kuangtung schools.[14] Hsieh referred to the work of Soviet psychologist Anayev on the relationship between self-evaluation and the ability to exercise moral judgment on the behavior of others.

[14] Hsieh Ch'ien-ch'iu, "Ch'ing-shao-nien tao-te p'ing-chia neng-li ti i-hsieh yen-chiu" (Studies on the ability of moral judgment in adolescents), *Hsin-li hsueh-pao*, No. 3 (1964).

Self-evaluation was seen, in turn, as essential to the cultivation of moral character. Hsieh's study was thus the most direct attack found in recent psychological writings on character training, while his specific problem, the relationship between the quality of moral judgment and intellectual levels, pointed to the mounting attention among psychologists on individual differences.

Hsieh asked his subjects to make moral judgments on the behavior of the main character in six written stories (one from the classic *Ch'un Ch'iu* and five contemporary episodes). Answers were classified according to four aspects of the moral judgments: (1) Did the subject see through superficial characteristics of behavior to reach the fundamentals? (2) Did he consider all angles of the situation? (3) Did he differentiate between the main point and subsidiary ones? (4) Did he apply concrete analysis to concrete problems? The experimenter found a parallel distribution between junior and senior middle-school students in all four aspects of judgment, leading him to conclude first of all that junior middle-school students had already developed their power of moral judgment, and that a certain proportion of senior middle-school students still had a comparatively low level of moral judgment. Of the four aspects of judgment, however, the biggest difference due to age was found in the ability to make analyses of concrete situations. Next came the ability to consider all angles and to see essentials of the situation; and the least difference was found to be in distinguishing main points of the moral situations. Over-all, a positive relationship was found between ability for moral judgment and level of intellectual attainment.

Unfortunately for the development of psychology as a science, Hsieh's promising investigation of moral judgment brought forth a year later a direct, ideological rebuttal by Ssu-ma Feng,[15] a name appearing in the journal for the first

[15] Ssu-ma Feng, "Te-yü hsien-li-hsueh ti yen-chiu pi-hsü kuan-ch'e chieh-chi fen-hsi yuan-che — Hsieh Ch'ien-ch'iu t'ung-chih shang-

time. This rebuttal was also the first time a politically based criticism, barely if at all tied in with psychological theory and aimed at a specific piece of work, was published in the journal. The very subtitle of this article reveals its political character: "a Discussion with Comrade Hsieh Ch'ien-ch'iu." Ssu-ma took basic issue with Hsieh for not using class struggle as the fundamental premise for evaluating all moral behavior, as the mode of analyzing its formation and differential development, and as the practical recommendation for remedying the lack of high attainment. Specifically, Hsieh was attacked for (1) using "abstract, supra-class" individual differences for examining moral judgment in children instead of using differences in political standpoint; (2) breaking down moral judgment into its intellectualized components; and (3) "obscuring" differences in class standpoint and political thinking of the children by differentiating them according to age and academic class. In short, all the variables that a psychologist would normally use in studying social behavior were ruled out by Ssu-ma as ideologically incorrect. Instead, he proposed class struggle as the only "valid" method for approaching all aspects of moral behavior. This critique, then, presaged the eclipse of this phase of development in scientific psychology, just at a time when the maturation of educational psychology as a branch led researchers to the brink of grappling with a strategic social problem: the formation, identification, and measurement of the different components of moral conduct. The denial of the relevancy of abstracted components of intelligence and the insistence on class viewpoint and political thinking as the main and sufficient explanation for children may also limit work in other parts of educational psychology, and not inconceivably in medical psychology and industrial psychology as well.

---

chueh" (The principle of class analysis must be applied in the research on psychology of moral education — a discussion with comrade Hsieh Ch'ien-ch'iu), *Hsin-li hsueh-pao,* No. 2 (1965), pp. 114–120.

The following three studies in moral character were published in the spring of 1966 and therefore belong to the era of the "cultural revolution." These papers, though submitted during 1965, foreshadowed the politicizing of psychology by defining their problems in terms of class factors, treating data along class lines, and drawing conclusions in accord with the progressive class viewpoint. In fact, beginning with the first issue of 1966, the entire tone and content of the *Hsin-li hsueh-pao* underwent a fundamental change. Thought-criticism articles aimed at specific psychologists, as well as clear political evaluations of research pieces, were in sharp contrast to the hitherto academic, highly professional, and nonpolitical kind of writing that had characterized this journal from its inception. The three 1966 studies reported here are full of quotes from and references to Chairman Mao. It might be added that all three projects were done at provincial normal institutions.

The study entitled "Children's aims and motivation for learning," by Wu I-ling and Li Cho-min,[16] reveals not only the way in which scientific research could be utilized to justify politically desirable conclusions but also how the latter could deflect attention away from unsolved problems contained in empirical findings. The particular way in which the concept of motivation or motivating force (*tung-chi*) was employed in this article clarifies, furthermore, the meaning of the term in psychological theory on the mainland.

This "motivation" study by Wu and Li might be classified by Western psychologists as a study in the formation of attitudes toward learning and toward laboring. A total of 350 children between the third and sixth grades, from regular schools and from half-study, half-work schools, were studied via questionnaires as well as by intensive participant-

[16] Wu I-ling, Li Cho-min, "Shao-nien erh-t'ung hsueh-hsi mu-ti yü tung-chi ti fen-hsi" (An analysis of the purpose and motivation for learning among youth), *Hsin-li hsueh-pao,* No. 2 (1966), pp. 137–145.

181

observation and informal interviews with parents, teachers, and so forth. This "total push" spirit of psychological investigation was reminiscent of the mental health survey during the Great Leap. The initial purpose of the investigation was to show the relation between work experience and "correctness of recognition" regarding the goal of education and the meaning of labor. When the children from the two types of schools — with and without work experience — did not show significant differences in recognition in the paper-and-pencil test, the research was expanded to include a wider source of data. The research team was enlarged to 74 and saturated the children's social environment as participant observers. The prolonged and intensive contact with the children yielded what was called "real recognition." By "real recognition" was meant that which is manifested in actual behavior in day-to-day living situations, including those outside the schoolroom. The result was that when a distinction was drawn between "test recognition" and "real recognition" of the purpose of education and meaning of labor, a wide difference was unearthed between children of regular schools and those of the work-schools. This finding was explained in terms of Marxist epistemology and Mao's writings that knowledge and thought must be based on actual experience and that "best knowledge" alone was not sufficient to produce desirable learning.

A second phase of this investigation turned its attention to the "causes of incorrect recognition" concerning one's educational goals and the meaning of labor. After interviewing and observing parents, teachers, and other relevant persons, and from analyzing the class origin and political attitude of the family, the following conclusions were reached: (1) Class origin of the family was correlated with "real recognition" of the children — a poor peasant and lower-middle peasant background produced a higher proportion of children with "correct real recognition," while upper-middle and rich peasant families produced more children with "incorrect real recognition"; (2) political thought of parents played the greatest role among family and social influences in producing "incorrect recognition" in children; (3) family and other social influences played a lesser role among work-school pupils than among regular-school pupils in producing children with "incorrect recognition"; and (4) class origin of family could not entirely determine the correctness of recognition in children.

We shall not present or evaluate the numerical data included in this research report, for without knowing the criteria upon which the categories were based, the figures are largely meaningless. It should only be noted that this study was written up with scientific-appearing charts, discussion of method of investigation, and publication of the questionnaire and observation instruments. However, the observation chart was so general as to permit the inclusion of any kind of subjective data, which could in turn lead to any kind of numerical results. Furthermore, the fourth conclusion, which should constitute the crux of the problem of attitude formation for psychologists, was dismissed with the recommendation of more education for parents. For the empirical data showed that parents with the proper class background who held proper political attitudes for their own lives could still transmit "incorrect" learning attitudes in their children.

A final conclusion of this study pointed to the relationship between age and recognition: among regular-school pupils, the gap between "test recognition" and "real recognition" increased with age, but among work-school pupils, the gap was negligible and remained so with increasing age. Thus, a nonpolitically derived variable was also shown to operate in the proper direction.

It became apparent from this study what was meant by the term *motivation* in Communist Chinese psychology and why, among other, more political reasons, it had not been an important subject for research. The concept of motivation in this research report appeared to be almost equivalent to and interchangeable with the concept of recognition, especially "real recognition." We can further infer that the concept of "recognition" as it was frequently used implied more than rational understanding, for as a component of the active consciousness, "recognition" partakes of the active aspect or the energy aspect of the latter. To "recognize" includes "to see the necessity of" or even "to want to." Thus, in this article, "test recognition" was also called "rational recognition" (*li-lun jen-shih*), to distinguish it from "real recognition," which included knowing the reason why. In much psychological writing from the mainland, there was the implicit assumption that "correct recognition leads to correct action." Little attention was paid to what intervenes between recognition and final behavior, a vast and problematical area that Western psychologists would label motivation. But with the consistent neglect of nonrational factors in psychological processes among Chinese Communist psychologists, the question of motivation in their scheme becomes a superfluous one.

Two other studies represented a more direct approach to the question of moral education — one by Nieh Shih-mou on "Function of the exemplar in student self evaluation" [17] and the other by Yuan Liang-tso and Li Tuan-wu on "Revolutionary hero stories and the formation of pupils' moral consciousness." [18] These two studies attempted a direct confrontation with the problems of the incorporation of moral standards and the relation between moral consciousness and moral conduct. Both contributed to our understanding of the gradual evolution of a Communist Chinese theory of

[17] Nieh Shih-mou, "Pang-yang tui-pi tui shao-nien hsueh-sheng tzu-wo p'ing-chia ti tso-yung" (Function of the examplar for student self-evaluation), *Hsin-li hsueh-pao,* No. 2 (1966), pp. 146–153.

[18] Yuan Liang-tso, Li Tuan-wu, "Ke-ming ying-hsiung ku-shih tui hsiao-hsueh-sheng tao-te i-shih hsing-ch'en ti tso-yung ti ch'u-pu yen-chiu" (Function of revolutionary hero stories for the formation of pupils' moral consciousness), *Hsin-li hsueh-pao,* No. 2 (1966), pp. 154–162.

thought and behavior and helped to illuminate the rationale behind much of the regime's policies in education and mass indoctrination.

Nieh divided 30 students between the ages of 13 and 17 from three half-work schools into experimental and control groups. Using a combination of questionnaire, interviews, written themes, discussion groups, and consultation with teachers, the investigator gave two tests of moral self-evaluation about a month apart. The experimental group, who received exemplar education in the form of story reading, lectures, and discussions, showed more critical remarks about self and more political standards, rather than simply general moral standards about everyday behavior. The second test of the experimental group (as well as group discussions) also revealed a heightened sense of "incorporated" standards of moral judgment, independent of reliance upon what teachers, classmates, and others demanded. From these results, the investigator concluded that self-evaluation in children could be changed with comparative ease, and that exemplar education could be utilized to increase the formation of independent standards of self-evaluation, thus shedding reliance upon the judgment of others. The author warned, however, that such verbal standards must not be equated with true advance in thought or with political awakening.

Perhaps the line of thinking behind this study could help to explain the inordinately heavy reliance upon learning from the thought of Chairman Mao in the cultural and educational revolution, that direct inspiration from a super hero could be even more efficacious than mutual criticism in instilling internal standards for moral behavior. And if moral consciousness is a major ingredient for moral conduct, as the previous study aimed to demonstrate, then the extreme form of hero worship arose out of a rationale — the concept of active consciousness, the same source from which Chinese psychological theory derived its impetus.

Another research effort tested the effectiveness of the

hero story in the formation of moral consciousness and in cementing the relationship between moral consciousness and moral conduct. Yuan and Li used a small sample of third graders and employed more intensive case methods. From the authors' discussion of their results, a theoretical stance is apparent on the relation between moral conduct on the one hand and its application to one's own behavior. Test data were presented to show that the experimental group, which had increased its knowledge of rules of moral conduct, also applied it in class behavior, in homework, and in conduct both at home and at school. The hero stories were further shown to have increased the self-awareness (*tzu-chueh-hsing*) of the motivation for moral conduct. While it was warned that moral behavior could also result from habit or external force, hero stories were said to "heighten moral recognition and to *create the wish* for emulating heroes," or to "*actively direct* their moral conduct" (italics added). The activating nature of recognition was clearly expressed here. In other words, the moving force for behavior is embodied in the concept of recognition; no separate concept of motivation was provided in this theory, for consciousness is *active*.

INDIVIDUALITY AND INDIVIDUAL DIFFERENCES

The concept of individuality had been a troublesome one for the mainland psychologists. Its content, which had never been clearly defined, shifted in focus in the decade after the new psychology took shape, due partly to terminological ambiguity and partly to ideological problems. There were dangerous political traps to be wary of when using the term. When talking about "individuality" (*ko-hsing*), the psychologists had to dissociate themselves from "individualism" (*ko-jen chu-i*), which was attributed to bourgeois societies and associated with genetic assumptions. If they

186

took a position on "individuality" and incorporated it in a general theory in psychology, they had to remember that it would automatically have implications for educational policy. As for "individual differences," it was not until the early sixties, when national focus turned to the cultivation of human resources, that psychologists faced the problem concretely or even used the concept to any extent at all in their publications.

In the early years of the new psychology, psychologists were preoccupied with an examination of isolated psychological processes; the whole individual was left unexplored. The concept of individuality began to be discussed during the criticism-debate meetings of 1958–1959. At that time, it was used primarily *in opposition* to something; that is, the scientifically oriented psychologists who concentrated on psychological processes with emphasis on functions of the brain and higher nervous system were criticized for *neglecting individuality*. In that context, individuality meant the whole individual as compared to abstract processes such as sensation, perception, memory, or even more minute problems in the nervous system. The critics, with ideological backing, insisted that psychology should study the "concrete individual," with his class background and class consciousness, and should employ the "class method of analysis." Beyond these requirements in focus, "method," and "point of view," there were no further explanations of what individuality meant or what it should include. The crucial question at stake at that time was whether the individual shared universal psychological processes (pan-human ones) with his fellowman or whether a person's class background colored and overrode all his psychological processes. Psychologists with the latter point of view were really arguing for the necessity to study the *wholeness* of the individual, without meaning, of course, that it was important to study the *uniqueness* of each individual, with all the idiosyncratic characteristics that made him different from other individuals, including

187

those with similar class background. In fact, they were really interested in the masses (or relevant classes) and their *common* problems, rather than in separate individuals. By individuality they meant group characteristics manifested in the individual. It was still the *sameness* of certain classes of individuals instead of the *differences* among individuals that formed the burden of the argument. The differences were either ignored as unimportant or held to be reduceable to a common level through deliberate effort.

The terminological difficulty of individuality actually presented more of a pressing problem to the education field than in psychology during the fifties. While psychologists debated on what aspect of the person to study, writers on education philosophy had to wrestle with the meaning of individuality within the then-current policy of the "total development of the individual." In a long discourse on this subject, Ma Chi-hsiung explored in the *Hua-tung Normal University Journal* [19] various definitions of the term individuality, including what little psychologists had to offer. This piece was illuminating because it spelled out the potential pitfalls and educational implications for any psychological stance on the subject. In tracing the historical definitions of the concept *ko-hsing*, Ma explained, "Our purpose in this minute differentiation of the meanings of *ko-hsing* is to unmask the deceitfulness of the principle of *ko-jen chu-i* [individualism] that has infiltrated the citadel of the science of education under the guise of *ko-hsing chu-i* [individuality]." Ma proceeded to give three different interpretations for educational policy based on the furtherance of individuality: (1) a well-designed program to call forth the optimum development of the aptitudes of the children, together with remedial measures to eliminate the deficiencies of the same children; (2) absolute freedom for pupils; and (3) the

[19] Ma Chi-hsiung, "T'an-t'an 'ko-hsing ti ch'uan-mien fa-chan'" (On the "total development of the individual"), *Hua-tung shih-ta hsueh-pao*, No. 1 (1958), pp. 97–112.

assumption that the great majority of school children are of average intelligence, with a small group above it of superior intelligence and another small group below it of feeble-minded children. Quite obviously, the first fitted in with the then-current policy. Optimum development of aptitudes, combined with raising the deficiencies of the *same* children, implied the assumption of a rough equality of endowments among all children and the feasibility of achieving a high level in all aspects of development in all children: the total development policy.

Ma also pointed out that there was no direct equivalent of the term *ko-hsing* in the Russian language. Apparently, various Chinese terms such as *ko-jen* (individual), *jen-ko* (character), or simply *jen* (man) have been used as well as *ko-hsing* interchangeably by translators. (The Chinese term *jen-ko*, character, is only an aspect of individuality and therefore narrower.) This linguistic ambiguity confounded the problem for Chinese educators and psychologists.

Among the psychologists, only a few attempted any definition of "individuality." Kuo Jen-ch'uan was one: "*Ko-hsing* is the psychological and physiological characteristics of a person, that is, the content and direction of development of the physiology and psychology of a person." Ma found this to be too narrow a definition. Yet a broader one in current use appeared to be too vague to him: "*Ko-hsing* is the sum total of the physiological, psychological, and cultural traits of a person."

One of the very few psychologists who discussed at any length the concept of individuality was Yang Ch'eng-chang. After quoting Mao Tze-tung's "On Understanding," Yang wrote in the official psychological journal in 1961:

> . . . Man's will, feeling, and the development of his entire individuality is also due to the function of the reflection of objective reality and active consciousness.
> . . . *As to man's individuality, it is the complete reflection* of the entire history of the change in his objective reality

189

and the realization of his active consciousness. As man continually remakes his subjective world and shapes his consciousness, he develops his individuality [italics added].[20]

Individuality for Yang was thus the end product at any given time of the process of "reflection" and functioning of the active consciousness, or in terms familiar to the West, the result of interactions between the conscious self and his environment. This is then more inclusive than the Western concept of personality, which does not have a materialistic base, the physiological organism. The key to the dynamics of this individuality lies in the concept of reflection, a term deeply imbedded in Marxist-Leninist ideology that psychologists have adopted without further definition or operational refinement for purposes of scientific analysis of behavior.

Another psychologist, Liu Fan, saw the foundation of individuality in the process of recognition. Recognition, Liu said, is characterized by self-consciousness (or recognition of one's own recognition) and goal orientation. When man develops a habitual attitude toward his reflection of objective reality, this becomes individual character. There are aspects of individuality besides recognition, Liu pointed out, and these are ability and temperament. The development of both ability and temperament depends upon experiences or reflection.[21] Individuality is not self-moving but is moved by reflection activity. Individuality, with its biological base, influences reflection activity and is influenced, in turn, by reflection. In a class society, Liu added, there is also class individuality (*chi-t'uan ti ko-hsing*), or a certain tendency of the consciousness formed by repeated reflection.[22]

[20] Yang Ch'eng-chang, "Shih-lun jen-ti hsin-li ti mao-tun ti t'e-shu-hsing" (Some considerations on the specificity of contraditions of mental activity). *Hsin-li hsueh-pao*, No. 3 (1961).

[21] Liu Fan, "Tui-yü hsin-li-hsueh tui-hsiang wen-t'i ti ch'u-pu k'an-fa" (Tentative views on the subject matter of psychology), *Kuang-ming jih-pao*, July 20, 1959.

[22] Ts'ao Jih-ch'ang, "Hsin-li-hsueh ti yen-chiu jen-wu yü hsueh-k'o hsing-chih" (Psychology, its responsibility and scientific nature),

In terms of research policy, individuality had always occupied a place in the statement of plans. It is recalled that the 12-year plan for psychology drawn up in 1956 included "the study of individuality." From its early days the Institute of Psychology mentioned individuality as one of its concerns, but no publication on the subject from this early period has come to light. Even amidst the heightened research activities of the Great Leap, the topic of individuality received no explicit attention. Individuality was to be studied under the Division of Medical Psychology, but neither here nor in labor and educational divisions did any new ideas on the subject emerge. In medical psychology, for instance, neurasthenia cases were discussed in terms of central tendencies, or mass types, without regard to the range of individual variability. This was true in the work on the origin of neurasthenia, methods of its treatment, or evaluation of the effectiveness of a therapeutic measure. Failures in treatment, for example, were not examined for clues to the problem of individual variations. Similarly, in labor psychology, even the process of creativity was placed in a group setting, blurring differences of creative capacity among individuals.

In the educational field, the policy in the fifties on the "total development of the individual" came under criticism for three reasons: (1) it interpreted total development as equal development by stressing the common characteristics of students at the expense of the different characteristics; (2) it overloaded the student academically, leaving little spare time for the development of individual interests and inclinations; and (3) it placed too much emphasis on group activities. By the mid-fifties, opinion was beginning to be expressed on the limitations of the total development policy. Obviously, the educational system had to confront the problem of individual differences in ability to grasp the material presented and to move at different rates toward fulfillment of

---

Hsin Chien-she, June 7, 1959; and "Hsin-li-hsueh yen-chiu she-mo" (What does psychology study), *Jen-min jih-pao,* July 9, 1959.

the educational goals. The Minister of Higher Education, Yang Hsiu-fung, pointed out in his speech to the third session of the All-China National Congress in 1956 that the pursuit of the three educational objectives of knowledge, health, and technical training "must be within the capability of the students" and that it must incorporate a "flexibility of approach," in which the capability of each student could be adapted to a study program or work assignment.[23]

By the sixties, when research in educational psychology really got under way, the climate of opinion had changed. Improvement in education and moral training became important, and that led to the question of raising the level of achievement of school children. Psychologists came face to face with the problem of individual differences, both intellectual and behavioral. Pan Shu wrote in 1962: [24]

> New instructional conditions are likely to produce differences in scholastic achievements in the same classroom. It is important to study, discover, and develop talents in various fields, and to analyze causes of bad behavior and poor learning.

Ts'ao Jih-ch'ang also began pointing out the same theme. He stated that the development of children's thinking ability on abstract things "is mainly determined by their education, teaching methods, and teaching progress. . . . The more you raise the teaching standard and progress of the class, the bigger the differences between the slow and fast students. The former problem involved the level of psychological development and the latter the problem of differences between the individuals." [25] In his address to the 1963 meeting of psychologists, Ts'ao Jih-ch'ang lamented

[23] Fang Hsun-i, "Ch'üan-mien fa-chan yin-ts'ai shih-chiao wen-t'i ti ch'u-pu t'an-t'ao" (Preliminary exploration of the problem of total development and flexibility of approach), *Hua-nan shih-fan hsueh-yuan hsueh-pao*, No. 2 (1957), pp. 8–11.

[24] *Kuang-ming jih-pao*, March 13, 1962.

[25] *Kuang-ming jih-pao*, June 2, 1961.

the lack of attention to individual differences and character development and stressed the complexity of the problem: [26]

> Individual differences is an urgent problem to study. In primary and secondary schools at present, some students with high learning ability lack discipline, making the atmosphere difficult for the slower students. Teachers, especially in primary schools, have to spend too much time either coping with discipline or helping slow ones catch up. In proceeding with educational reform, we must first be clear about laws of intellectual development. Today we are carrying on many experiments. Can we not also select a group of children with high learning ability (*hsueh-hsi neng-li kao*) for testing? Perhaps they can use (and more urgently need) the four suitable measures in educational reform, especially that of raising standards of accomplishment.

Another psychologist made a similar plea. Shan Yu, in talking about the educational psychology meeting of 1962 remarked that most projects had been carried out in entire classes, neglecting the individual case study of model types. Also neglected, he said, was the study of the individual superior child.[27] The focus in the sixties was clearly on the *differences* among individuals, in both their positive and negative aspects, and not on *sameness*, even in a potential sense.

In the new research on moral education reported in previous pages, it is obvious that both in the acquisition of moral norms and in the actual behavioral responses to them, individual and group variations received close attention. Furthermore, researchers raised the question of the psychological dynamics of individuality: *how* the individual, any individual, reconciles his needs, wishes, previous experience, and so forth, with the current situation requiring behavioral response that involves moral judgment. The question was no longer *whether* individuality is or is not class determined, but

[26] Ts'ao Jih-chang, "Kuan-ch'e li-lun. . . ."
[27] *Kuang-ming jih-pao,* March 14, 1962.

in what manner individuality (the end product of past experiences) is brought to bear in current behavior.

Perhaps the time was not far away for this relatively young psychological tradition to include some attention to the problem of individual deviations in a broader sense. The work on neurasthenia was one type of social deviation. The whole range of problems covered by the Soviet branch of defectology (for example, their work on mental defectives, the physically handicapped, etc.) was yet untouched. The biggest problem of deviation was, of course, in the moral dimension, the starting point of the moral education campaign. These directions were, in a sense, logical evolutions of a science of behavior, partly independent of the particular ideological foundation of the science. But at the same time, actualization would have depended a great deal on a favorable political climate.

The next logical step for psychologists to have taken would have been a serious look at the problem of psychological testing, in order to measure the differences by some means and to assess the effectiveness of appropriate programs. For recognizing the fact of individual differences and measuring these differences are two different affairs. Individual differences can be measured in different dimensions, some of which are aptitude, intelligence, or achievement in various areas. Intelligence testing as such has been condemned as capitalistic from the very beginning of the development of mainland psychology, as a method seen as based on the assumption of native, inborn aptitudes that would not allow for change as the result of classroom teaching or other environmental factors.

However, a new note was sounded at the 1963 annual meeting; the topic of intelligence and other testing came in for some discussion. Wu Chiang-lin, Ph.D. from Syracuse University and a professor at Kuangtung Normal University, presented a report on "some problems of intelligence" under one of the "four special topics introducing new directions." According to the summary of the meetings by Ch'en Ta-jou, Wu "introduced some definitions and opinions on intelligence." If intelligence was to be viewed as an individual characteristic, Wu said, then it must be approached from the point of view of historical materialism. She criticized idealism in the capitalist approach to intelligence, but pointed out that some "useful methods" could be adopted. Chen noted that the question "whether to use intelligence tests or not brought about debate." [28]

Ts'ao Jih-ch'ang also called for more attention to the development of measuring procedures for capabilities. In discussing how concrete research in education must be linked with theory, he raised the problem of ability (*neng-li*): "There are many studies on the physiological foundation and special characteristics of ability. If, at the same time, we can measure and analyze the ability to learn, and the selection and training of special worker types and soldier types, we can raise the scientific level and also help education, production, and defense." [29]

The fact that there are observable differences in people's behavior, that some children do better than others in school, and so forth, is incontrovertible. But how shall these differences be understood, what should be done about them, and how does one fit these differences into the needs of a socialist society? That problem became salient in the early sixties. Great need was then felt for trained manpower in many jobs of different levels, and since the educational system did not allow every one to continue on into higher levels of education, the problem of selection on the basis of some criteria of achievement and potential for achievement posed immense problems for psychology and education. The approach to the question of individual differences in children's abilities and

[28] Ch'en Ta-jou, "Chung-kuo Hsin-li-hsueh hui 1963 nien. . . ."
[29] Ts'ao Jih-ch'ang, "Kuan-ch'e li-lun. . . ."

capabilities became crucial but potentially controversial. The problem was at once political and intellectually challenging to psychological research and educational practices.

Before this line of inquiry into individual differences could be fully developed, the political wind changed its course in 1965, and equalitarianism of the most fundamental sort became the reigning value. Educational psychology, with its talk of testing and other tools for analyzing differences in psychological processes, became at best superfluous. The only differences that remained relevant were class differences, obliterating all other considerations about individual differences. Another phase in the development of the science of psychology came to an end. It is not yet known what theoretical issues in psychology may have been brought forth by the cultural revolution.

EDUCATION AND THE INDIVIDUAL

Despite a late beginning, educational psychology showed signs of incorporating in its research some of the problems in the mainstream of social concerns. The total range of interest in educational psychology extended from the study of separate mental processes, such as memory and learning, to developmental stages and investigation of the whole individual. The former type of interest, more experimental in nature and requiring more sophisticated methodology and laboratory equipment, had been dominated by the Institute of Psychology. But some of the concrete curriculum studies, as well as the observation of the "whole individual," could be undertaken by provincial psychologists working in normal institutions. Thus, the broadening of research concerns of educational psychology meant increased publications by provincial, and perhaps also younger psychologists.

The development of educational psychology took place in three areas: the psychology of learning certain school subjects, research into age levels and developmental stages, and characteristics of moral judgment and moral behavior. Curriculum research was largely restricted to mathematics and language, both approached basically from the standpoint of abstract thought processes influencing the learning of concrete material. This theoretical foundation stemmed from the continued dominance of the Pavlovian second signal system. The methodology and approach for the study of arithmetic and geometry remained heavily Soviet in nature; but Pavlovianism did not prevent language research, especially work on memory, from being affected by Western sources, particularly American ones. Another source of academic dissemination from the United States was the initial exploration into teaching machines.

The psychology of curriculum subjects, however, could potentially include a much wider range of subject matter than that actually tackled. The study of written Chinese could logically lead to investigation into language structure and thought and into the role of literature and art in the learning process. Starting from the science subjects, another obvious direction would be the teaching of technical and industrial problems. As far as we know, both areas of broadened work are yet to be developed.

The study of age levels and development of the young child was focused on psychological stages rather than chronological age or physiological maturation, although more work in the latter may well be done by neurologists. While initial interest in age-level study was sparked by the issue of readiness for school as a result of education reform, the interests of the psychologists included wider questions of the acquisition of different kinds of knowledge at various stages of psychological development. Coming from Soviet theoretical as well as local ideological sources, psychological knowledge was viewed in terms of the polarities of concrete versus abstract, theoretical versus practical, and sensory versus rational. Conspicuous by contrast with the current emphasis in the West was the lack of explicit interest on the emotional aspect of learning. Such interest was potentially there, as shown by an awareness of the role of the teacher as authority figure in facilitating learning or supplementing the role of rational understanding of the goal and its requirements, just as in medical psychology the role of the therapist in the recovery process of the mentally ill led medical psychologists into the realm of interpersonal relations. By policy, the first phase of developmental study was devoted to the early school years; thus, there was no work on adolescence as a psychological stage, although some of the work on moral education was done on middle-school students.

Uneven rates of child development naturally pointed to the question of differences among individuals and the factors determining these differences. This trend of research interest, together with the political concern of the early sixties over the lack of revolutionary fervor of youth, opened up questions concerning the "causes of bad behavior and poor learning" and how to discover and develop talents in different fields. But before this line of inquiry could proceed very far, it landed the psychologists back in the old dilemma of the proper object of psychological study: the brain and its mechanisms *or* the individual as a social animal — in other words, the controversy of natural science versus social science. It is ironic that an intellectual tradition based on philosophical monism should continue to be bedeviled by this split, while in the "dualistic" West this particular dichotomy has been blurred and psychology has proceeded on a multiphased front to study the individual as a whole. A second and more formidable obstacle to the study of individual differences appeared in the form of the cultural revolution. By the end of 1965, and certainly in 1966, the class viewpoint, or the class factor, became the foremost and almost the sole acceptable variable in psychological research. The use of other variables came under vehement attack, being politically suspect. The first such encounter was in connection with a promising line of inquiry on the acquisition of moral judgment in children, a subject matter closest to Party interests. Yet this ideological confrontation might have occurred in almost any line of developmental study, sooner or later, given the upward trend in ideological supremacy in recent years. Thus, the most challenging goal in educational psychology was doomed by the ultimate ideological dictum of the class struggle theory.

CHAPTER SEVEN

CONCLUSIONS AND OBSERVATIONS

The science of psychology has had more than a decade to function and to grow in the new soil of Communist Chinese society, but it is still too young to have developed a distinctive school of thought. Since its importation from the Soviet Union in the early fifties, this psychology has not departed from its philosophical base of dialectical materialism or the political orthodoxy of Marxism-Leninism and has stood in firm opposition to the "idealism" of Western psychology. So far the new science has largely followed the lead of Soviet psychology, although some differences in emphasis and in directions of application are discernible. Certainly one could not conclude that psychology on mainland China has established theoretical independence from the Soviet tradition or raised a challenging voice to Soviet leadership commensurate to the challenge on the ideological front.

As this Soviet-inspired discipline becomes imbedded in the context of Communist China's institutions of teaching and research and as it carries out its work in response to the scientific and academic requirements of the field and the demands and assignments from the authorities, psychology is gradually acquiring characteristic usages and interpretations of the basic concepts of the field, and more or less unique ways of applying them to the solution of concrete problems. Some of the new developments can be understood in terms of what is inherited from the Soviet Union, such as the old controversy over whether psychology is a natural or a social science; others may reveal preferences in thinking characteristic of pre-Communist China, which supplied the fertile soil for Dewey's pragmatism and functionalism; and still others arise out of the fundamental dilemma in the dialectical-materialist approach to psychology, that is, between the universalism of psychological processes and the historicism of the class theory. As the discipline develops in the context of Maoist Communism, responding and adjusting to the fluctuating demands of a society in which politics periodically takes firm command, a strain is felt against the logical scientific working out of the materialist position and toward the primacy of class determination of psychological phenomenon. The latter tendency is partly in evidence during periods of activism such as the Great Leap, but is particularly marked in the ideological ascendancy of the Great Proletarian Cultural Revolution. Since mainland psychologists have not been given much to theorizing, especially of a synthesizing variety, no claim or explicit statement of a "Chinese theory of man" has appeared.

In the past two decades, the rapidly expanding field of psychology in the rest of the world, especially in the United States, Europe, and Japan, has been characterized by increasing professionalization and bifurcation from a common center to become either biological or social in emphasis. Soviet psychology has tended to become biotropic, placing physiological and experimental psychology with physiology. In the United States, there has been a growing separation of biological and social psychology in both teaching and practice.

Beyond these common tendencies, the question of national differences in the development of psychology and its relationship to national cultures or political situations is a

201

complex one about which we have very little knowledge of a systematic sort. The notable exception is Bauer's study of Soviet psychology.[1] Thus, the present inquiry, while it benefits greatly from Bauer's precedent, has no other study for comparison across national boundaries, especially in the category of a secondary or derivative school of the major Soviet tradition.

In mainland China, psychology has maintained its existence as a distinctive field academically and professionally, with a continuity of professional leadership and organizational framework and with some measure of unity in its theoretical assumptions and methodological outlook. We shall outline four phases that psychology passed through from the early fifties to the beginning of the Cultural Revolution in 1966, and we shall look at this emerging tradition of psychology in light of the pre-1949 Western root of Dewey's pragmatism and functionalism and of some Chinese views about man and his world.

The phases that psychology passed through from 1949 to mid-1966, the beginning of the Cultural Revolution, may be labeled (1) the introductory-Soviet phase, from 1949 through the mid-fifties; (2) the Great Leap phase in the latter part of the fifties; (3) the phase of consolidation and exploration in the first half of the sixties; and (4) the phase of ideological ascendancy, beginning in 1965.

As we characterize the state of psychology through these phases, we shall discuss the ebb and flow of four opposing, overlapping sets of principles: centralism versus localism, scientism versus activism, a biophysiological emphasis versus a sociopsychological one, and psychology as an independent science versus psychology as an applied field of the historical process of class struggle. Each position contains loosely connected theoretical stances in psychology, several of which, couched in the lingo of Marxist polemics, were aired

[1] Raymond Bauer, *The New Man in Soviet Psychology* (Cambridge, Mass.: Harvard University Press, 1952).

at the criticism-debate meetings in 1958–1959. The issue of centralism-localism is one of the pattern of professionalism and institution-building. As the field organizes itself to accomplish the tasks of teaching, research, and practical work, how does it distribute its personnel and resources, take care of the training of future leaders, and arrive at decisions affecting the fate of the profession? The second issue is one of conceptual orientation. Since psychology is linked on the one hand with the organism and on the other hand with society, toward which system should its theory be oriented? Third, psychology may tend to emphasize its scientific aspect or its practical implications. And finally, should the purpose of psychology be to study universal principles, or should psychology be a subsidiary of politics?

SOVIET PHASE

During the first half-decade of this new science, the importation of the Soviet brand of psychology, with Pavlov as the historical authority, resulted in a phase of scientism and universalism. The necessity of combating the Western "idealistic" tradition in Chinese psychology favored the adoption of a new approach that stressed the "materialist," that is, psychologically, based experimental science. Since the conditioned-reflex theory is explicit and unified, the Pavlovian doctrine was well suited to this purpose of reindoctrination. Consequently, the new psychology began with a firm scientific underpinning, an alliance with medicine and physiology, Soviet-inspired texts, and a number of teaching and research laboratories for the study of the conditioned reflex. Also in line with the Soviet model and following pre-Communist tradition, advanced research was entrusted to a centralized organ, the Institute of Psychology of the National Academy of Sciences. This national concentration of science-oriented research was to create rival, provincial centers of politically oriented psychologists who eventually challenged scientism

203

and centralized leadership. In teaching, too, the available personnel and equipment were concentrated in the few top universities, while the professional organization was also firmly in the hands of older psychologists. In fact, an early list of psychologists included mostly those with Ph.D.'s from the Western countries. (Here, of course, one must keep in mind the distinction between psychologists and "psychological workers.")

In this early phase, there was no concern about the question of physiological bases *versus* the psychological and social bases of the mind. After all, the great academician Pavlov had already solved it by grounding learning and thought processes in the physiological functioning of the organism. It is to be remembered that this introductory phase in psychology coincided with the phase of political and economic collaboration and assistance between the Soviet Union and Mao's fledgling regime.

GREAT LEAP FORWARD

No sooner had a new foundation been established in psychology than voices began to be heard arguing for a more activist, pragmatically oriented individuality based on class analysis rather than a process-centered field. Arguments on both sides of the theoretical dilemma were spelled out most clearly in the debate-criticism meetings during the Great Leap years of 1958–1959.

That the scientism-universalism position had a fair amount of strength could be seen in the tenacity of its defenders in debate meetings, which ended without satisfactory resolution in either direction. The appeal of science has always carried great weight in modern China. This may account for the fact that although Soviet influence began to wane after 1957, this science-oriented strand of work persisted through the Great Leap period to make a resurgence in the early sixties.

The force competing with scientism for the allegiance of psychology during the Great Leap period was activism. Psychologists were called out of their laboratories, institutes, and debate forums to apply their theories in actual situations of "work, study, and living."

Established psychologists from the national centers of learning and research mingled with politically zealous psychological workers: nurses, students, industrial representatives. Especially in the data collection campaigns, such as in mental health surveys, a large number of such persons were mobilized and exposed to short-term training in research methods. Thus, some of the old lines of authority were disrupted as professional personnel were dispersed into the field and mingled with mass-type organizations. Traditional boundaries of psychology were dissolved in the name of studying the concrete, whole individual: a spirit of eclecticism pervaded the discipline, and research began to cross national and ideological lines.

Once in the field and confronted with pressing, concrete problems, there was little evidence of hard questioning of ideological correctness of theory. In the spirit of maximizing the use of available human and technical resources, theoretical issues were temporarily blurred. The all-out enthusiasm required of every productive enterprise during that period brought about a kind of practical inventiveness among psychologists, resulting in a moderate amount of conceptual clarification and scientific advance. The laboratory-trained, methodology-conscious scientists applied their craft to more practical problems, such as the study of sensory perception in the factory or classroom or the measurement of brain waves on the normal and the mentally ill. At the same time, less precise but more action-oriented studies were launched by teams of workers in the medical, labor, and educational branches of psychology to apply the concept of active consciousness to a variety of actual human situations.

In the course of focusing attention on the whole individual, questions that had not been in the foreground previously now became pressing: What makes one individual produce more than another? What accounts for the optimistic attitude of one person and the pessimistic attitude of another? What, indeed, makes one individual *want to change* in the desirable socialist direction and another backslide into, for example, the state of neurasthenia? These questions were not yet couched in the concept of motivation, which did not become prominent in research vocabulary till the sixties.

In answering these questions, psychologists began with the socialist axiom that the ultimate and primary source of motivation lies in the socialist society itself. This is where the key concept of active consciousness comes in, for through it the movement of society toward its socialist goal is transplanted into motivation of the individual who participates in history. The critical issue is thus the extent to which the individual "reflects" in his active consciousness this march of history. The problem was how to mobilize this positive spirit. Within this global concept of active consciousness, by far the most important function and the one receiving explicit and almost exclusive research attention was the role of recognition, which implicitly includes goal orientation. (The other aspects, will and emotion, were mentioned only in passing.)

The psychologists pursued this assignment energetically and, from a scientific point of view, rather conscientiously, if not always thoroughly. The teams of psychologists posed this central question in the various contexts of mental illness, industrial productivity, and creativity, and in the classroom learning situation as well as in the formation of moral character of children. In every research setting, the studies concluded with the demonstration that active consciousness, or the recognition aspect within it, plays a decisive role in affecting the functioning of the individual: the neurasthenia patient improved, the worker produced more or became more inventive, the student learned his arithmetic or language or moral lesson better. In short, the more the individual understands, the more he does what society wants of him.

As the concept of active consciousness and the recognition aspect become clarified in actual research, their central place in a theory of behavior becomes apparent. This direct and almost simple relationship between collective goals and the motivating force of the individual submerges conceptually the importance of the group. Thus, we make the ironic discovery that Communist China, which makes such extensive, thorough, and fundamental use of groups, has not developed any theory on the relationship between the individual and the group. In fact, in case after case in this most activist phase of psychological research, there was no adequate theoretical tool to handle the group's effect upon the individual. For that matter, the relationship between one individual and another was also only minimally explored. In several studies, the data point unmistakably to these two areas. Yet the areas were either ignored or inadequately treated because of the bias in favor of the direct relationship of the individual consciousness to the goals of the large collectivity. In medical psychology, the doctor-patient relationship was examined only for its critical role in recovery from neurasthenia. In the factory setting, unexplained factors in production records as well as in the phenomenon of group creativity did not lead to even tentative theorizing. Nevertheless, because of a certain degree of scientific eclecticism and relatively slack ideological demands in the Great Leap spirit of research, psychologists were beginning to be led by their data to push at the limits of their existing theoretical assumptions.

CONSOLIDATION AND EXPLORATION

As life regained a more normal pace after the excesses of the Great Leap, psychologists also slowed down their frenzied research activities. The action-oriented teams were apparently dissolved while psychologists of various persuasions returned to their former lines of investigation. Lead articles in the journal were again under the signature of senior psychologists. The scientifically oriented, methodologically sophisticated studies again appeared: measurements of EEG, PGR, and sensory perception in connection with classroom learning and the aviation industry. Other interests of a pure science sort emerged, such as work on modern information theory involving coding and semantic noise, an area that the Soviets call "man and technology" — what is known in the United States as "human engineering."

In studies of the moral character of children, research in this period continued the momentum begun during the Great Leap years by explicitly pursuing the central question of motivation. Such inquiry began, as before, by stating the problem in terms of the effect of rational understanding on learning moral principles or on practicing moral conduct. Soon, however, the research results themselves pointed to the inadequacy of recognition as the single factor explaining behavior. Psychologists began to talk about the teacher-pupil or parent-child relationship in learning or about "temporary motivation" supplied by the presence of the teacher and acting on the pupil via "self-reinforcement of language."

Again, in finding a discrepancy between moral knowledge and actual moral conduct, psychologists were on the brink of "discovering" other than recognition factors. Children did not live up to their own moral beliefs, not because of lack of understanding or of the wrong class background but as the result of such mental processes as compromises and rationalizations. In other words, here were causes for antimoral behavior that were inherent in the psychological functioning of the individual already living in socialist society. No amount of knowledge-building would eradicate this kind of cause. Psychologists dealt with this phenomenon by differentiating between "recognition motivation" and "reality motivation." By coining this pair of concepts, the researcher of course identifies the discrepancy without pointing to the origin.

An additional issue raised during this phase of consolidation and exploration was that of individuality and individual differences. Again the problem was not a new one: it was unimportant or irrelevant when psychology focused its attention on abstract, universal processes; and it lay submerged when mass mobilization during the Great Leap aimed at mass results. Now that psychology was looking at the whole individual and beginning to ask questions about how he got to be what he is, the inescapable question of stages of development and of individual differences came to the fore. Instead of the earlier belief that all individuals could be raised to essentially the same level of excellence or of health, it was now permissible to look at the unequal potentials and uneven development of a given person.

In examining these aspects of the functioning of the whole individual, psychologists were straining the limits of the ideological dictum that class position determines psychological phenomenon, for nonclass factors appeared in different research contexts. This kind of relatively unhampered inquiry was possible because this was a period of comparative ideological relaxation. But before these fruitful lines of inquiry could be pursued to their logical-scientific ends, the political winds of the country changed abruptly, and psychology felt this impact suddenly and unmistakably.

IDEOLOGICAL ASCENDANCY

This study was originally intended to cover the period up to the Cultural Revolution, but what we could find out about the new direction in late 1965 and early 1966 was significant enough to warrant this brief treatment.

Signs of the tightening of ideological reins were felt early in psychology. Beginning in 1965, the whole tone of the journal changed sharply from a professional to a political one. Whereas before there was seldom mention of political figures or Maoist sayings, now articles of a thought-reform type and even reprints of lead pieces in the *People's Daily* appeared. Scientific issues that had hitherto been discussed on intellectual grounds now became targets of attack on grounds of correct or incorrect class position. The work of individual psychologists was singled out and examined retrospectively and in detail, including definition of the problem, selection of test material, use of variables, and nature of conclusions. Tendencies deviating from the newly declared orthodoxy of class analysis were criticized. The new direction set for psychology was clear, and the pressure was strong and definite, although the material available is too skimpy to permit the study of detailed patterns at this time.

Another abrupt change was in the pattern of leadership. The voice of authority in the journal now came not from the established psychologists in the top institutions but from unknown authors in provincial normal schools or even secondary schools. This trend away from centralism to localism was accompanied by further signs of "democratization": an entire academic class of students would write an article attacking its professional seniors. We do not know what other changes were taking place in the organizations dealing with psychology, for sources of information were being cut off; but the new direction was clear even before the Red Guards revolutionized all established hierarchies and institutions.

At this time, some of the old issues that plagued the field in the criticism-debate meetings resurfaced. The scientific branch of psychology again was attacked for its "abstractism" and "biologism," in other words, for emphasizing the physiological basis of psychological phenomenon, a tendency now specifically linked to the "capitalist concept of the nature of man." This did not mean that the work of Pavlov himself came under attack, at least not in this early stage of the Cultural Revolution. The new orthodox position merely wished to dissociate psychology from Pavlov's theory of the higher nervous system, which was still described as an "undoubtedly great physiological discovery." What mainland psychologists were accused of was the "forceable transfer" of higher nervous functions from physiology to psychology, so that "temporary nervous connections *become the same as* psychological phenomena" (italics added). This criticism was retrospective for the past ten years and covered theoretical work as well as popularized psychology in teacher-training schools. The new order was out: abandon "naturalism" so that psychology can "march forward toward dialectical materialism." [2]

What, then, was the new correct position for psychology? Continuity with natural science was apparently being sacrificed for increased emphasis on the qualitatively different characteristics of psychological activity. A main focus on active consciousness remained, only now the action output of the human organism was being stressed rather than brain functions. Psychological phenomena arc grounded in materialism in the sense that the human consciousness propels an individual to carry out the social act. His efforts to understand society and change society are his other link with material reality, now the chief object of psychological study.

There is an obvious connection here to the position that class analysis is the main method of and only correct standpoint for psychology. Whether a person's or a group's active consciousness can be developed, or how fully it can be developed is declared to be entirely dependent upon class position. Since Marxism-Leninism and the thought of Mao constitute a revolutionary theory, only persons, groups, or nations with the correct class standpoint can grasp it and thus activate their active consciousness. Capitalists, reactionaries, and revisionists cannot discover the law of social development and are unable and unwilling to promote the march of history. It therefore follows that the function of will or volition, an unexplored aspect of the active consciousness, is also said to be a function of class position.

[2] Chou Tso-yun, "Kuan-yü hsin-li-hsueh chung ti tzu-jan chu-i kuan-tien" (On the naturalistic point of view in psychology), *Hsin-li hsueh-pao,* No. 1 (1966), pp. 11–15.

211

The germ of this new orthodoxy could be found in the 1958 debate. Then, the arguments in favor of psychology being a social science and using class analysis were simply declarations of doctrine. At the time of the Cultural Revolution, the full implications of the dichotomous positions were clearer. Perhaps even the hints as to where unhampered research might lead psychology became apparent. In any case, the new task for psychology was the practical question of understanding the laws of the functioning of the active consciousness in order to stimulate the voluntary development of moral, intellectual, and physical capacities of the citizens. The constant assignment in education in China was that the children know not only what they learn but also for whom they learn and why they learn. In accomplishing this task, emulation of heroes was turned to as the primary aid to rational learning.

We see here the psychological justification for extensive memorization of Mao's sayings, for this exercise reflects the primacy of ideas, the stimulation of the active consciousness, and the emulation of the hero of heroes. How *this* theoretical stance has worked out in actual research, teaching, and other activities in psychology we do not know. Sources of information for this field, as for many others, have not been reopened.

GLOSSARY

CHINESE TERMS FROM THE TEXT*

an-shih 暗示
cheng-feng 整風
chi-chi hsing 積極性
ch'i-fa 啓發
chi-i neng-liang 記憶能量
chi-t'uan ti ko-hsing 集團的個性
chih-li ti shih-yen 智力的實驗
chou-chi 週記
chu-tung hsing 主動性
chu-kuan neng-tung-li 主觀能動力
ch'uang-chao hsing 創造性
Ch'un Ch'iu 春秋
Chung-hua chao-yü 中華教育
fan-she 反射
fu-po-shih 副博士
hsi t'ing Mao hua ti chu 席聽毛話的主
hsia-fang 下放

---

* These terms have been indexed, and the English translations are given
at their first appearance in the text.

hsiang-hsiang 想像
hsiao-tsu 小組
hsin-li chi-shu hsueh 心理技術學
hsin-li chuang-k'uang 心理狀況
hsin-li-hsueh chiao-hsueh 心理學教學
hsin-li kai-tsao 心理改造
hsin-yin-hsing 心因性
hsueh-hsi 學習
hsueh-hsi huo-tung 學習活動
hsueh-hsi neng-li kao 學習能力高
Hsun-tzu 荀子
i-chih 意志
i-shih 意識
jen 人
jen-ko 人格
Jen-min Chung-kuo 人民中國
jen-shih 認識
jen-shih-hsing tung-chi 認識性動機
ko-hsing 個性
ko-hsing chu-i 個性主義
ko-jen chu-i 個人主義
k'uai-su tsung-ho liao-fa 快速綜合療法
k'uang 狂
kung-yeh hsin-li hsueh 工業心理學
kuo-yü 國語
lao-shih 老師
lao-tung 勞動
lao-tung tsu-chih 勞動組織
li-lun jen-shih 理論認識
lien-hsiang 聯想
lien-so 聯鎖
ling-huo hsing 靈活性
ling-ken 靈根
liu-ch'ing 六情
liu-chih 六志
ma-hu 馬虎

mu-ti hsing 目的性
neng-li 能力
pai-hua 白話
ping-tien 病點
she-hui kai-tsao 社會改造
shen-ching shuai-jo cheng 神精衰弱症
shih-chi tung-chi 實際動機
Shih-fan chuan-k'o hsueh-hsiao 師範專科學校
Shih-fan hsueh-yuan 師範學院
Shih-fan ta-hsueh 師範大學
shih-yeh hsin-li hsueh 實際心理學
shuo-li 說理
su-chih 素質
t'ai-chi-ch'üan 太極拳
tao-te chiao-yü 道德教育
ti-erh-hao hsin-hsi 第二号信系
t'ing Mao-chu-hsi ti hua 聽毛主席的話
to-hsing 惰性
to-mien-shou 多面手
Tso Chuan 左傳
tsung-ho ta-hsueh 綜合大學
t'ui-tung hsing-wei ti li-liang 推動行爲的力量
tung-chi 動機
tun-wu 頓悟
t'ung-kuo 通過
tzu-chueh-hsing 自覺性
tzu-chueh neng-tung-li 自覺能動力
wen-yen 文言
yü-chien hsing 預見性

ADDITIONAL TERMS FROM MAINLAND JOURNALS*

active consciousness 自覺能動力
amount of information 信息量
Bender visual-motor gestalt test 賓德氏視學—動作格式塔
case study 個例研究
chronic schizophrenia 慢性精神分裂症
clinical psychology 診查心理學
concept 觀念，概念
control group 控制組
defectology 欱陷學
experience 体驗
figure drawing test 人形繪画測驗
figure painting test 指画測驗
free association 聯想
function 機能
Gestalt 格式
group dynamics 群体動學
group individuality 集團的個性
level of aspiration 慾求水平

* Some of these terms have different characters from those given in the text.

mosaic test 鑲嵌測驗
motion 運動行程
neurasthenia 神經衰弱
orienting reflex 朝向反射，定向反射
  (exploration reflex) 探究反射
projective psychology 投射心理學
psychodiagnosis 心理診察學
psychosynthesis 心理綜合
psychotherapy 心理治療
rate of efficiency 效率
Rorschach test 羅夏墨跡測驗
sentence completion test 語句完成測驗
social climate 社會氣氛
social contract 社會制約性
subjective initiative 主觀能動力
thematic apperception test 主旨統覺測驗
threshold 閾限
visual movement 運動知覺
Watson 華生

BIBLIOGRAPHY

BOOKS AND ARTICLES IN ENGLISH

"Articles on Psychology in Communist China." Translation of selected articles from *Hsin-li hsueh-pao*, No. 3 (1959), pp. 146–149. Joint Publications Research Service No. 3424.

Bauer, Raymond A. *New Man in Soviet Psychology*. Cambridge, Mass.: Harvard University Press, 1952.

Brière, O., S. J. "Philosophy in the New Regime. " *Soviet Survey*, No. 24 (April–June 1958), Special China Issue.

Brozek, Josef. "Contemporary Soviet Psychology." *Transactions of the New York Academy of Sciences*, Ser. II, Vol. 27, No. 4 (Feb. 1965), pp. 422–438.

Brackbill, Yvonne. "Research and Clinical Work with Children," in Raymond Bauer (ed.), *Some Views on Soviet Psychology*. Washington, D. C.: American Psychological Association, 1962, pp. 94–164.

Cerny, Jan. "Chinese Psychiatry." *International Journal of Psychiatry*, Vol. I, No. 2 (1965), pp. 229–247.

Chan Wing-tsit. "Trends in Philosophy," Chapter XX in Harley MacNair (ed.), *China*. Berkeley, Calif.: University of California Press, 1946.

Chou Hsien-keng and Ch'en Han-piao, "The rise of industrial psychology in China," *Tsing-hua hsueh-pao*, Vol. 1 (1936). Joint Publications Research Service No. 3424.

Chu Chih-hsien. "The Nature of Psychology." *Kuang-ming jih-pao*, July 18, 1961. Joint Publications Research Service No. 12524.

Dewey, John. "Psychology and Social Practice," in Joseph Ratner (ed.), *Philosophy and Social Practice*. New York: Putnam Brothers, 1963, pp. 295–315.

———. "The Reflex Arc Concept in Psychology," *Psychology Review*, July 1896, pp. 357–370.

"The educational psychology research section of the Kuangtung Educational Association discussed the problem of the object of study of educational psychology." *Kuang-ming jih-pao*, Jan. 29, 1962, 2. Joint Publications Research Service No. 13039.

Feuerwerker, Albert (ed.). *History in Communist China*. Cambridge, Mass.: The M. I. T. Press, 1968.

———, and Sally Cheng. *Chinese Communist Studies of Modern Chinese History*. Cambridge, Mass.: Harvard University Press, 1961.

Field, Mark G. "Mental Illness in Soviet Society." *Social Problems*, No. 4 (1960), pp. 277–297.

———. "Soviet and American Approaches to Mental Illness: A Comparative Perspective." *Review of Soviet Medical Sciences*, Vol. 1, No. 1 (1964), pp. 1–36.

Freedman, Maurice. "A Chinese Phase in Social Anthropology," *British Journal of Sociology*, No. 14 (March 1963), 1–19.

———. "Sociology in China: A Brief Survey," *China Quarterly*, No. 10 (April–June 1962), pp. 166–173.

Goldman, Merle. *Literary Dissent in Communist China*. Cambridge, Mass.: Harvard University Press, 1967.

Hsu, Yang Te-chuang, and Wang Tsi-chih. "Stimulus Response Compatibility and Efficiency of Information Transmission." *Scientia Sinica*, Vol. XIII, No. 6 (June 1964), pp. 1015–1017.

International Directory of Psychologists. Washington, D. C.: National Academy of Sciences, National Research Council, Publication 520, 1958.

Lasure, Denis. "Politics and Mental Health in New China." *The American Journal of Orthopsychiatry*, Vol. XXXIV, No. 5 (October 1964), pp. 925–933.

Levenson, Joseph R. *Modern China and Its Confucian Past*. Garden City, N. Y.: Doubleday Anchor, 1964.

Lewis, John L. "China's Secret Military Papers: 'Continuities' and 'Revelations,'" in Roderick MacFarquhar (ed.), *China Under Mao: Politics Takes Command*. Cambridge, Mass.: The M. I. T. Press, 1966.

Li Cho-ming. *Economic Development of Communist China*. Berkeley, Calif.: University of California Press, 1959.

Li Ch'ung-p'ei, Hsu Yu-hsin, Keng Chen-mei, Wang Ming-te, Graduate Study Group, Mental Health Department, Peking College of Medicine. "Some Problems Concerning the Cause of Psychasthenia and Attempts to Find Quick Treatments," in *Collections of Theses on Achievements in the Medical Sciences in Commemoration of the 10th National Foundation Day of China*. Vol. II, "Mental Health," pp. 652–670. Joint Publications Research Service No. 14829.

Lin Ch'ung-hsien. "Psychological Disposition Necessary for the Study of Flying." *Hang-k'ung chih-shih* (Aviation Knowledge), No. 3 (Mar. 8, 1960), pp. 24–25. Joint Publications Research Service No. 2973.

Lindbeck, John M. H. "The Organization and Development of Science," in "Science in Communist China." *The China Quarterly*, No. 6 (April–June 1961), pp. 98–132.

———. "An Isolationist Science Policy." *Bulletin of the Atomic Scientist*, February 1969, p. 70.

Liu Ch'ing-ho, "A Preliminary Discussion on Some of the Problems Regarding the Learning Process of Children," *Jen-min jih-pao*, March 26, 1961. Joint Publications Research Service No. 9398.

London, Ivan D. "Therapy in Soviet Psychiatric Hospitals." *American Psychologist*, No. 2 (February 8, 1953), pp. 79–82.

Mainland China Organizations of Higher Learning in Science and Technology and Their Publications. Washington, D. C.: U. S. Government Printing Office, 1961.

Mintz, Alexander. "Introduction to Contemporary Soviet Psychology," in Raymond Bauer (ed.), *Some Views on Soviet Psychology*.

Washington, D. C.: American Psychological Association, 1962.

Nivison, David S. "The Problem of 'Knowledge' and 'Action' in Chinese Thought since Wang Yang-ming," in Arthur Wright (ed.), *Studies in Chinese Thought*. Chicago: Chicago University Press, 1953.

Orleans, L. A. *Professional Manpower and Education in Communist China*. Washington, D. C.: National Science Foundation, 1961.

P'an Shu. "Ideas about Expanded Research in Educational Psychology." *Kuang-ming jih-pao*, Mar. 13, 1962. Joint Publications Research Service No. 13531.

Razran, Gregory. "Growth, Scope, and Direction of Current Soviet Psychology." *American Psychologist*, No. 19 (1964), pp. 324–349.

Rudik, P. A. *Psicologia* (Psychology), Moscow Fizkul'turai Sport, 1958, as reported by Josef Brozek, "Soviet Psychology," in Melvin Marx and William Hillix (ed.), *Systems and Theories in Psychology*. New York: McGraw-Hill, 1963.

Shinkuro Iwahara. "Oriental Psychology," Appendix C in Melvin Marx and William Hillix (ed.), *Systems and Theories in Psychology*. New York: McGraw-Hill, 1963.

Su Hsiang-yu. "Development of Psychology in China in the Last Decade" (in Chinese), *Acta Psychologica Taiwanica: Science Reports of National Taiwan University*, pp. 112–115.

T'ao Kuo-t'ai. "Healing and Preventative Work in the Field of Childhood Mental Diseases," in *Collection of Theses on Achievements in the Medical Sciences in Commemoration of the 10th National Foundation Day of China*. Vol. II, "Mental Health," pp. 683–699. Joint Publications Research Service No. 14829.

Teplov, B. M., and V. D. Nebylitzyn. "The Study of the Basic Properties of the Nervous System and Their Significance for the Psychology of Individual Differences." Translation in *Soviet Psychology and Psychiatry*, Vol. IV, No. 3-4 (Spring–Summer 1966), pp. 80–85.

Ts'ao Jih-ch'ang. "Why Should We Discuss the Nature of Psychology?" *Kuang-ming jih-pao*, June 2, 1961. Joint Publications Research Service No. 4937.

Wang Chi. *Mainland China Organizations of Higher Learning in Science and Technology and Their Publications—A Selected Guide.* Washington, D. C.: Library of Congress Reference Department, Science and Technology Division, 1961.

Wu Cheng-i. "New China's Achievements in Psychiatry," in *Collection of Theses on Achievements in the Medical Sciences in Commemoration of the 10th National Foundation Day of China.* Vol. II, "Mental Health," pp. 594–617. Joint Publications Research Service No. 14829.

BOOKS AND ARTICLES IN CHINESE

Chang Chih-kuang 章志光 "Tsai-t'an hsin-li-hsueh ti tui-hsiang yü hsing-chih"
再談心理學的對象與性質 (Further comments on the subject matter and nature of psychology). *Hsin-li hsueh-pao*, No. 1 (1959), pp. 22–31.

Chang Chih-kuang, Chu Wen-pin 章志光, 朱文彬 "Hsiao-hsueh-sheng k'o-yeh tse-jen-hsin hsing-ch'eng ti shih-yen yen-chiu"
小學生課業責任心形成的實驗研究 (Research on the formation of primary school students' sense of responsibility toward homework). *Hsin-li hsueh-pao*, No. 2 (1964), pp. 194–202.

Chang Shu-tsu, Chan Lung-tse, Shen Te-li 張述祖, 詹龍澤, 沈德立 "Tz'u tsai erh-t'ung kai-kua jen-shih chung ti tso-yung"
詞在兒童概括認識中的作用 (The effect of words in children's generalized cognition). *Hsin-li hsueh-pao*, No. 1 (1957).

Chang Tseng-chieh, Huang Hsi-t'ing 張增杰, 黃希庭 "Liu-ch'i-sui erh-t'ung shih-chien chih-chueh ti ch'u-pu yen-chiu"
六七歲兒童時間知覺的初步研究 (An experimental study on the time perception in 6–7 year old children). *Hsin-li hsueh-pao*, No. 3 (1963), pp. 214–221.

Chang Tseng-chieh, Wang P'an-hsia 張增杰, 汪盼霞 "Ying hsiang erh-t'ung kan-chih suan-shih ti liang-ko yu-kuan-yin-ssu ti shih-yen"
影響兒童感知算式的兩個有關因素的實驗 (An experimental

222

study of the factors influencing the comprehension of arithmetical problems). *Hsin-li hsueh-pao*, No. 4 (1963). pp. 304–311.

Chang Tseng-hui, Li Chiu-lin, Feng Heng-ts'an 張噌慧，李久林，馮恆燦 "Kuan-yü shen-ching shuai-jo tsung-ho k'uai-shu chih-liao chung ping-jen chu-kuan neng-tung-hsing ti ch'u-pu t'an-t'ao"
關于神經衰弱綜合快速療中病人主觀能動性的初步探討 (The role of active consciousness of neurasthenic patients in the speedy synthetic treatment). *Hsin-li hsueh-pao*, No. 3 (1961), pp. 163–178.

Chao Li-ju, Ts'ao Jih-ch'ang 趙莉如，曹日昌 "Ch'u-chung hsueh-sheng ti shih-chi fang-fa I. tui ssu-tzu tuan-chü ti chi-i fang-fa"
初中學生的識記方法 I. 對四字短句的識記方法 (Studies on the methods of memorization used by junior middle-school pupils I. Methods for memorizing four-word sentences). *Hsin-li hsueh-pao*, No. 4 (1963), pp. 312–320.

Ch'en Chung-keng 陳仲庚 "Shen-ching shuai-jo ti tzu-chüeh cheng-chuang yü p'i-fu-tien hsien-hsiang"
神經衰弱的自覺症狀與皮膚電現象 (Psychogalvanic reflex and the subjective states of neurasthenics). *Hsin-li hsueh-pao*, No. 1 (1964) pp. 103–108.

Ch'en Chung-keng 陳仲庚 "Tso Chuan chung ti pin-li hsin-li-hsueh ssu-hsiang"
左傳中的病理心理學思想 (Some psychological thoughts in the book of *Tso Chuan*). *Hsin-li hsueh-pao*, No. 2 (1943), pp. 156–164.

Ch'en Li, Ts'ao Jih-ch'ang 陳立，曹日昌 "Te-i-chih Ming-chu Kung-ho-kuo ti lao-tung hsin-li hsueh"
德意志民主共和國的勞動心理学 (Industrial psychology in the German Democratic Republic). *Hsin-li hsueh-pao*, No. 2 (1957), pp. 107–116.

Ch'en Li and Chu Tso-jen 陳立，朱作仁 "Hsi-sha-kung p'ei-hsun chung ti chi-ko hsin-li-hsueh wen-t'i"
細紗工培訓中的幾個心理學問題 (Some psychological prob-

lems in the training of fine textile weavers). *Hsin-li hsueh-pao*, No. 1 (1959), pp. 42–50.

Ch'en Ta-jou 陳大柔 "Chung-kuo Hsin-li-hsueh Hui ti-erh-tz'u tai-piao hui-i"
中國心理學會第二次代表會議 (Second Congress of the Chinese Psychological Society), *Hsin-li hsueh-pao*, No. 2 (1960), pp. 128–131.

Ch'en Ta-jou 陳大柔 "Chung-kuo Hsin-li-hsueh Hui 1963 nien hsueh-shu nien-hui"
中國心理學會 1963 年學術年會 (The 1963 annual academic meeting of the Chinese Psychological Society). *Hsin-li hsueh-pao*, No. 1 (1964), pp. 109–112.

Ch'en Ta-jou 陳大柔 "Hsin-li hsueh tsen-yang wei she-hui chu-i chien-she fu-wu ti"
心理學怎樣為社會主義建設服務的 (How psychology serves socialist construction). *Hsin-li hsueh-pao*, No. 3 (1959), pp. 142–145.

Cheng Chün-chieh 鄭俊杰 "Tui pien-ting p'u-t'ung hsin-li-hsueh chiao-hsueh ta-kang ti ch'u-pu i-chien"
對編訂普通心理學教學大綱的初步意見 (Preliminary sugges-tions on preparing an outline for the teaching of general psychology). *Shansi shih-fan hsueh-yuan hsueh-pao* 山西師範學院學報 (Shansi Normal College Journal), No. 1 (1957), pp. 85–97.

"Chiao-yü yen-chiu" 教育研究 (Educational Research). *Kuang-ming jih-pao*, May 16, 1955.

Ching Ch'i-ch'eng and Fang Yun-ch'iu 荆其誠，方芸秋 "Fu-ho tsai ta-hsiao chih-chueh heng-ch'ang-hsing chung ti tso-yung"
輻合在大小知覺恆常性中的作用 (The role of convergence in size constancy). *Hsin-li hsueh-pao*, No. 4 (1963), pp. 260–270.

Ching Ch'i-ch'eng, P'eng Jui-hsiang, Fang Yun-ch'iu 荆其誠，彭瑞祥，方芸秋 "Chü-li, kuan-ch'a tzu-shih tui ta-hsiao chih-chueh ti ying-hsiang"
距離，觀察姿勢對大小知覺的影響 (The effect of distance

and posture of observer on the perception of size). *Hsin-li hsueh-pao*, No. 1 (1963), pp. 20–30.

Ching Ch'i-ch'eng, P'eng Jui-hsiang, Fang Yun-ch'iu, Lin Chung-hsien 荆其誠，彭瑞祥，方芸秋，林仲賢 "Tui-hsiang tsai pu-t'ung yang-fu ti chüeh-t'u ti ta-hsiao p'an-tuan" 對象在不同仰俯的角度的大小判断 (Size judgments of an object in elevation and in descent). *Hsin-li hsueh-pao*, No. 3 (1963).

Ching Ch'i-ch'eng, Yeh Hsuan 荆其誠，葉絢 "Yun-tung chih-chüeh k'uo-hsien ti shih-yen yen-chiu" 運動知覺闊限的實驗研究 (Thresholds of visual movements). *Hsin-li hsueh-pao*, No. 1 (1957), pp. 158–164.

Chiang Ch'i-pin 蔣起斌 "Cheng-mien yao-ch'iu yü kai-ts'o tui hsueh-sheng tso-yeh hsiao-kuo ti ying-hsiang" 正面要求與改錯對學生作業效果的影響 (The effects of reproduction and correction in the exercise on achievements). *Hsin-li hsueh-pao*, No. 1 (1965), pp. 57–62.

"Ching-tao Sun Kuo-hua hsien-sheng" 敬悼孫國華先生 (Obituary for Mr. Sun Kuo-hua). *Hsin-li hsueh-pao*, No. 1 (1958), p. 1.

Ch'iu Hsueh-hua 邱學華 "Erh-t'ung hsing-ch'eng chu-suan yun-suan hsu-lien ti yen-chiu" 兒童形成珠算運算熟練的研究 (A study of the skill of calculation with abacus in school children). *Hsin-li hsueh-pao*, No. 2 (1963), pp. 106–112.

Chou Tso-yun 周作雲 "Kuan-yü hsin-li-hsueh chung ti tzu-jan chu-i kuan-tien," 關于心理學中的自然主義觀點 (On the naturalistic point of view in psychology), *Hsin-li hsueh-pao*, No. 1 (1966), pp. 11–15.

Chu Chih-hsien 朱智賢 "Kuan-yü jen-ti hsien-li ti chieh-chi-hsing wen-t'i" 關于人的心理的階級性問題 (On the question of the class nature of human psychology). *Kuang-ming jih-pao*, June 23, 1959.

Chu Chih-hsien, Ch'en Kuo-mei, Wu Feng-Kang 朱智賢，陳

幗眉，吳鳳崗 "Erh-t'ung tso-yu kai-nien fa-chan ti shih-yen yen-chiu"
兒童左右概念發展的實驗研究 (Experimental study on children's conceptions of left and right), *Hsin-li hsueh-pao*, No. 3 (1964), pp. 229–236.

Chung-kuo k'o-hsueh-yuan, Hsin-li yen-chiu-so, Lao-tung hsin-li-tsu 中國科學院心理研究所，勞動心理組 (Division of Labor Psychology, Institute of Psychology, Academy of Sciences), "Kai-chin ch'ung-ya kung tso fang-fa ti ch'u-pu yen-chiu"
改進冲壓工作方法的初步研究 (A preliminary study in methods for improving operations on punch). *Hsin-li hsueh-pao*, No. 1 (1959), pp. 51–56.

Chung-kuo k'o-hsueh-yuan, Hsin-li yen-chiu-so, Lao-tung hsin-li-tsu 中國科學院心理研究所，勞動心理組 (Division of Labor Psychology, Institute of Psychology, Academy of Sciences), "Chuan-lu lien-kang-kung huo-yen shih-chieh p'an-tuan ti ch'u-pu yen-chiu"
轉炉練鋼工火焰視界判斷的初步研究 (A preliminary study on the visual judgment of flames by steel workers operating the converters), *Hsin-li hsueh-pao*, No. 3 (1959), pp. 161–167.

Chung-kuo k'o-hsueh-yuan, Hsin-li yen-chiu-so, Lao-tung hsin-li-tsu 中國科學院心理研究所，勞動心理組 (Division of Labor Psychology, Institute of Psychology, Academy of Sciences). "Ts'u-chin fa-ming ch'uang-tsao ti ch'ang-shih chin-yen"
促進發明創造的嘗試經驗 (Some experiences in attempt at promotion of invention and creation). *Hsin-li hsueh-pao*, No. 1 (1959), 36–41.

Fang Hsun-i 方惇頤 "Ch'üan-mien fa-chan yin-ts'ai shih-chiao wen-t'i ti ch'u-pu t'an-t'ao"
全面發展因材施教問題的初步探討 (Preliminary exploration of the problem of total development and flexibility of approach). *Hua-nan shih-fan hsueh-yuan hsueh-pao*, No. 2 (1957), pp. 8–11.

Fang Yun-ch'iu, Ching Ch'i-ch'eng 方芸秋，荆其誠 "Shuang-yen fu-ho tui ta-hsiao chü-li p'an-tuan ti ying-hsiang" 双眼輻合對大小距離判斷的影響 (The influence of convergence on size-distance judgments). *Hsin-li hsueh-pao*, No. 4 (1963), pp. 251–259.

Feng Ken-ch'uan, Yang Te-chuang 封根泉，楊德庄 "Shih-chueh huan-tung ti shih-yen yen-chiu" 視覺幻動的實驗研究 (An experimental study of autokinetic illusion). *Hsin-li hsueh-pao*, No. 5 (1959), pp. 303–316.

Ho Pao-yuan 赫葆源 "Hsiang-wei ch'a-tui shan-kuang hsin-hao pien-jen ho szu-tung hsien-hsiang ti ying-hsiang" 相位差對閃光信号辨認和似動現象的影響 (The influence of phase differences on the discrimination of flash signals and apparent movement). *Hsin-li hsueh-pao*, No. 2 (1964), pp. 121–130.

Ho Pao-yuan, Ma Mou-ch'ao 赫葆源，馬謀超 "Kuang-p'ing tui t'ung-shih-hsing shan-kuang hsing-hao pien-jen ti ying-hsiang" 光坪對同時性閃光信号辨認的影響 (Bright vs. dim, instead of dark phase, of simultaneous flash signals and their discrimination), *Hsin-li hsueh-pao*, No. 1 (1965), pp. 63–75.

Hsieh Ch'ien-ch'iu 謝千秋 "Ch'ing-shao-nien tao-te p'ing-chia neng-li ti i-hsieh yen-chiu" 青少年道德評价能力的一些研究 (Studies on the ability of moral judgement in adolescents). *Hsin-li hsueh-pao*, No. 3 (1964).

"Hsin-li chih-liao tsai shen-ching shuai-jo k'uai-su tsung-ho liao-fa chung ti tso-yung" 心理治療在神經衰弱快速合療法中的作用 (Function of psychotherapy in a speedy and synthetic treatment of neurasthenia). *Hsin-li hsueh-pao*, No. 3 (1959), pp. 151–160.

Hsin-li-hsueh chiang-i 心理學講義 (Lectures in psychology). K'ai-feng shih-fan hsueh-yuan hsin-li-hsueh chiao-yen-tsu pien 開封師範學院心理學教研組編 (edited by the Psychology Study Group of K'ai-feng Normal College). Wuhan, 1957.

"Hsin-li-hsueh hui chao-k'ai chiao-yü hsin-li chuan-yeh hui-i" 心理學會召開教育心理專業會議 (Psychology Society calls meeting on educational psychology). *Kuang-ming jih-pao*, Mar. 9, 1962.

"Hsin-li-hsueh li-lun lien-hsi shih-chi shou-ch'eng-hsiao" 心理學理論聯系實際收成効 (Unification of theory and practice in psychology brings results). *Wen-hui pao* (Shanghai), Dec. 21, 1959.

Hsu Lien-ts'ang 徐聯倉 "Hsin-hsi to-yü-hsing tui chang-wo hsin-hao chieh-ko kuo-ch'eng ti ying-hsiang" 信息多余性對掌握信号結构過程的影響 (The role of redundancy in the learning of signal patterns). *Hsin-li hsueh-pao*, No. 3 (1963), pp. 230–238.

Hsu Lien-ts'ang 徐聯倉 "Shui-p'ing p'ai-li hsin-hao ti tsu-ho t'e-tien tui hsin-hsi ch'uan-ti hsiao-lü ti ying-hsiang" 水平排列信号的組合特點對信息傳遞効率的影響 (Information transmission of horizontally arranged signal patterns). *Hsin-li hsueh-pao*, No. 4 (1963), pp. 321–329.

Hsu Lien-ts'ang 徐聯倉 "Su-lien hsin-li-hsueh chieh tsai yen-chiu she-mo" 蘇聯心理學界在研究什么 (What is Soviet psychology studying?). *Hsin-li hsueh-pao*, No. 4 (1959), pp. 276–278.

Hsu Lien-ts'ang 徐聯倉 "Tsai fu-ho tz'u-chi chung hsin-hsi-liang yü fan-ying shih ti kuan-hsi" 在複合刺激中信息量與反應時的關係 (The amount of information as a determinant of reaction time to complex stimuli). *Hsin-li hsueh-pao*, No. 1 (1963), pp. 42–47.

Hsu Shu-lien, K'uang P'ei-tzu 許淑蓮,匡培梓 "Yung yen-yü ch'iang-hua ti yun-tung t'iao-chien fan-she fang-fa yen-chiu 8–10 sui erh-t'ung chieh-t'ung chi-neng lei-tien t'e-hsing ti i-tien chin-yen" 用言語強化的運動條件反射方法研究 8–10 歲兒童接通机能類點特性的一點經驗 (Note on types characterized by the coupling of the highest nervous activity in children by means of verbally reinforced motor conditioning method). *Hsin-li hsueh-pao*, No. 1 (1958), pp. 53–64.

Hsu Yu-hsin 許又新 "Liang-Chin Nan-pei-ch'ao chi Sui-T'ang shih-tai wo-kuo ching-shen-hsueh chien-chiai" 兩晉南北朝及隋唐時代我國精神病學簡介 (Introduction to psychiatry from Chin to Sui-T'ang Dynasties), *Chung-kuo shen-ching ching-shen k'o tsa-chih*, No. 1 (1959), pp. 14–19.

Jen-min Chung-kuo (People's China), Japanese edition, No. 3 (1964), pp. 65–66.

Jen-min shou-ts'e 1958 人民手冊 (Handbook on People's China). Peking: Ta-kung-pao Publishing Co.

Kan Feng 敢峯 "T'an-t'an chi-i ho li-chieh ti pien-cheng kuan-hsi" 談々記憶和理解的辨証關係 (On the controversial relationship between memory and understanding). *Kuang-ming jih-pao*, Sept. 25, 1963.

"Kuan-yü shih-yen hsin-li-hsueh ti chi-ko wen-t'i ti shang-ch'üeh" 關于實驗心理學的幾個問題的商確 (Some questions on experimental psychology). *Kuang-ming jih-pao*, May 16, 1955.

"Kuang-tung hsin-li-hsueh chiao-shih hsia-hsiang hsia-ch'uang tiao-ch'a yen-chiu" 廣東心理學教師下鄉下廠調查研究 (Kuangtung teachers of psychology go down to villages and factories for investigation and research). *Kuang-ming jih-pao*, June 12, 1959.

Kung Yao-hsien 龔耀先 "Lien-hsiang shih-yen chi-ch'i lin-ch'uang ying-yung, I, II" 聯想實驗及其臨床應用 (Free association test and its clinical application, I, II). *Hsin-li hsueh-pao*, No. 2 (1963), pp. 130–145.

Kung Yao-hsien 龔耀先 "Shen-ching shuai-jo huan-che p'i-ts'eng kuo-ch'eng chang-ai ti nao-tien-t'u yü lin-ch'uang ti yen-chiu" 神經衰弱患者皮層過程障礙的腦電圖與臨床的研究 (An EEG and clinical study of the cortical function of neurasthenics). *Hsin-li hsueh-pao*, No. 1 (1963), pp. 65–74.

Li Cheng 李錚 "Liu-sui tso-yu erh-t'ung ti han-tzu tzu-hsing chih-chueh hsing-wei ti ch'u-t'an" 六歲左右兒童的漢字字形知覺形位的初探 (A preliminary study on the perception of Chinese characters by six year old children). *Hsin-li hsueh-pao*, No. 2 (1964), pp. 178–184.

Li Chia-chih 李家治 "Kuan-yü shan-kuang hsin-hao yü-i kan-jao ti ling-i-hsieh shih-yen yen-chiu"
關于閃光信号語義干擾的另一些實驗研究 (Further studies on the semantic noise in coding flash signals). *Hsin-li hsueh-pao*, No. 2 (1964), pp. 113–120.

Li Chia-chih 李家治 "Shan-kuang hsin-hao ti yü-i kan-jao"
閃光信号的語義干擾 (Semantic noise in coding flash light signals). *Hsin-li hsueh-pao*, No. 3 (1963), pp. 165–174.

Li Chia-chih, Hsu Lien-ts'ang 李家治, 徐聯倉 "Kung-yeh shih-ku yuan-yin ti ch'u-pu fen-hsi"
工業事故原因的初步分析 (Causation of industrial accidents). *Hsin-li hsueh-pao*, No. 1 (1957), pp. 184–193.

Li Hsin-t'ien 李心天 "Hsin-li chih-liao tsai man-hsing ching-shen fen-li cheng chung ti ying-yung"
心理治療在慢性精神分裂症中的應用 (The application of psychotherapy in the treatment of chronic schizophrenia). *Hsin-li hsueh-pao*, No. 1 (1963), pp. 55–64.

Li Hsin-t'ien 李心天 "Jen-shih huo-tung tsai shen-ching shuai-jo chih-liao shang ti tso-yung"
認識活動在神經衰弱治療上的作用 (The effect of recognition in the treatment of neurasthenia). *Hsin-li hsueh-pao*, No. 1 (1960), pp. 36–45.

Li Po-shu, Chou Kuan-sheng 李伯黍, 周冠生 "Shao-nien erh-t'ung tao-te hsing-wei tung-chi t'e-cheng ti hsin-li fen-hsi"
少年兒童道德行為動机特征的心理分析 (Motivational characteristics of moral behavior in children). *Hsin-li hsueh-pao*, No. 1 (1964), pp. 25–32.

Li Yi 李沂 "Hsiao-hsueh kao-nien-chi hsueh-sheng ts'an-chia nung-yeh lao-tung chung so piao-hsien ti i-hsieh hsin-li t'e-tien ti ch'u-pu fen-hsi"
小學高年級學生參加農業勞動中所表視的一些心理特點的初步分析 (An analysis of the psychological characteristics of primary school 5–6th grade students participating in agricultural

work). *Hsin-li hsueh-pao*, No. 5 (1959), pp. 293–302.

Lin Chung-hsien 林仲賢 "Shih-chueh ho tung-chueh tsai ting-wei chung ti hsiang-wu tso-yung" 視覺和動覺在定位中的相互作用 (A study on interaction between visual and kinesthetic localization). *Hsin-li hsueh-pao*, No. 3 (1964), pp. 211–222.

Lin Chung-hsien 林仲賢 "Tsui-sui yun-tung yü pu-t'ung chih-yeh hsun-lien ti kuan-hsi ti shih-yen yen-chiu" 追隨運動與不同職業訓練的關係的實驗研究 (The relationship between pursuit movement and professional training). *Hsin-li hsueh-pao*, No. 3 (1963), pp. 222–229.

Lin Chung-hsien 林仲賢 "Ying-hsiang pu-t'ung fang-wei tz'u-chi kuan-ch'a ti jo-kan yin-ssu ti ch'u-pu yen-chiu" 影響不同方位刺激觀察的若干因素的初步研究 (Some factors affecting the observation of stimuli from different directions). *Hsin-li hsueh-pao*, No. 2 (1963), pp. 113–120.

Liu Ching-ho 劉静和 "Tsai hsiao-hsueh shih-chiao tai-shu ti shih-yen yen-chiu" 在小學試教代数的實驗研究 (A psychological study on experimental teaching of algebra to primary school children), *Hsin-li hsueh-pao*, No. 1 (1960), pp. 13–27.

Liu Fan 劉范 "Tui-yu hsin-li-hsueh tui-hsiang wen-t'i ti ch'u-pu k'an-fa" 對于心理學對象問題的初步看法 (Tentative views on the subject matter of psychology). *Kuang-ming jih-pao*, July 20, 1959.

Liu Fan, Kung Wei-yao 劉范，龔維瑤 "Yu-kuan chung-hsueh-sheng sheng-ch'an lao-tung shih-chien ho chang-wo li-lun chih-shih ti kuan-shi ti ch'u-pu fen-chi" 有關中學生生產勞動實踐和掌握理論知識的關係的初步分析 (An analysis of the relationship between practice in productive labor and acquisition of theoretical knowledge in middle-school students). *Hsin-li hsueh-pao*, No. 5 (1959), pp. 279–292.

Liu Shih-i 劉世熠 "Nao-tien-t'u yü hsin-li ti ta-nao sheng-li chi-chih yen-chiu ti chi-ko wen-t'i" 脳電圖與心理的大脑生理机制研究的幾個問題 (Some problems of EEG and brain mechanism). *Hsin-li hsueh-pao*, No. 3 (1961), pp.141–154.

Liu Shih-i, Wu Ch'in-o 劉世熠，鄔勤娥 "Jen-lei chan-shih lien-hsi ti nao-tien-t'u yen-chiu" 人類暫時聯系的腦電圖研究 (An electroencephalographic study of the formation of temporary connections in man). *Hsin-li hsueh-pao*, No. 1 (1963), pp. 11–19.

Liu Shih-i, Wang Nai-i 劉世熠，王乃怡 "Chih-li fa-yü pu-ch'üan wei-che ti nao-tien-t'u yen-chiu" 智力發育不全患者的腦電圖研究 (An electroencephalographic study of mentally deficient patients). *Hsin-li hsueh-pao*, No. 3 (1963), pp. 194–202.

Lü Ching, Wang Wen-chün 呂靜，汪文鋆 "Ti nien-chi erh-t'ung chang-wo ying-yung-t'i kai-nien ti ssu-wei ling-huo-hsing" 低年級兒童掌握應用題概念的思惟靈活性 (The thinking processes in arithmetical operation in lower-grade school children). *Hsin-li hsueh-pao*, No. 2 (1960), pp. 121–135.

Lü Ching, Wang Wen-chün, Cheng Yü-tan 呂靜，汪文鋆，鄭月旦 "Hsiao-hsueh ti-nien-chi erh-t'ung chang-wo suan-shu k'o-ni t'ui-li yü ssu-wei ti ling-huo hsing" 小學低年級兒童掌握算數可逆推理與思想的靈活性 (The mastery of reverse operation and flexibility of thinking in arithmetic in school children). *Hsin-li hsueh-pao*, No. 3 (1964), pp. 237–247.

Lu Chung-heng, Chu Hsin-ming 盧仲衡，朱新明 "Wai-chou hsien-tuan tui t'u-hsing chih-chueh chieh-kou ho ssu-hsiang kuo-ch'eng ti ying-hsiang (III)" 外周幾段對圖形知覺結構和思想過程的影響 (The effect of outer shape on the perceptive structure of geometric figures and thought processes). *Hsin-li hsueh-pao*, No. 3 (1964), pp. 248–257.

Lu Chung-heng, Mao Yü-yen, Ying Yü-yeh, Ma Chieh-wei, Chang Mei-ling 盧仲衡，茅于燕，應玉業，馬佶爲，張梅玲 "Chiao-hsueh kai-ke chung ch'u-chin hsueh-sheng chang-wo shu-hsueh chih-shih ti i-hsieh hsin-li yin-su"

教學改革中促進學生掌握数學知識的一些心理因素 (Some psychological factors in promoting the students' grasp of arithmetical knowledge, as found in recent educational reforms). *Hsin-li hsueh-pao*, No. 3 (1961), pp. 190–201.

Lu Chung-heng, Ying Yü-yeh, Chang Mei-ling, Hung T'ieh-lun, Yen Hui-fen 廬仲衡, 應玉葉, 張梅玲, 洪鉄倫, 閻慧芬 "Pu-t'ung chiao-hsueh fang-fa tui hsueh-sheng chang-wo chi-ho chi-pen kai-nien ti ying-hsiang ti shih-yen yen-chiu" 不同教學方法對學生掌握幾何基本概念的影響的實驗研究 (An experimental study of the effects of different methods of teaching on the formation of fundamental geometrical concepts). *Hsin-li hsueh-pao*, No. 2 (1963), pp. 88–97.

Ma Chi-hsiung 馬驥雄 "T'an-t'an 'ko-hsing ti ch'uan-mien fa-chan'"
談談「個性的全面發展」 (On the "total development of the individual"). *Hua-tung shih-ta hsueh-pao*, No. 1 (1958), pp. 97–112.

Mao Yü-yen, Kung Wei-yao, Ch'en P'ei-lin 茅于燕, 龔維瑤, 陳沛霖 "Fu-ho ying-yung-t'i chieh-ko ti ch'u-pu t'o-t'ao" 複合應用題結構的初步探討 (Preliminary study on the structure of complex arithmetic problems). *Hsin-li hsueh-pao*, No. 1 (1964), pp. 57–71.

Nieh Shih-mou 聶世茂 "Pang-yang tui-pi tui shao-nien hsueh-sheng tzu-wo p'ing-chiai ti tso-yung" 榜樣對比對少年學生自我評价的作用 (Function of the exemplar for student self-evaluation). *Hsin-li hsueh-pao*, No. 2 (1966), pp. 146–153.

P'an Shu 潘菽 "Chung-kuo hsin-li-hsueh ti hsien-chuang ho fa-chan ch'ü-hsiang" 中國心理學的現狀和發展趨向 (A general review of psychology in China). *Hsin-li hsueh-pao*, No. 2 (1958), pp. 3–8.

P'an Shu 潘菽 "Fa-hui chi-t'i li-liang wei fa-chan fu-wu yü wo-kuo wei-ta ti she-hui chu-i ti k'o-hsueh erh fen-tou" 發揮集体力量爲發展服務于我國偉大的社會主義建設的科學心理學而奮鬥 (Develop group strength, struggle to expand scientific psychology to be of service to our great socialist construction). *Hsin-li hsueh-pao*, No. 1 (1956), pp. 1–10.

P'an Shu 潘菽 "Mien-tui keng-ta ti yueh-chin hsing-shih, p'an-teng hsin-li-hsueh ti kao-feng"
面對更大的躍進形勢，攀登心理學的高峯 (Responding to the Big Leap, scaling the peaks of psychological science). *Hsin-li hsueh-pao*, No. 2 (1960), pp. 63–66.

P'an Shu 潘菽 "Wo-kuo hsin-li-hsueh ti hsien-chuang ho fa-chan fang-hsiang"
我國心理學的現狀和發展方向 (A review of psychology in our country). *Jen-min jih-pao*, July 2, 1957. The title of this news article is almost exactly the same as that of the journal article by the same author, but the contents are not the same.

P'eng Jui-hsiang, Fang Yun-ch'iu, Ching Ch'i-ch'eng ，
方芸秋，荆其誠 "Mu-piao-wu ta-hsiao ying-hsiang chü-li p'an-tuan ti shih-yen yen-chiu"
目標物大小影響距離判斷的實驗研究 (Target size as a cue to distance judgment along a ground strip). *Hsin-li hsueh-pao*, No. 1 (1963), pp. 31–41.

Shan Yü 山羽 "Feng-wei chih-kuo k'o yü-ch'i—Chung-kuo Hsin-li-hsueh Hui Chiao-yü hsin-li Chuan-yeh hui-i sui-kan"
丰蔚之果可預期 — 中國心理學會教育心理專業會議隨感 (Fruitful results can be predicted—impressions of the Educational Psychology Specialty Conference of the Chinese Psychological Society). *Kuang-ming jih-pao*, Mar. 14, 1962.

"Shang-hai hsin-li-hsueh chieh chan-k'ai cheng-lun" 上海心理學界展開爭論 (Shanghai psychologists open debate meeting), *Wen-hui pao*, Apr. 14, 1959.

Shen Nai-chang 沈廼璋 "Cheng-chang ch'eng-jen ti hsing-chung ts'o-chueh"
正常成人的形重錯覺 (The size-weight illusion of normal adults). *Hsin-li hsueh-pao*, No. 3 (1963), pp. 186–193.

Ssu-ma Feng 司馬烽 "Te-yü hsin-li-hsueh ti yen-chiu pi-hsü kuan-ch'e chieh-chi fen-hsi yuan-che—yü Hsieh Ch'ien-ch'iu t'ung-chih shang-chueh"
德育心理學的研究必須貫徹階級分析原則 — 與謝千秋同志商榷
(The principle of class analysis must be applied in the

research on psychology of moral education—a discussion with comrade Hsieh Ch'ien-ch'iu). *Hsin-li hsueh-pao*, No. 2 (1965), pp. 114–120.

Sun Shih-lu 孫世路 "Pu-t'ung nien-ling pei-shih ti Müller-Lyer ts'o-chueh"
不同年齡被試的謬勒萊依爾錯覺 (Age differences in Müller-Lyer illusion). *Hsin-li hsueh-pao*, No. 3 (1964), pp. 223–228.

Sun Wei-chen, Cheng Fu-sheng, Li Hsin-t'ien 宋維眞, 鄭福生, 李心天 "Ts'ung tui liang-chung ch'iang-tu sheng-yin tz'u-chi ti chien-tan fan-ying k'an ching-shen fen-lieh-cheng huan-che ti ta-nao chi-neng t'e-tien"
從對兩種強度聲音刺激的簡單反應看精神分裂症患者的大腦机能特點 (Characteristics of the cerebral functions of schizophrenics as shown in simple reactions to sound stimuli). *Hsin-li hsueh-pao*, No. 4 (1964), pp. 381–387.

Ting Ts'an 丁瓚 "K'ai-chan wo-kuo i-hsueh hsin-li-hsueh ti kung-tso"
開展我國醫學心理學的工作 (Developing a program in Chinese medical psychology). *Chung-hua shen-ching ching-shen k'o-hsueh ts'a-chih* (Chinese journal of neuropsychiatry), No. 4 (1956), pp. 322–325.

Ting Ts'an 丁瓚 "Lun hsin-li-hsueh tui-hsiang chi ch'i k'o-hsueh hsing-chih"
論心理學對象及其科學性質 (On the subject matter and scientific nature of psychology). *Hsin-li hsueh-pao*, No. 1 (1960), pp. 7–12.

Ting Ts'an "Tsen-yang tsai wo-kuo k'ai-chan i-hsueh hsin-li-hsueh ti kung-tso"
怎樣在我國開展醫學心理學的工作 (How to develop medical psychology in China). *Hsin-li hsueh-pao*, No. 3 (1959), pp. 146–150.

"Ts'an-chia hsin-li-hsueh hsueh-shu t'ao-lun ti t'i-hui" 參加心理學學術討論的体會 (Ideas from participation in academic discussion meetings in psychology). *Jen-min jih-pao*, June 10, 1959.

Tsang Yü-hai 臧玉海 "Kuan-yü hsin-li-hsueh tui-hsiang ti

chi-ko chung-yao wen-t'i"
關于心理學對象的幾個重要問題 (Some important questions on the object of psychology). *Hsin-li hsueh-pao*, No. 1 (1956), pp. 21–25.

Ts'ao Chuan-yung 曹傳詠 "I-ko tien-tzu tien-lu k'ung-chih ti ch'eng-shih ch'i"
一個電子電路控制的呈示器 (An electronic tachistoscope), *Hsin-li hsueh-pao*, No. 3 (1963), pp. 247–250.

Ts'ao Chuan-yung, Shen Yeh 曹傳詠, 沈曄 "Hsiao-hsueh erh-t'ung fen-hsi, kai-k'uo ho pien-jen han-tzu tzu-hsing neng-li ti fa-chan yen-chiu"
小學兒童分析，概括和辨認漢字字形能力的發展研究 (Developmental studies on the recognition and generalization of Chinese characters in primary-school children I. Development of recognition under tachistoscopic conditions). *Hsin-li hsueh-pao*, No. 1 (1965), pp. 1–9.

Ts'ao Chuan-yung, Shen Yeh 曹傳詠, 沈曄 "Tsai su-shih t'iao-chien hsia erh-t'ung pien-jen han-tzu tzu-hsing ti shih-t'an hsing yen-chiu"
在速視條件下兒童辨認漢字字形的試探性研究 I, II, III (The recognition of Chinese characters under tachistoscopic conditions in primary-school children, I, II, III). *Hsin-li hsueh-pao*, No. 3 (1963), pp. 203–213; No. 4 (1963), pp. 271–279 and 280–286.

Ts'ao Jih-ch'ang 曹日昌 "Chi-i ti fa-chan ho shih-chi hsiao-lü"
記憶的發展和識記效率 (Memory and efficient recognition). *Kuang-ming jih-pao*, Apr. 4, 1964.

Ts'ao Jih-ch'ang "Hsin-li-hsueh ti yen-chiu jen-wu yü hsueh-k'o hsing-chih"
心理學的研究任務與學科性質 (Psychology, its responsibility and scientific nature). *Hsin Chien-she*, June 7, 1959.

Ts'ao Jih-ch'ang "Hsin-li-hsueh yen-chiu she-mo"
心理學研究什么 (What does psychology study). *Jen-min jih-pao*, July 9, 1959.

Ts'ao Jih-ch'ang 曹日昌 "Kuan-ch'e li-lun lien-hsi shih-chi, k'o-hsueh yen-chiu wei she-hui chu-i chien-she fu-wu ti

fang-chen, t'i-kao hsin-li-hsueh kung-tso ti shui-p'ing"
貫徹理論聯係實際，科學研究爲社會主義建設服務的方針，提高心理學工作的水平 (Raising the scientific level of psychological research: address to the 1963 annual meeting of the Chinese Psychological Society). *Hsin-li hsueh-pao*, No. 1 (1964), pp. 1–18.

Ts'ao Jih-ch'ang 曹日昌 "Yu hsueh-shu p'i-p'an ming-ch'ueh hsin-li-hsueh ti yen-chiu jen-wu"
由學術批判明確心理學的研究任務 (From academic discussion to the research responsibility of psychology). *Kuang-ming jih-pao*, April 14, 1959.

Ts'ao Jih-ch'ang, Ching Ch'i-ch'eng, Lin Chung-hsien 曹日昌，荆其誠，林仲賢 "Yü-ts'e yun-tung hsing-ch'eng ti ch'u-pu yen-chiu"
預測運動行程的初步研究 (Preliminary study on the prediction of motion). *Hsin-li hsueh-pao*, No. 1 (1957), pp. 142–157.

Ts'ao Jih-ch'ang, Li Chia-chih 曹日昌，李家治 "Chung-kuo lao-tung hsin-li-hsueh kai-k'uang"
中國勞動心理學概況 (Industrial psychology in China). *Hsin-li hsueh-pao*, No. 4 (1959), pp. 204–214.

Tseng Ch'eng-jui 曾呈瑞 "Hsi-sha hsien-chin sheng-ch'an-che ts'ao-tso t'e-tien ti ko-li yen-chiu"
細紗先進生產者操作特點的個例研究 (A case study of the characteristics of working of an advanced textile worker). *Hsin-li hsueh-pao*, No. 1 (1963), pp. 75–80.

Tuan Hui-fen, Ts'ao Jih-ch'ang 段蕙芬，曹日昌 "Ch'u-chung hsueh-sheng ti chi-i fang-fa III. Wen-yen-wen ho pai-hua wen ti chi-i fang-fa yü kuo-ch'eng"
初中學生的識記方法 Ⅲ. 文言文和百話文的識記方法與過程 (Studies on the methods of memorization used by junior middle school pupils III. Methods and courses of memorizing classical and modern prose). *Hsin-li hsueh-pao*, No. 1 (1965), pp. 10–27.

Wang Ching-ho and Li Hsin-t'ien 王景和，李心天 "Shen-ching shuai-jo ping-yin wen-t'i ti ch'u-pu t'an-t'ao"

神經衰弱病因問題的初步探討 (Preliminary study of the etiology of neurasthenia). *Hsin-li hsueh-pao*, No. 1 (1960), pp. 46–52.

Wang Pai-yang 王伯揚 "Che-chiang erh-t'ung sheng-t'i fa-yü ti i-hsieh kuei-li"
浙江兒童身体發育的一些規律 (Physical development of Chekiang children). *Hsin-li hsueh-pao*, No. 4 (1963), pp. 336–346.

Wang Pai-yang 王伯揚 "Che-chiang erh-t'ung ti wo-li ti fa-chan"
浙江兒童的握力的發展 (Growth of grip strength of Chekiang children). *Hsin-li hsueh-pao*, No. 3 (1963), pp. 239–246.

Wang Shu 王甦 "Shou-pu chi-jo kung-tso tui hsing-chung ts'o-chueh ti ying-hsiang"
手部肌關工作對形重錯覺的影響 (The effect of muscular work of hands on the size-weight illusion). *Hsin-li hsueh-pao*, No. 2 (1963), pp. 81–87.

Wu I-ling, Li Cho-min 吳益令，李卓民 "Shao-nien erh-t'ung hsueh-hsi mu-ti yü tung-chi ti fen-hsi"
少年兒童學習目的與動机的分析 (An analysis of the purpose and motivation for learning among youth). *Hsin-li hsueh-pao*, No. 2 (1966), pp. 137–145.

Yang Ch'eng-chang 楊成章 "Shih-lun jen-ti hsin-li ti mao-tun ti t'e-shu-hsing"
試論人的心理的矛盾的特殊性 (Some considerations on the specificity of contradictions of mental activity). *Hsin-li hsueh-pao*, No. 3 (1961).

Yeh Hsuan, Fang Yun-ch'iu 葉絢，方芸秋 "Hsueh-ch'ien erh-t'ung fang-wei chih-chueh ti ch'u-pu shih-yen yen-chiu"
學前兒童方位知覺的初步實驗研究 (A preliminary experimental study on spatial orientation in preschool children). *Hsin-li hsueh-pao*, No. 1 (1958), pp. 65–71.

Yeh Hsuan, Ts'ao Jih-ch'ang 葉絢，曹日昌 "Shih, t'ing yü-wen ts'ai-liao t'ung-shih shih-chi ti kan-jao yü hsiang-tui yu-shih"
視，聽語文材料同時識記的干擾與相對優勢 (Interference and

dominance in simultaneous memorization of different visual and aurally presented materials). *Hsin-li hsueh-pao*, No. 2 (1964), pp. 131–142.

Yuan Kung-wei 袁公韋 *Hsin hsin-li-hsueh*
新心理學 (A new psychology). Shanghai, 1953.

Yuan Liang-tso, Li Tuan-wu 源良佐，李端吾 "Ke-ming ying-hsiung ku-shih tui hsiao-hsueh-sheng tao-te i-shih hsing-ch'en ti tso-yung ti ch'u-pu yen-chiu"
革命英雄故事對小學生道德意識形成的作用的初步研究 (Function of revolutionary hero stories for the formation of pupils' moral consciousness). *Hsin-li hsueh-pao*, No. 2 (1966), pp. 154–162.

*A MAINLAND COMPILATION OF CHINESE PSYCHO-
LOGICAL TERMS (HSIN-LI HSUEH MING-TZ'U)*

The following list of Chinese psychological terms was published by the Chinese Academy of Sciences in 1954, with a foreword by Kuo Mo-jo. Its preface explained that this was a preliminary list after the reform of psychology according to Marxism and Pavlovianism. In principle, therefore, the list included as many Pavlovian terms as possible and left out terms from old, "reactionary" psychology. Since this list is generally inaccessible and since no later list has been found, we reprint it here for the convenience of interested scholars.

Compilation of Terms, Chinese Academy of Science

英 文 名 詞	中 文 名 詞
A	
A. D. = average deviation	平均差
A. M. = arithmetic mean	算術平均〔數〕
aberration of light	光行差
ability	能力
ability distribution	能力分配
abnormal	變態的
abnormal psychology	變態心理學
absolute brilliance limen (absolute brilliance threshold)	絕對明度閾限
absolute limen (absolute threshold)	絕對閾限
absolute pitch	絕對音高
absolute refractory period	絕對不應期
absolute sensitivity	絕對感受性
absolute threshold (absolute limen)	絕對閾限
abulia	喪志症
accessory sense-apparatus	感官附屬組織
accommodation	調節
achievement age	成就年齡
achievement test (accomplishment test)	成就測驗
Achilles reflex (Achilles tendon reflex)	跟腱反射
achromatic	無色調的, 無色彩的
achromatic vision	無色視覺
achromatism (total color blindness)	全色盲
acoumeter (audiometer)	聽覺計
acoustic shadow	聲影
acquired	1. 習得的, 2. 獲得的
acromegaly	肢端肥大症
action current	動作電流

action potential	動作電位
active attention	主動注意
active recall	主動回憶
activity-cage	動作記錄籠
activity-wheel	動作記錄輪
acuity	敏銳度
adaptability	適應性
adaptation	適應
adaptation time	適應時間
adaptometer	〔網膜〕適應測時計
adequate stimulus	適當刺激
adjustment	順應
adjustment mechanism	順應機構
adjustment system	順應系統
adjustor	順應器
adolescence	青年期
adrenal gland (suprarenal gland)	腎上腺
adrenalin	腎上腺素
Adrian principle (all-or-none law)	全或無定律
aerial perspective	空氣透視
aesthesiometer (esthesiometer)	觸覺計
affect	感情
affection	感情
affective tone (feeling tone)	情調
affectivity	情感性
afferent	內導的
after discharge	後放
after-effect	後效
after-image	後像
age scale	年齡量表
age-norm	年齡常模
ageusia	失味症
agitated depression	激動性沉鬱
agitated melancholia	激動性憂鬱症
agnosia	失知覺症

241

agraphia	失寫症	antagonistic color	對抗色
Aktpsychologie	意向心理學	anterograde amnesia	遠事遺忘〔症〕
albedo	反照率	anthropometry	人體測量
alcoholic psychosis	酒毒精神病	anthropomorphism	擬人說
alexia (word blindness)	詞盲	(anthropomorphic	
algesia	痛覺過敏	hypothesis)	
algesthesis	痛覺	anticipation method	預料法
algometer	痛覺計	anxiety hysteria	焦慮性歇斯底里
alienation	精神錯亂	anxiety neurosis	焦慮性神經病
alienist (psychiatrist)	精神病學家	aphasia	失語症
allied reflex (synergic reflex)	協合反射	aphemia (motor aphasia)	運動性失語症
all-or-none law	全或無定律	apnoea	呼吸暫停
(Adrian principle)		apparatus	1. 儀器; 2. 器官
alpha rhythm (alpha wave)	甲種腦電波（伯	apparent movement	似動〔現象〕
(Berger rhythm)	格氏波）	apperception	統覺
alternating personality	更替性人格	apperceptive mass	統覺團
alternating psychosis	更替性精神病	applied psychology	應用心理學
(alternating insanity)		apprehension	領會
alternating reflex	更替反射	apraxia	失動症
ambidexterity (ambidextral-	兩手均能性	aptitude	能力傾向
ity)		aptitude test	能力傾向測驗
ambiguous figure	交變圖形	Aristotle's illusion	亞里斯多德錯覺
ambilaterality	兩側均能性	arithmetic mean (A.M.)	算術平均〔數〕
ambivalence	情緒矛盾	articular sensation (joint	關節覺
ambivert	〔內外〕兩向者	sensation)	
amentia (mental deficiency)	智力缺陷	articulate speech	有聲語言
amnesia	遺忘症	assimilation	1. 同化; 2. 吸收
anaesthesia (anesthesia,	麻木	associate points	聯合點
anaesthesis)		association	1. 聯想; 2. 聯合
analgesia	失痛症	association area	聯合區
analytic psychology	分析心理學	association by contiguity	接近聯想
analyzer (analysator)	分析器	association by contrast	對比聯想
anatomical age	骨骼年齡	association by similarity	類似聯想
anecdotal method	軼事法	association center	聯合中樞
angular displacement	角移	association fibres	聯合纖維
anima	靈氣	association of ideas	觀念聯合
animal magnetism	動物磁性說	association time	聯想時間
animal psychology	動物心理學	associationism	聯想主義
animism	靈氣說	associative inhibition	聯合抑制
anorexia	食欲缺乏	astasia	站立不穩
anosmia	失嗅症	astasia-abasia	不能步行症
anoxemia	缺氧症	astereognosis (stereoagnosis)	觸物失知症

asthenia	無力	autonomic reflex	自律神經反射
astigmatism	1. 像散性; 2. 像散現象	autosuggestion	自我暗示
		avalanche conduction	雪崩式〔神經〕傳導
ataxia	動作失調		
atrophy (atrophia)	萎縮	average deviation (mean deviation) (A.D.)	平均差
attack psychosis	發作性精神病		
attensity	注意度	axon (axone)	軸突. 軸索
attention	注意		
attention span	注意廣度	**B**	
(span of attention, range of attention)		backward association	倒行聯合
attitude	態度	backward conditioning	倒行條件〔反射〕作用
attitudinal reflex	體態反射	balancing response	平衡反應
attribute	屬性	bar	巴 (壓力單位即 10^6 barye)
audibility	可聽度		
audibility range	可聽廣度	basal ganglia	基底神經節
(range of hearing)		basal metabolism	基底代謝
audile (auditory type)	聽像型	basilar membrane	基膜
audio frequency	〔成〕聲頻〔率〕	beat	拍 (音的升沉)
audiometer (acoumeter)	聽覺計	beat-tone	升沉音, 拍音
audition	聽覺	behavior	行為
auditory area	聽覺區	behavior pattern	行為型式
auditory flicker	聽覺閃爍	behaviorism	行為主義
auditory localization	聲源定位	behavioristic psychology	行為主義心理學
auditory oculomotor reflex	聽聲動眼反射	bel	貝〔耳〕
auditory sensation	聽覺	Bell-Magendie law	柏爾、馬戎第定律
auditory space	聽覺空間		
auditory type (audile)	聽像型	benign psychosis	良性精神病
Aufgabe	課題	Berger rhythm (alpha rhythm, alpha wave)	甲種腦電波〔伯格氏波〕
aura	病兆		
Ausfrage method	詢問法	beta hypothesis	學習乙說
Aussage test	口述測驗	Bewusstseinslage	意識態度
autistic	我向的	(conscious attitude)	
auto-eroticism (auto-erotism)	自淫	bilateral transfer (cross transfer)	左右遷移
autokinetic sensation	遊動錯覺	bimodal	雙峰的
(autokinetic illusion, Charpentier's illusion)		binaural	雙耳的
		binaural fusion	雙耳〔音〕融合
automatic writing	1. 不由自主的書寫; 2. 扶乩	Binet-Simon scale	比納、西蒙量表
(mediumistic writing)			
automatism	不由自主的動作	binocular	雙眼的
autonomic nervous system	自律神經系〔統〕	binocular color mixture	雙眼色混合

binocular contrast	雙眼對比
binocular fixation	雙眼注視
binocular flicker	雙眼視閃動
binocular fusion	雙眼〔視像〕融合
binocular parallax	雙眼視差
binocular perspective	雙眼透視
binocular rivalry	雙眼〔視像〕競爭
biometry	生物統計
biophysical	生物物理的
biosocial	生物社會的
blank experiment	插入實驗
blend	混合
blind alley (cul de sac)	盲路
blind-spot	盲點
blockage (blocking)	阻滯
bond	聯結
brain (encephalon)	腦
brain stem	腦幹
brain wave	腦電波
brightness (brilliance)	1. 亮度; 2. 明度
brightness constancy	明度常性
brightness contrast	明度對比
brightness induction	1. 亮度誘導; 2. 明度誘導
brilliance (brightness)	1. 亮度; 2. 明度
Broca's area	卜洛卡區
bulb (medulla oblongata)	延髓
bulky color	厚色
buzzer	蜂音器

C

C. A. = chronological age	實足年齡（實齡）
C. N. S. = central nervous system	中樞神經系〔統〕
campimeter (perimeter)	視野測量器
cancellation test	劃消測驗
capacity	能量
card sorting test	分卡片測驗
cardiograph	心動描記器
case history method (case method)	個案法
catalepsy	僵直

catatonia	緊張症
catharsis (katharsis)	宣洩
cenesthesis (coenesthesia)	一般機體覺
censor	稽查者
center	中樞
central canal	中央管
central fissure (fissure of Rolando)	中央裂
central nervous system (C.N.S.)	中樞神經系〔統〕
central tendency	集中趨勢
cephalic index	頭顱指數
cerebellar cortex	小腦皮質
cerebellum	小腦
cerebral cortex (cortex)	大腦皮質
cerebral dominance	大腦半球優勢
cerebral hemispheres	大腦半球
cerebral lobe	大腦葉
cerebral localization	大腦皮質定位
cerebral nerve (cranial nerve)	腦神經
cerebration	大腦作用
cerebrospinal nervous system	腦脊系〔統〕
cerebrum	大腦
chain reflex	連鎖反射
character	性格
characterology	性格分析〔學〕
Charpentier's illusion (autokinetic illusion, autokinetic sensation)	遊動錯覺
chemical sense	1. 化學感官; 2. 化學感覺
chemoreceptor	化學感受器, 化學受納器
child psychology	兒童心理學
choc (shock)	休克
choice reaction	選擇反應
choice reaction time	選擇反應時間
choleric	膽汁質
chorea (St. Vitus' dance)	舞動症
chroma (hue, color tone)	色調
chromaesthesis (color hearing)	色聽聯覺

chromatic	1. 色調的, 色彩的; 2. 半音階的
chromatic aberration	色[像]差
chromatic adaptation	色調適應, 色彩適應
chromatic contrast	色調對比, 色彩對比
chromatic zone (color zone)	[網膜]感色區
chronaxie (chronaxy)	時值
chronological age (C.A.)	實足年齡 (實齡)
chronometer	時計
chronoscope	計時器
circular psychosis	循環性精神病
clairvoyance	千里眼
clang (Klang)	樂音
clearness	清楚
clinical psychology	診療心理學
clonus	陣攣
closure	趨合
cochlea	[耳]蝸
co-consciousness	並存意識
coefficient of correlation	相關係數
coefficient of multiple correlation	複相關係數
coefficient of partial correlation	淨相關係數
coefficient of reliability	信度係數
coefficient of validity	效度係數
coenaesthesis (cenesthesia)	一般機體覺
cognition	識知
cold sensation	冷覺
cold spot	冷點
color	1. 彩色; 2. 色
color blindness (Daltonism)	色盲
color circle	色圈
color constancy	彩色常性
color contrast	色對比
color disc	色盤
color equation	配色公式
color induction	色誘導
color mixer	混色器

color mixture	色混合
color pyramid	色稜錐
color sensation	色覺
color spindle	色紡錘
color tone (hue, chroma)	色調
color triangle	色三角
color weakness	色弱
color wheel	混色輪
color zone (chromatic zone)	[網膜]感色區
colored hearing (chromaesthesia)	色聽聯覺
coma	昏迷
combination tone	差合音
comparative psychology	比較心理學
comparison stimulus (variable stimulus)	變量刺激
compensation	補償
compensatory movement	補償動作
complementary color	補色
completion test	填空測驗
complex	1. 情結; 2. 複合
compulsion	強迫[動作]
compulsion neurosis (obsessional neurosis)	強迫性神經病
concentration	集中
concept	概念
conception	1. 概念作用; 2. 概念
concomitant learning	附件學習
conditioned inhibition	條件抑制
conditioned inhibitor	條件抑制物
conditioned reflex	條件反射
conditioned reflex of second order (secondary conditioned reflex)	二級條件反射
conditioned reflex of third order (tertiary conditioned reflex)	三級條件反射
conditioned response	條件反應
conditioned stimulus (conditional stimulus)	條件刺激
conditioning	條件作用

conduction	傳導	cortical blindness	皮質盲
cone (retinal cone)	〔網膜〕錐體	cortical deafness	皮質聾
cone vision	錐體視覺	co-twin control method	孿生比較法
configuration (Gestalt)	完形	counter-suggestion	抵消暗示
conflict	衝突	covert response (implicit response)	內隱反應
congenital	生來的	
conjugate movement	協同運動	cranial nerve (cerebral nerve)	腦神經
connectionism	聯結主義	
connector	聯結器	cranio-sacral division	頭薦部分
conscious	意識的	creative ability	創造性能力
conscious attitude (Bewusstseinslage)	意識態度	creative imagination	創造性想像
		cretinism	呆小症
consciousness	意識	critical flicker frequency	閃爍臨界頻率
consonance	諧和	cross education	左右轉移訓練
constancy	常性	cross transfer (bilateral transfer)	左右遷移
constancy hypothesis	常性假設	
constant error	常差	crystal gazing	圓光
constellation	叢	cue	線索
constitutional	體質的	cul de sac (blind alley)	盲路
constitutional types	體質類型	cumulative frequency	累積次數
consummatory response	完成反應	curve of conditioning	條件〔反射〕建立曲線
content psychology	內容心理學	
contiguous receptor	接觸感受器，接觸受納器	curve of extinction	〔條件反射〕消退曲線
contrast	對比	cutaneous sensation (skin sensation)	皮膚覺
contrast illusion	對比錯覺	
contra-suggestion (negative suggestion)	反暗示	cutaneous sense (skin sense)	1. 皮膚感官; 2. 皮膚覺
control experiment	參校實驗	cyclothymia	循環性精神病
control group	控制組，參校組	

D

controlled association	控制聯想	D.L. = difference limen	差別閾限
convergence	會合〔眼動〕	Daltonism (color blindness)	色盲
conversion	轉變性	dark adaptation (scotopic adaptation)	對暗適應
convolution (gyrus)	〔腦〕回	
convulsion	抽風	day blindness	晝盲
coördination	協調	day-light vision (photopic vision)	強光視覺
cornea	角膜	
correlation	相關	db = decibel	分貝〔耳〕
corresponding points (corresponding retinal points)	〔網膜〕相稱點	decerebrate rigidity	大腦切除癱直
		decerebration	大腦切除
cortex (cerebral cortex)	大腦皮質	decibel (db)	分貝〔耳〕

decortication	皮質毀除	inhibition)	的抑制）
deep pressure sensibility	深部壓覺	disintegration	解體
deep sensibility	深部覺	disorder	1. 錯亂; 2. 失常
defense mechanism	自衞機構	disorientation	迷向
defense reflex	自衞反射	disparate points (disparate	〔網膜〕不相稱點
delayed conditioned reflex	延遲條件反射	retinal points)	
delayed instinct	遲熟本能	disparate sensations	不同感官感覺
delayed response (delayed	遲發反應	dispersion	離中趨勢
reaction)		dissimilation	異化
delirium	昏譫	dissociated personality	分裂的人格
delirium tremens	顫動性昏譫	dissociation	分裂
delusion	妄念	dissonance	不諧和
delusion of grandeur	誇大妄念	distance receptor	距離感受器，距
delusion of persecution	受難妄念	(teleoceptor)	離受納器
dementia	智力衰失	distraction	分心
dementia praecox	早發精神衰失症	distributed learning (spaced	間時學習
dendrite	樹突	learning)	
depression	沉鬱	distribution	分配
depth perception	深度知覺	dizygotic twins (fraternal	異卵孿生兒
desire	欲望	twins)	
determining tendency	決定趨勢	double images	雙像
determinism	定決論	double personality (dual	雙重人格
deuteranopia	乙型色盲	personality)	
dextrality	右偏性	double-aspect theory	兩相說
dichoglottic stimulation	二味同時刺激	double-point aesthesiometer	兩點觸覺計
dichorhinic stimulation	二鼻同時刺激	drainage theory (drainage	挹注說
dichotic stimulation	兩耳同時刺激	hypothesis)	
dichromatic vision	二色視覺	dream work	夢的造作
(dichromatism)		drive	內驅力
diencephalon (interbrain)	間腦	dual personality (double	雙重人格
difference limen (difference	差別閾限	personality)	
threshold) (D.L.)		duplicity theory	兩重作用說
difference tone	差音	duration	久暫
differential inhibition	分化抑制	dynamic psychology	動的心理學
differential psychology	差別心理學	dynamic stereotypy	動的定型
differentiation	分化	dynamometer	握力計
digit span	數字廣度		
discord	不諧和	**E**	
discrimination	辨別		
discrimination box	辨別箱	E.A. = educational age	教育年齡
discrimination time	辨別時間	E.E.G. = electroencephalo-	腦電波圖
disinhibition (inhibition of	抑制解除 （抑制	gram	
		eclectic psychology	折衷心理學

Edipus complex (Oedipus complex)	戀母情結
educational age (E.A.)	教育年齡
educational psychology	教育心理學
effective stimulus	有效刺激
effector	反應器
efferent	外導的
ego	自我
egocentric	自我中心的
eidetic image	遺覺像
eidetic type	遺覺型
Einstellung	定向
electroencephalogram (E.E.G.)	腦電波圖
elementarism (elementism)	原素主義
emotion	情緒
emotional expression (expression of emotion)	情緒表現
empathy	神入
empirical psychology	經驗心理學
encephalon (brain)	腦
end spurt	結束奮進
end-brain (telencephalon)	端腦
endocrine gland	內分泌腺
end-organ	末梢器官
engram	印跡
enteroceptor (interoceptor)	內感受器，內受納器
entoptic	眼內的
epicritic sensibility	後起精覺
epilepsy	癲癇症
epileptoid	1. 似癲癇的; 2. 似癲癇者
episcotister	節光器
equipotentiality	等功性
ergograph	〔肌肉〕疲勞記錄器
erogenous zone	動慾區
escape mechanism	逃避機構
esthesiometer (aesthesiometer)	觸覺計
excitability	1. 興奮性; 2. 激動性

excitation	1. 興奮; 2. 激動
exhaustion psychosis	疲竭性精神病
exhibitionism	裸露癖
existential psychology	現象心理學
experience	經驗
experimental error	實驗誤差
experimental neurosis	實驗性神經病
experimental psychology	實驗心理學
explicit response (overt response)	外現反應
expression of emotion (emotional expression)	情緒表現
extensity	延展
external inhibition	外抑制
exteroception	外受作用
exteroceptor	外感受器，外受納器
extinction	消退
extinctive inhibition	消退抑制
extrinsic behavior	外現行為
extroversion	外傾
extrovert	外傾者
eyedness	偏眼性

F

facial expression	面部表情
facilitation	助長
factor theory of intelligence	智力因素說
faculty psychology	官能心理學
fatigue	疲勞
Fechner's law	費希訥律
feeblemindedness	低能
feeling	1. 情感; 2. 感
feeling of familiarity	熟識感
feeling tone (affective tone)	情調
fetichism	物戀
field observation	現場觀察
field of attention	注意域
field of consciousness	意識域
field of vision (visual field)	視野
figure-ground structure	形基結構
film color	泛色
final common path	最後總路

248

fissure	〔腦〕裂	mental)	
fissure of Rolando (central fissure)	中央裂	fusion of disparate images	異像融合

G

fissure of Sylvius (lateral fissure)	外側裂	g = general factor	普通因素
fixation	1. 注視；2. 固結；3. 固戀	Galton whistle	哥爾頓哨
		galvanic skin reflex (psychogalvanic reflex)	皮膚電反射，心理電反射
fixation point	注視點	ganglion	神經節
fixed idea	固執觀念	general factor (g)	普通因素
flicker	閃爍	general paralysis (general paresis)	全身癱瘓
flicker photometry	閃爍量光法		
flight of colors	色的流變	general psychology	普通心理學
flight of ideas	觀念奔馳	generalization	泛化
fluctuation of attention	注意起伏	genetic method	發展法
forebrain	前腦	genetic psychology	發展心理學
forgetting	遺忘	genius	天才
forgetting curve	遺忘曲線	geometrical illusion	幾何形錯覺
form board	形板	Gestalt (configuration)	完形
form constancy	形式常性	Gestalt psychology	完形心理學
form quality (Gestaltqualtät)	形式性	Gestaltqualität (form quality)	形式性
formal discipline	形式訓練		
forvea (fovea centralis)	中央凹	gesture language	手勢語言
fraternal twins (dizygotic twins)	異卵孿生兒	gifted children	聰明兒童
		gigantism	體格巨大症
free association (uncontrolled association)	自由聯想	globus hystericus	〔歇斯底里性〕窒喉覺
frequency	1. 次數；2. 頻率	glove anaesthesia	手套式麻木
frequency distribution	次數分配	gonad	生殖腺
Freudianism (Freudism)	佛洛伊德學派，佛洛伊德學說	grand mal	〔癲癇〕大發作
		graphology	字相學
fringe of consciousness	意識邊緣	grasping reflex	抓握反射
frontal lobe	額葉	gustatory sensation	味覺
frustation	挫折	gyrus (convolution)	〔腦〕回
fugue	浮客症		

H

functional disorder	機能錯亂	habit	習慣
functional psychology	機能心理學	hair sensibility	毛髮覺
functional psychosis	機能性精神病	hallucination	幻覺
functionalism	機能主義	handedness	偏手性
fundamental color (primary color)	基色	harmony	諧和
fundamental tone (funda-	基音	hebephrenia	青春期癡呆

Helmholtz theory (three-component theory)	海姆霍茲三色說
hemiplegia	半身不遂
Hering theory	赫陵視覺說
hierarchy of habits	習慣階層
higher-order conditioned reflex	高次條件反射
highest audible tone	最高可聽音
hind-brain	後腦
Holmgren's test	彩線色盲測驗
homing behavior	回窩行爲
horizontal-vertical illusion	橫豎錯覺
hormic psychology	策動心理學
horopter	〔相稱點〕外投域
hue (color tone, chroma)	色調
hydrocephalic idiot	水腦白癡
hyperaesthesia (hyperesthesia)	感覺過敏
hyperalgesia	痛覺過敏
hypnagogic hallucination (hypnagogic image)	入睡前影像
hypnagogic state	入睡狀態
hypnosis	1. 催眠; 2. 催眠狀態
hypnotism	催眠術
hypochondria	疑病症
hypothalamus	丘腦下部
hysteria	歇斯底里, 癔病

I

I.Q. = intelligence quotient	智力商數 (智商)
id	伊特
idea	觀念
ideation	觀念作用
ideational learning	觀念學習
identical elements	相同分子
identical twins (monozygotic twins)	同卵孿生兒
identification	自居作用
ideo-motor activity	〔觀〕念〔運〕動活動
idiot	**白癡**

idiot-savant	低能特才
illusion	錯覺
illusion of motion	運動錯覺
illusion of rever'sible perspective	交替透視錯覺
image	意像. 像
imageless thought	無像思惟
imagery type	意像類型
imagination	想像
imbecile	愚笨
imitation	模倣
immediate experience	直接經驗
implicit response (covert response)	內隱反應
impulse (impulsion)	衝動
inadequate stimulus	不適當刺激
inarticulate speech (inner speech, subvocal speech)	無聲語言
incentive	誘因
individual difference	個別差異
individual psychology	1. 個別心理學; 2. 個性心理學; 3. 個人心理學
individuality	個性
induced color	誘起色
inducing color	誘導色
induction	誘導
industrial psychology	工業心理學
infancy	嬰兒期
infantile	幼稚的
infantilism	1. 幼稚病; 2. 幼稚行爲
inferiority complex	自卑情結
inhibition	1. 抑制; 2. 抑制作用
inhibition of delay	遲延抑制
inhibition of inhibition (disinhibition)	抑制解除 (抑制的抑制)
inhibitory stimulus	抑制性刺激
inhibitory stimulus of the second order	二級抑制性刺激

250

initial spurt	起始奮進
ink-blot test	墨跡測驗
innate	先天的
inner speech (inarticulate speech, subvocal speech)	無聲語言
insanity	精神錯亂
insight	頓悟
insomnia	失眠症
instinct	本能
integration	整合
intelligence	智力
intelligence quotient (I.Q.)	智力商數（智商）
intelligence scale	智力量表
intelligence test	智力測驗
intensity	強度
interactionism	〔身心〕交感論
interbrain (diencephalon)	間腦
interest	興趣
interference	干擾
internal inhibition	內抑制
interoception	內受作用
interoceptor (enteroceptor)	內感受器，內受納器
interocular distance (interpupillary distance)	瞳孔間距
interruption tone	間歇音
intertone	中間音
interval timer	報時鐘
intrinsic behavior	內隱行為
introspection	內省
introspective psychology	內省心理學
introversion	內傾
introvert	內傾者
intuition	直覺
investigatory reflex (orienting reflex)	探索反射
involuntary response	不隨意反應
involutional melancholia	初老期憂鬱症
irradiation	擴散
irritability	激應性
Ishihara test	石原氏色盲測驗

J

j.n.d. = just noticeable difference	最小〔可〕覺差〔別〕
James-Lange theory of emotion	詹姆士 郎格情緒說
joint sensation (articular sensation)	關節覺
judgement	判斷
just noticeable difference (least noticeable difference) (j.n.d.)	最小〔可〕覺差〔別〕
juvenile delinquent	少年違法者

K

katharsis (catharsis)	宣洩
kinaesthesis (kinesthesis)	動覺
Klang (clang)	樂音
kleptomania	偷竊癖
kymograph	記紋鼓

L

labyrinth	迷路
labyrinthine sense	迷路感官
Ladd-Franklin theory	拉德佛蘭克林色覺說
lag	時滯
lag of sensation	感覺時滯
language	語言
latent content	夢意
latent period	潛伏期
lateral fissure (fissure of Sylvius)	外側裂
law of association	聯想律
law of contiguity	接近律
law of contrast	對比律
law of disuse	失用律
law of effect	效果律
law of exercise	練習律
law of frequency	頻因律
law of primacy	首因律
law of recency	近因律
law of similarity	類似律

law of use	使用律	(average deviation)	
law of vividness	顯因律	meaning	意義
learning	學習	measurement	測量
learning curve	學習曲線	mechanism	機構
least noticeable difference	最小〔可〕覺差	median	中數
(just noticeable difference)	〔別〕	mediumistic writing	1.不由自主的書
left-handedness	左手性	(automatic writing)	寫;2.扶乩
libido	里比多	medulla oblongata (bulb)	延髓
light adaptation (photopic	對光適應	melancholia	憂鬱症
adaptation)		melancholic	憂鬱質
light induction	光誘導	memory	記憶
light sensation	光覺	memory after-image	記憶後像
limen (threshold)	閾限	memory curve	記憶曲線
liminal sensitivity	下閾感受性	memory image	記憶像
liminal stimulus	下閾刺激	memory span	記憶廣度
line of fixation	注視線	memory system (mnemonics,	記憶術
line of regression	迴歸線	mnemonic device)	
linear correlation	直線相關	mental	心理的
linear perspective	線條透視	mental aberration	心理失常
lip key	唇鍵	mental age (M.A.)	智力年齡(智齡)
local sign (local signature)	部位記號	mental chemistry	心理化學
localization	定位	mental compound	心理代合
loudness	響度	mental defective	心理缺陷者
lowest audible tone	最低可聽音	mental deficiency (amentia)	智力缺陷
		mental element	心理原素
M		mental hygiene	心理衛生
M.A. = mental age	智力年齡(智齡)	mental process	心理過程
maladjustment	順應不良	mental set	心〔理定〕向
mania	瘋狂	mental test	心理測驗
manic-depressive psychosis	狂鬱精神病	mesencephalon (midbrain)	中腦
manifest content	夢境	metencephalon	後腦
manoptoscope	手眼相關器	method of average error	均差法
marginal consciousness	邊緣意識	(method of mean error)	
marginal contrast	邊緣對比	method of constant stimuli	固定刺激法
masking	掩蓋	(method of right and	
masochism	受虐色情狂	wrong cases)	
mass activity	整體活動	method of equal-appearing	感覺等距法
massed learning	密集學習	intervals (method of mean	
maturation	成熟	gradation)	
maze	迷律津	method of equivalents	等值法
mean	平均數	method of just noticeable	最小覺差法
mean diviation	平均差	difference (method of	
		minimal changes)	

252

method of limits	極限法
method of mean error (method of average error)	均差法
method of mean gradation (method of equal-appearing intervals)	感覺等距法
method of minimal changes (method of just noticeable difference)	最小覺差法
method of order of merit (ranking method)	等第法
method of paired associates	對聯法
method of paired comparison	成對比較法
method of right and wrong cases (method of constant stimuli)	固定刺激法
metronome	節拍器
midbrain (mesencephalon)	中腦
milli-micron ($m\mu$)	毫微米
mimetic respone	摹擬反應
mind	1. 心, 心理; 2. 精神
mirror drawing	鏡畫
mnemonic device (mnemonics, memory system)	記憶術
mode	衆數
monaural (uniaural)	單耳的
monochromatic	單色的
monocular (uniocular)	單眼的
monozygotic twins (identical twins)	同卵孿生兒
mood	心境
morbid	病態的
moron	蠬憧
mosaic	羅列, 鑲嵌式
motile (motor type)	運動型
motivation	動機的引起
motive	動機
motor	運動的
motor aphasia (aphemia)	運動性失語症
motor area	運動區
motor nerve	運動神經

motor sense	1. 運動感官; 2. 動覺
motor type (motile)	運動型
multiple choice apparatus	多方選擇器
multiple correlation	複相關
multiple personality	多重人格
muscle sensation	肌覺
muscle sense	1. 肌肉感官; 2. 肌覺
muscle spindle	肌梭
muscle tone (tonus)	肌肉緊張
myelin sheath	髓鞘

N

narcissism	影戀
native	先天的
natural conditioned reflex	自然條件反射
negative adaptation	消極適應
negative after-image	負後像
negative conditioned reflex	負條件反射
negative conditioned stimulus	負條件刺激
negative induction	負誘導
negative suggestion (contra-suggestion)	反暗示
negative transfer	負遷移
negativism	抗拒性
neonate	新生兒
neopallium	新〔腦〕皮質
nerve	神經
nerve center	神經中樞
nerve conduction (neural conduction)	神經傳導
nerve current (neural current)	神經流
nerve ending	神經末梢
nerve fiber	神經纖維
nerve impulse (neural impulse)	神經衝動
nervous system	神經系〔統〕
neuraesthenia	神經衰弱症
neural	神經的
neural conduction (nerve conduction)	神經傳導

neural current (nerve current)	神經流
neural impulse (nerve impulse)	神經衝動
neuron (neurone)	神經原
neurosis	神經病
neurotic	1. 神經病的; 2. 神經病者
night blindness	夜盲
noise	噪聲
nonsense syllable	無意義音節
norm	常模
normal curve (normal distribution curve, probability curve)	常態〔分配〕曲線; 幾率曲線
nucleus	1.〔神經〕核; 2.〔細〕胞核
nystagmus	〔眼球〕廻動

O

object color (surface color)	表面色
obsession	強迫〔觀念〕
obsessional neurosis (compulsion neurosis)	強迫性神經病
obstruction method	阻礙法
occipital lobe	枕葉
odor	臭
odor prism	臭覺三稜圖
Oedipus complex (Edipus complex)	戀母情結
oestrus cycle	性慾週期
olfactie	臭單位
olfaction	臭覺
olfactometer	臭覺計
olfactory area	臭覺區
olfactory lobe	臭葉
one-way vision screen	單向視幕
ontogeny	個體發生
ophthalmotrope	眼動儀
optic chiasm	視〔神經〕交叉
optical illusion	視錯覺
organ of Corti	螺旋器

organic psychosis	機體性精神病
organic sensation	機體覺
organic sense	1. 機體感官; 2. 機體覺
organism	〔有〕機體
orientation	朝向
orienting reflex (investigatory reflex)	探索反射
overlearning	過度學習
overt response (explicit response)	外現反應
overtone	倍音

P

p.e. = probable error	幾誤
pain sensation	痛覺
pain spot	痛點
paired associates	聯合對偶
paracentral vision	周中視覺
paradoxical cold	詭冷覺
paradoxical phase	反常相
paralysis	癱瘓
paranoia	妄想狂
parapsychology	靈學
parasympathetic nervous system	副交感神經系〔統〕
parathyroid gland	甲狀旁腺
paresis	輕癱
parietal lobe	頂葉
parotid gland	腮腺
part learning	分段學習
partial (partial tone)	分音
partial color-blindness	部份色盲
partial correlation	淨相關
percentile	百分位
percentile rank	百分等級
perception	知覺
performance test	操作測驗
perimeter (campimeter)	視野測量器
peripheral nervous system	周圍神經系〔統〕
peripheral vision	邊緣視覺
personal equation	個人差別

personality	人格	pressure sensation	壓覺
perspective	透視	primary color (fundamental color)	基色
perversion	反常	primary sex character	性別主特徵
petit mal	〔癲癇〕小發作	primary signaling system	第一信號系統
phantasy	幻想	probability	幾率
phase	位相, 相	probability curve (normal curve, normal distribution curve)	常態〔分配〕曲線, 幾率曲線
phase difference	位相差		
phase of equalization	均等相		
phi-phenomenon (ø-phenomenon)	φ〔似動〕現象	probable error (p.e.)	幾誤
phlegmatic	黏液質	problem box	問題箱
phobia	〔病態〕恐怖	process	過程
photochromatic interval	光色距	projected pain	投射痛覺
photometer	光度計	projective technique	投射診斷法
photopic adaptation (light adaptation)	對光適應	proprioceptor	本體感受器, 本體受納器
photopic vision (day-light vision)	強光視覺	prosencephalon	前腦
		protanopia	甲型色盲
photoreceptor	光感受器, 光受納器	protopathic sensibility	先起粗覺
		pseudoscope	反位鏡
phrenology	骨相學	psychaesthenia	精神衰弱症
phylogeny	種族發生	psyche	心靈
physiological limit	生理極限	psychiatrist (alienist)	精神病學家
physiological psychology	生理心理學	psychiatry	精神病學
physiological zero	生理零度	psychical research	心靈研究
pitch	音高	psychoanalysis	精神分析
pituitary gland	垂體	psychobiology	心理生物學
plateau	高原	psychodiagnostics	心理診斷術
pleasantness	愉快	psychogalvanic reflex (galvanic skin reflex)	皮膚電反射, 心理電反射
pneumograph	呼吸描記器		
point scale	積點量表		
position habit	位置習慣	psychogenic disorder	精神性錯亂
positive after-image	正後像	psychology	心理學
positive conditioned reflex	正條件反射	psychometrics	心理測量學
positive conditioned stimulus	正條件刺激	psychoneurosis	精神神經病
positive induction	正誘導	psychopath	心理病者
post-hypnotic suggestion	後催眠暗示	psychopathology	心理病理學
practice curve	練習曲線	psychophysical parallelism	身心並行論
practice limit	練習極限	psychophysics	心理物理學
Prägnanz	完形趨向	psychophysiology	心理生理學
precocity	早熟	psychosis	精神病
prepotent	優勢的	psychosomatic medicine	心身醫學
		psychotechnology	心理技術學

psychotherapeutics	精神治療術
psychotherapy	精神治療
psychotic	1, 精神病者; 2. 精神病的
puberty	發身
punctiform distribution	點狀分佈
Purkinje phenomenon	樸金耶現象
purple	紫
purposive psychology	目的心理學
pursuitmeter	〔手眼〕協調測量器
puzzle box	迷箱

Q

quartile	四分值
quartile deviation (semi-interquartile range)	四分位差
questionnaire	問卷

R

random movement (random activity)	散漫活動
random sampling	隨機取樣
range of attention (attention span, span of attention)	注意廣度
range of hearing (audibility range)	可聽廣度
rank correlation	等級相關
ranking method (method of order of merit)	等第法
rapport	感通
rationalization	文飾〔作用〕
reaction (response)	反應
reaction key	反應鍵
reaction time	反應時間
reasoning	推理
recall	回憶
recapitulation theory	復演說
receptor	感受器, 受納器
reciprocal induction	相互誘導
reciprocal innervation	交互神經支配
recognition	認識

recurrent image	復現後像
recurrent psychosis	重發性精神病
red-green blindness	紅綠盲
redintegration (reintegration)	重整作用
reduction screen	減光屏
referred pain	移位痛覺
referred sensation	移位感覺
reflex	反射
reflex arc	反射弧
reflex circuit	反射環
reflexology	反射學
refractory period	不應期
regression	倒退
reinforcement	強化
reintegration (redintegration)	重整作用
relapse	復發
relative refractory period	相對不應期
relearning	再學習
reliability	可靠性
remembering	記憶
reminiscence	記憶恢復
remote association	遠距聯想
repression	壓抑
reproduction	復現
resonance box	共鳴箱
resonance theory	〔聽覺〕共鳴說
response (reaction)	反應
retention	保持
retention curve	保持曲線
retina	視網膜
retinal cone (cone)	〔網膜〕錐體
retinal disparity	雙像差
retinal image	網膜像
retinal rod (rod)	〔網膜〕棒體
retroactive amnesia (retrograde amnesia)	倒攝遺忘
retroactive association	倒攝聯想
retroactive inhibition	倒攝抑制
retrograde amnesia (retroactive amnesia)	倒攝遺忘

retrospection	回省	sense data	感覺資料
reversible figure	兩可圖形	sense limen (sense threshold)	感覺閾限
reversible perspective	交替透視		
revery (reverie)	遐想	sense modality	感覺模
rhinencephalon	鼻腦	sense organ	感〔覺器〕官
rhodopsin (visual purple)	視紫	sense threshold (sense limen)	感覺閾限
rhythm	節奏		
righthandedness	右手性	sensitivity	感受性
rod (retinal rod)	〔網膜〕棒體	sensorimotor	感覺運動的
rod vision	棒體視覺	sensory acuity	感覺敏銳度
Rorschach test	〔羅夏氏〕墨跡測驗	sensory aphasia	感覺性失語症
		sensory area	感覺區
rote memory	强記	sensory nerve	感覺神經
		sentiment	情操

S

s = specific factor	特殊因素	set	定向
S.D. = standard deviation	標準誤差	sex difference	兩性差異
saccadic eye movement	眼球跳動	sham feeding	假餵
sadism	殘暴色情狂	shape	形狀
sampling	取樣	shock (choc)	休克
sanguine	多血質	shock therapy	休克治療
saturation	濃度	sigma (δ)	1. 毫秒; 2. 標準誤差
saving method	省時法		
schizophrenia	精神分裂症	signal	信號
scotopic adaptation (dark adaptation)	對暗適應	simultaneous contrast	同時對比
		sinistrality	左偏性
scotopic vision (twilight vision)	微光視覺	situation	情境
		size constancy	大小常性
secondary conditioned reflex (conditioned reflex of second order)	二級條件反射	size-weight illusion	形重錯覺
		skill	技巧
		skin sensation (cutaneous sensation)	皮膚覺
secondary extinction	繼發消退	skin sense (cutaneous sense)	1. 皮膚感官; 2. 皮膚覺
secondary law of association	聯想副律		
secondary sex character	性別副特徵	sleep walking (somnambulism)	睡遊
secondary signaling system	第二信號系統		
self	自我	smell compensation	嗅覺抵消
semicircular canal	半規管	smooth muscle (unstriated muscle)	平滑肌
semi-interquartile range (quartile deviation)	四分位差		
		social psychology	社會心理學
senescence	衰老	somaesthesis	軀體覺
sensation	感覺	somaesthetic area	體覺區
sense	1. 感官; 2. 感覺	somatic	軀體的

somatic sense	1. 軀體感官; 2. 軀體覺
somnambulism (sleep walking)	睡遊
sound cage	音籠
space error	位置誤差
space perception	空間知覺
spaced learning (distributed learning)	間時學習
span of apprehension	領會廣度
span of attention (attention span, range of attention)	注意廣度
span of perception	知覺廣度
specific factor (s)	特殊因素
spectral color	光譜色
sphygmograph	脈搏描記器
spinal cord	脊髓
spontaneous	自發的
St. Vitus' dance (chorea)	舞動症
stammering	結舌
standard deviation (S.D.) (δ)	標準誤差
static sense	1. 平衡感官; 2. 平衡覺
statistical error	統計誤差
steadiness tester	穩定測量器
stereoagnosis (astereognosis)	觸物失知症
stereoscope	實體鏡
stereoscopic vision	立體視覺
Stilling's test	希第陵色盲測驗
stimulus	刺激
stimulus error	刺激執誤
stimulus limen (stimulus threshold)	刺激閾限
stocking anaesthesia	襪子式麻木
strabismus	斜視
stream of consciousness	意識流
striated muscle	橫紋肌
stroboscope	動景器
structural psychology	構造心理學

structuralism	構造主義
stupor	昏呆
stuttering	口吃
subconscious	下意識
subject	被試人
sublimation	昇華作用
subliminal	閾下的
subnormal	遜常的
subvocal speech (inner speech, inarticulate speech)	無聲語言
successive contrast	先後對比
suggestibility	暗示感受性
suggestion	暗示
summation tone	合音
supernormal	超常的
supraliminal	閾上的
suprarenal gland (adrenal gland)	腎上腺
surface color (object color)	表面色
sympathetic ganglion	交感神經節
sympathetic nervous system	交感神經系〔統〕
symptom	症狀
synaesthesia (synesthesia)	聯覺
synapse	〔神經原〕觸處
syndrome	症狀羣
synergic reflex (allied reflex)	協合反射
systematic error	系統誤差
systematic psychology	系統心理學

T

tachistoscope	速示器
tactual sensation (tactile sensation)	觸覺
tactual space	觸覺空間
talent	天資
tambour	氣鼓
tapping board	扣擊板
taste bud	味蕾
taste sensation	味覺
telencephalon (end-brain)	端腦
teleoceptor (distance receptor)	距離感受器, 距離受納器

258

telepathy	心靈交通術
telephone theory	〔聽覺〕電話說
temperament	氣質
temperature sensation	溫度覺
temperature sense (thermal sense)	1. 溫度感官；2. 溫度覺
tempo	快慢
temporal lobe	顳葉
temporal maze	時間迷津
temporary connection	暫時聯繫
tendency	趨勢
tendon sensation	腱覺
terminal sensitivity	上閾感受性
tertiary conditioned reflex (conditioned reflex of third order)	三級條件反射
thalamus	丘腦
theory of specific energy of nerves	神經〔特〕殊能〔力〕說
therbligs	微動作單元
thermal sense (temperature sense)	1. 溫度感官；2. 溫度覺
thinking	思考
thought	1. 思惟；2. 思想
three-component theory (Helmholtz theory)	海姆霍茲三色說
threshold (limen)	閾限
thymus gland	胸腺
thyroid gland	甲狀腺
tic	肉跳
timbre (tone-color)	音色
time error	時間誤差
time marker	標時器
time perception	時間知覺
time-motion study	時動研究
tonal fusion	音融合
tonal gap (tonal lacuna)	音隙
tonal island	音島
tonal lacuna (tonal gap)	音隙
tonal sensation (tone sensation)	音覺
tone	1. 音；2. 純音

tone deafness	樂音聾
tone sensation (tonal sensation)	音覺
tone-color (timbre)	音色
tonus (muscle tone)	肌肉緊張
topological psychology	形勢心理學
total color blindness (achromatism)	全色盲
touch sensation	觸覺
touch spot	觸點
trace	痕跡
trace reflex	痕跡反射
tracing board	循軌板
tract	通路
trait	品質
transfer	遷移
transfer of training	訓練遷移
transference	移情
transmarginal inhibition	超限抑制
transparent color	透明色
transposability	關係轉移性
trauma	創傷
trial-and-error learning	嘗試錯誤學習
trichromatism	三色視覺
tropism	向動
tuning fork	音叉
twilight vision (scotopic vision)	微光視覺
two-factor theory of intelligence	智力二因說
two-point discrimination	兩點辨別
two-point threshold	兩點閾限
type	類型, 型
type of nervous system	神經系〔統〕類型

U

ultra-paradoxical phase	超反常相
unconditioned reflex	無條件反射
unconditioned stimulus	無條件刺激
unconscious	無意識
uncontrolled association (free associati)	自由聯想

uniaural (monaural)	單耳的	visual purple (rhodopsin)	視紫
uniocular (monocular)	單眼的	visual space	視覺空間
unpleasantness	不愉快	visual type (visile)	視像型
unstriated muscle (smooth muscle)	平滑肌	voice key	語音鍵
		volition	意志
		volley theory	排發說
		voluntary response	隨意反應
V		Vorstellung	表象
variability	變異性		
variable stimulus (comparison stimulus)	變量刺激	**W**	
vector psychology	向量心理學	warm sensation	溫覺
verbal report method	口頭報告法	warm spot	溫點
vernier chronoscope	微差計時器	Weber's law	韋柏律
vestibule	前庭	Wever-Bray effect	維佛、伯萊效應
vibration sensation	振動覺	whole learning	全部學習
violet	菫	will	意志
visceral	內臟的	wish	願望
visceral sense	1. 內臟感官; 2. 內臟覺	wish fulfillment	願望滿足
		word association	詞聯想
visile (visual type)	視像型	word blindness (alexia)	詞盲
vision	視覺	word deafness	詞聾
visual angle	視角	work curve	工作曲線
visual area	視覺區	Würzburg school	符茲保學派
visual field (field of vision)	視野		

INDEX